# CONNECTING THEORY AND PRACTICE IN MIDDLE SCHOOL LITERACY

Bringing together the voices of researchers and teachers, this volume addresses how teachers connect theory to practice in the middle school English Language Arts education setting and explores how to teach and engage with young adults in a way that treats them as ethical and thoughtful citizens. The book bridges the gap between educational theory and real-world implementation and covers a range of timely topics in middle level education through a focus on text choice, identity, and practice. Contributors acknowledge and balance the challenges associated with the reality of teaching, including time constraints, sudden shifts, and fast-paced work, with real-world guidance on key topics, such as supporting multilingual students, queering middle grade pedagogies, teaching diverse texts, examining racial bias in the classroom, and critical digital literacy.

Ideal for courses on middle level education and literacy education, this book encourages and equips pre-service teachers to engage in meaningful conversations with their students that foster reflection and transformative learning.

**Jason DeHart** is Assistant Professor of Reading Education and Special Education at Appalachian State University, USA.

**Carla K. Meyer** is Associate Professor of Literacy Education at Duquesne University, USA.

**Katie Walker** is Assistant Professor of Literacy, Language, and Culture at the University of Southern Maine, USA.

# CONNECTING THEORY AND PRACTICE IN MIDDLE SCHOOL LITERACY

## Critical Conversations

*Edited by Jason DeHart, Carla K. Meyer, and Katie Walker*

Routledge
Taylor & Francis Group

NEW YORK AND LONDON

© Getty Images

First published 2022
by Routledge
605 Third Avenue, New York, NY 10158

and by Routledge
2 Park Square, Milton Park, Abingdon, Oxon, OX14 4RN

*Routledge is an imprint of the Taylor & Francis Group, an informa business*

© 2022 Jason DeHart, Carla K. Meyer, and Katie Walker

The right of Jason DeHart, Carla K. Meyer, and Katie Walker to be identified as the authors of the editorial material, and of the authors for their individual chapters, has been asserted in accordance with sections 77 and 78 of the Copyright, Designs and Patents Act 1988.

*Library of Congress Cataloging-in-Publication Data*
*A catalog record for this title has been requested*

ISBN: 978-0-367-77461-5 (hbk)
ISBN: 978-0-367-77182-9 (pbk)
ISBN: 978-1-003-17150-8 (ebk)

DOI: 10.4324/9781003171508

Typeset in Bembo
by SPi Technologies India Pvt Ltd (Straive)

# CONTENTS

# AUTHOR BIOGRAPHIES

**Arianna Banack** is a Doctoral Candidate at the University of Tennessee, Knoxville, specializing in children's and young adult literature. She is currently one of the assistant editors of *The ALAN Review*. Her research interests focus on adolescent reading engagement and YAL. Prior to enrolling at UTK, Arianna was a ninth-grade English teacher in a large, urban district in Connecticut. Arianna has published in several peer-reviewed journals, including *English Journal, The ALAN Review, Voices from the Middle,* and *Tennessee Literacy Journal.*

**Kim O'Donnell** currently serves as the Assistant Superintendent of Schools in Westbrook, Maine. She has taught grades K-6 and served in multiple administrative roles. A Maine native, LGBTQ community member and lifelong learner, she is deeply embedded in the recognition of marginalized groups within curriculum and in public schools. Her professional research interests include leadership development, inclusion and equity, especially for students who are transgender or non-gender conforming. Dr. O'Donnell is also affiliated with the University of Southern Maine, having completed her doctoral studies at the Muskie School, serving on their Education Leadership Advisory Board.

**Fatima van Hattum** is a PhD Candidate in the Language, Literacy, and Sociocultural Studies Program at the University of New Mexico and works as a Program Director at NewMexicoWomen.Org, the statewide women's foundation. She holds an MSc in Globalization and Development Studies from SOAS University of London. Her academic writing, poetry, and satirical comics have been published in: *Intersections: Critical Issues in Education; Chicana/Latina Studies: The Journal of MALCS; Critical Inquiry in Language Studies: An International Journal; CALYX Journal; apt;* and *New Moons: Contemporary Writing by North American Muslims.* Her research interests are Muslim identity, intersectional feminisms, and visual representation.

**Johnathan Hill** is a PhD Student at Texas A&M University – Corpus Christi. His focus is on Curriculum and Instruction with an emphasis in literacy. He also has eight years of teaching experience in public schools at the middle school level. He has taught 8th grade English Language Arts as well 6th–8th grade reading intervention and was a certified English as a Second Language teacher.

**Dani Kachorsky** is an Assistant Professor of Literacy in the Department of Curriculum, Instruction, and Learning Sciences at Texas A&M University – Corpus Christi. As a middle and high school English teacher, she had positive experiences incorporating comic books, graphic novels, and picture books into her classroom. These experiences have led her to research how readers transact with multimodal texts and the pedagogical approaches that support the use of such texts in classrooms and other contexts.

**Alexandria Perez** is a PhD Student and Graduate Assistant at Texas A&M University – Corpus Christi in the Department of Curriculum, Instruction, and Learning Sciences. As a former middle school teacher, she has experience in teaching students at varying levels from minority backgrounds in low-socioeconomic areas. Alexandria has an interest in teaching and researching in the areas of social semiotics and multimodalities, comics and graphic novels, and pop culture in education.

**Stephanie F. Reid** is an Assistant Professor of Literacy Education at the University of Montana. She studied English Literature at the University of Cambridge and Education at the University of Oxford before graduating from Arizona State University with a PhD in Learning, Literacies, and Technologies. Prior to pursuing her doctoral degree, Stephanie was a middle school English Language Arts and Reading teacher for 15 years. She taught students in both England and the United States. Stephanie's research focuses on children's and young adult literature and on understanding how students make and interpret multimodal texts in K-8 school spaces.

**Amanda Rigell** is a Doctoral Student at the University of Tennessee, Knoxville, specializing in literacy education. Her research interests include instructional decision-making, reading engagement, and the reading-writing connection. She taught middle school ELA for nine years and high school English for four years. She is a licensed Reading Specialist. Amanda has authored or co-authored publications in *English Journal, American Educational Research Journal, Voices from the Middle,* and *Journal of Language and Literacy Education.*

**Rachelle S. Savitz** is an Assistant Professor of Adolescent Literacy at Clemson University having been a K-12 literacy coach/interventionist and high school reading teacher. She is the recipient of the Association of Literacy Educators and Researcher's Jerry Johns Promising Researcher Award, American Reading Forum's Gary Moorman Early Career Literacy Scholar Award, a finalist for the International Literacy Association's Timothy and Cynthia Shanahan Outstanding Dissertation Award, as well as Secondary Reading Council of Florida's Reading Teacher of the Year award. She has published articles on inquiry-based learning, analysis and use of young adult literature, teacher self-efficacy, and culturally sustaining pedagogy. She also has co-authored a book with Drs. Douglas Fisher and Nancy Frey entitled *Teaching Hope and Resilience for Students Experiencing Trauma: Creating Safe and Nurturing Classrooms for Learning.*

Followed by earning a BA in English at Michigan State University, **Mary Roe** began her teaching career at Gardner Junior High in Lansing, Michigan, where she taught English and Latin. During that time, she completed an MA in educational psychology, also at Michigan State. Those experiences directed her future focus on literacy attainment and its instruction alongside issues of equity. She subsequently received an MEd in literacy education at Eastern Washington University and, following years of teaching and serving as a reading specialist, obtained a PhD from the University of Illinois. She is currently Professor Emerita at Washington State University.

**Kristie White Smith, PhD** is an Assistant Professor of Middle Grades Teacher Education at Columbus State University in Columbus, GA. She is a long-time middle grades educator, having served in the field as a teacher of English/ Language Arts, a teacher of English Language Learners, a middle grades Project Based Learning teacher, and a middle grades/secondary Literacy Instructional Specialist. Kristie's scholarship and research interests include curriculum and instruction, middle grades literacy education, and creative, equitable, socially just teaching practices aligned with 21st-century pedagogies.

**Daniel Stockwell** was a high school English language arts teacher in South Carolina. Now, he is a Ph.D. student in the Literacy, Language, and Culture program at Clemson University. Daniel's research interests include critical literacy, disciplinary literacy, and social justice pedagogies.

**Matthew Thomas–Reid** (he/him/his pronouns) is an Associate Professor of Educational Foundations and Affiliate Faculty with Gender, Women's and Sexuality Studies at Appalachian State University. Matthew is Faculty Advisor for GAPP (Gay and Progressive Pedagogy) and a member of the university Inclusive Excellence Team. His areas of research include philosophy of education, social justice education, and queering pedagogies. His current research projects focus on utilizing LGBTQIA histories and narratives with a view toward "queering" pedagogy, praxis, and digital literacies.

# INTRODUCTION

Jason DeHart, Katie Walker, and Carla K. Meyer

## The Challenges of Keeping Theory and Practice (Jason)

I vividly recall the feeling of stepping into a middle school classroom for the first time. I had taken a general methods course, loads of English courses, an educational philosophy class, and at least one course in secondary English methods – but here was the overwhelming task of recognizing my essential foundations in educational theory in a new space, far away from the comforts of a syllabus and teacher education course reading list. Specifically, teachers are granted the opportunity to incorporate knowledge into practice to support students in physical and virtual spaces. This notion of "knowledge-*in*-practice" is essential to the framing of this text and speaks to connections that are sometimes present beyond a conscious acknowledgment, but which educators draw on to build inquiry and engage in problem-solving (Cochran-Smith & Lytle, 1999, p. 263). It is the process of drawing on learning in the moment, and in the midst of the numerous decisions and interactions that occur in teaching practice; theory and practice are hardly a dichotomy, but rather a seamless and on-going engagement of thought and action that are embodied in each moment.

On top of the general intimidation I felt at this daunting work, I was in the midst of finishing a Master's thesis to complete my degree, and balancing the other demands of life. In short, it felt as though all of the theories I had learned about took a cognitive backseat as I attempted to put together a plan that would help me address the learning standards, manage my students, and send the message to my colleagues that, although I was only in my early twenties, I could tackle the challenge of being a teacher. I was focused on learning names, making sure to take attendance, and coming up with a fresh lesson plan each day, tailored to the needs of my 120 young adolescent learners. The moments where my beliefs were forefront and shaped my interactions were evident at times but often effected as a kind of muscle memory that are only most evident in hindsight. Sometimes we must be reminded of what we already know, and sometimes we must be brave enough to learn about new theories that may lead us forward.

Teaching is a challenging profession and we know that teacher education programs are often criticized for failing to equip educators for their many roles and tasks. As a teacher-insider (that is, someone who spent almost ten years in the classroom and who has now spent fifteen years in the world of education), I am all too familiar with the mounting demands placed on teachers that make the profession even more challenging.

These demands include, but are not limited to, curriculum mandates, restrictive pacing guides, adherence to value-added models that tell us precious little about the work teachers actually do (Berliner, 2013), getting to know and work with students who come from a wide range of backgrounds with a variety of support systems, and a general lack of teacher autonomy. All of this has led to a movement to reclaim the teaching profession – for teachers (Hatch, 2015). The demands do not end there, as teachers must also tackle real-life behavior management issues, as well as the duties and processes that are added in real classroom and school practice. No wonder new teachers may be tempted to engage in a kind of survival mode.

It is my hunch that many of the theoretical and philosophical conversations that take place in teacher education programs still have value, and that these ideas are an important part of practice. The best instructional strategies and moves in the classroom are rooted in thoughtful reflection and a focus on what works to maximize the experience and voice of all learners. Sometimes the interactions between theory and practice occur in split-second decisions, as well. Indeed, every moment of teacher practice is rooted in one kind of philosophical foundation or another – in the blitz that is classroom practice, that foundation may be overlooked as teachers sometimes simply do not have the time to be metacognitive about their work or the autonomy to design instruction based on philosophical understandings.

What we propose in this text is a reclaiming of theory and practice for meaningful pedagogy, particularly within literacy instruction in the middle grades classroom. In essence, we hope that this text will inspire professional educators to carry the conversation about what teachers do in practice that works, along with why teachers do what they do, beyond the cap and gown and into professional learning communities and classroom discussion. Theory need not be elusive or written in a mode that is indecipherable; educational insights and ideas should be available and accessible. Yet, we know that theories can present as complicated as thinkers offer much to challenge our worldviews, shape our practice, and push back on or reaffirm both situated notions and larger norms.

In order to accomplish this work, we are considering a particular slice of educational practice, both in terms of content focus and educational level – literacy education in the middle school classroom. This sense of focus resonates with our experiences and gives us direction in this inquiry.

Each of the editors of this volume has served as a middle grades teacher and can attest to the capability of this age group to hang with difficult conversations and abstract thinking. The theories that are advanced in teacher education programs have the potential to be transformative not only for educators, but for the students with whom they work. In fact, this capacity for abstract thinking is a notion that has been suggested by the Association for Middle Level Education's description of this age group, as well as research focused on adolescents (Moje, 2010). Within the pedagogical space of literacy, we have invited a number of contributors to speak to issues of critical theory. The story we unfold, chapter by chapter, is one that works on many levels, but I will identify at least two.

First, we honor the voices of the students who find their experiences and world-views reflected in thoughtful classroom practice. This is the foundational belief we share that leads us to consider religious freedom, gender identity and gender expression, critical race theory, and other stances of social justice and pedagogical inquiry. All of the voices in our classrooms matter, and all students are our students. What is more, we advocate for a wide range of literature within middle grades classrooms so that students can see themselves, as well as catch a glimpse into the experience of others.

In addition to honoring the voices of students, part of the work we have sought to accomplish in this book, through the multitude of authors we have invited, is to honor the work of teachers who enter our programs, work diligently, graduate, and then enter a profession in which they have the task of building thinking with young people. As we stated at the outset, this is not easy work, and it is our hope that the theories that engage learners in teacher education programs continue to shape our future classrooms – and, in turn, our future society.

One of my colleagues, in particular, is a person I return to in my teaching reflection as I think about people who shaped me into the practitioner I wanted to become. This colleague would often say to me, "May the conversation continue," and we quite agree.

## Keeping House in the Middle-Grades (Katie)

During my first year of teaching, I remember lamenting the never-ending tasks that I had to accomplish. It seemed like no matter how hard I worked, my desk was never "clear." That was when my mentor, a veteran teacher, and administrator said to me, "Katie, teaching is like housework. You accomplish a little bit each day and continue the rest tomorrow." While that advice seems very simplistic, it gave me an incredible sense of relief. This was a message I could easily wrap my head around: the work is on-going, prioritizing tasks is important, to-do lists are important, and, at the end of the day, if I did what was right by kids and accomplished as much as I could, it was okay to pack it in for the day and get back to it tomorrow. What this message really told me was that teaching is more than a profession or a craft, it's a way of life.

Since then, the concept of "keeping house" in the middle-grades has been ever present in my professional life. What is important in your house? For me, it is serving children and their families, perpetuating knowledge about best practice, and honoring the expertise of educators. These values fit well with the conceptualization of the middle-grades initiative and their subsequent Schools to Watch program.

## A Brief History of the Middle School Movement

The Middle School Movement began in the 1960s as a response to the Elementary and Secondary Education Act under President Johnson (Schaefer, Malu, & Yoon, 2016). The Elementary and Secondary Education Act of 1965 called for "full educational opportunity," by increasing funding for low-income schools and special education centers and focusing on increasing the quality of elementary and secondary schools in the United States (U.S. Department of Education, 2015). Though he was not the first person to note the unique needs of early adolescents, William Alexander was named the "father of the middle school movement" (Lounsbury, 1982) after his call to change junior high school models to middle school models (Alexander, 1968; Alexander, 1969; Lounsbury, 2009; Manning, 2000; Schaefer, Malu, & Yoon, 2016). Alexander argued that junior high schools that followed traditional college-preparatory courses found in high schools were not responsive to the development needs of young adolescents (Alexander, 1968; Beane, 1999).

The movement continued to develop in sophistication into the 1980s, as middle school advocates began to identify specific characteristics of what they believe to be appropriate instruction at the middle-level. Teachers and administrators working on middle-level curriculum development were encouraged to incorporate developmentally responsive, interdisciplinary, exploratory, and engaging lessons (Arnold, 1985; Arhar, Johnston, & Markle, 1989; Schaefer et al., 2016). The basis for these curricular foci was the position statement of the National Middle School Association (NMSA)'s *This We Believe* (1982), which outlined the fundamental beliefs of middle-level education, as well as the Carnegie Council's *Turning Points: Educating Adolescents in the 21ˢᵗ Century* (1989), which provided a call to action for middle-school policy and education, serving as a platform for a broader conversation regarding middle-level reform (Feldman & Ouimette, 2004; Schaefer et al., 2016).

In the 1990s, the middle school movement began to see reforms in the restructuring of middle schools and the increased attention of administrators and teachers (Schaefer et al., 2016). By this time, the middle school movement had developed the "middle-school concept" which is an educational philosophy founded on a holistic and humanistic perspective of education. The movement concerns itself with schools that are responsive to the developmental needs of young adolescents, design learning that is engaging to both the teacher and the students, and develop a democratic environment (Lounsbury, 2009). These beliefs were typically envisioned in practice as cooperative learning, teaming, exploratory and interdisciplinary courses, and block scheduling (Schaefer et al., 2016).

The National Forum to Accelerate Middle-Grades Reform (NFAMGR) was developed by a reform-oriented group who split from the American Middle School Association. The organization strives to unite stakeholders in a common voice to advance the middle school movement using research, policy, and leadership to produce replicable models of middle schools that are developmentally responsive, academically excellent, and socially responsible (NFAMGR, 2015a). The key initiatives of NFAMGR are to improve school and classroom practice through (STW*), Comprehensive School Reform (CSR)*, and *Transformation Network* and to engage key stakeholders through advocacy, policy statements, postsecondary access, and national conferences (NFAMGR, 2014). This organization is currently funded by The Fry Foundation, Stuart Foundation, J.P. Morgan Chase Foundation, The Rural School & Community Trust, Z Smith Reynold's Foundation, NEA Foundation, Raikes Foundation, Association for Middle Level Education (AMLE), Edmodo, and the National Association of Secondary School Principals (NASSP) (NFAMGR, 2015b). The NFAMGR works in collaboration with AMLE, NASSP, and the National Association for Elementary School Principals (NAESP) to further its mission to reform middle level education (NFAMGR, 2014).

The National Forum to Accelerate Middle Grades Reform launched the STW initiative in 1999, which is intended to identify schools that are on the path to exemplary status through the implementation of the criteria of high-performing middle schools (NFAMGR, 2016). To participate in the initiative, a State can apply to the NFAMGR. There are currently 17 participating states.

## The Modern Middle School Movement

Significant work has been done to distill and advocate for best practices in middle-grades instruction. However, to fully understand current issues in the middle school movement, it is important to understand that the movement itself was based in the flawed and highly criticized theory of adolescence as defined by G. Stanley Hall (1904). Hall's work relied on the recapitulation theory, in which he argued that early adolescence is a period of development in which humans transition from a savage state to a civilized state. This work is highly problematic in that it was centered in the white male experience (Hughes, 2012; Lesko, 2001) and argued that other genders and races were not capable of fully completing the transition from "savage" to "civilized."

These ideas have gone largely unchallenged by middle grades educators and while significant work has been done to examine best practices for the education of early adolescents, little has been done to fully integrate notions of how middle grades educators can best serve early adolescents from marginalized populations. Harrison, Hurd, & Brinegar (2019) argued that middle level educators must "disrupt an essentialized view of young adolescents" and "embrace an intersectionality lens" (p. 15) as a way to acknowledge and honor the importance of gender, culture, race, language, and experience in the development of early adolescents.

I would argue that in "keeping house" in the middle grades, we have kept our spaces clean and tidy, but that the foundation has been neglected and is in great need of repair. Many of the authors featured in this text have adopted the intersectionality lens, as suggested by Harrison et al., (2019) and will provide the audience with relevant theories and practical strategies for rebuilding a strong foundation that will serve to contextualize the work of middle grades educators as asset-based and complex. Just like keeping house is embroiled in the historical and current family matters, so is keeping house in the middle grades embroiled in the historical and current issues of middle-grades education.

## An Overview of the Book's Contents

At the outset of this exploration of theory and practice, a team of contributors, Dani Kachorsky, Alexandria Diaz, and John Hill, speak to a relevant and timely issue as teachers have moved to online instruction – and, indeed, may continue to find practice rooted in digital spaces and in hybridized classrooms. These authors consider the affordances of digital and multimodal texts, namely comic books and graphic novels, and elaborate on the ways these texts lend themselves to reading instruction, emphasizing practice around the theory of multimodality.

This embedding in considerations of text leads to the second contributor team, Rachelle Savitz and Daniel Stockwell, and their work on the connection between critical literacy theory and practice. The use of young adult literature as a textual space for exploring controversial, or "taboo topics," will pair with Kachorsky, Perez, and Hill's focus on pedagogical affordances for materials that have been considered controversial for classroom instruction. Stephanie Reid then returns to multimodal theory in the presentation of a study's findings focused on the pedagogical practices of a middle school teacher who reconfigures classroom practice based on the implementation of complex texts that communicate in a variety of ways.

Unfolding thematically from this conversation about text-centered controversy and identity in the classroom, Kim O'Donnell speaks to the assumptions and practices of school leadership when addressing students with unique needs – in particular, O'Donnell shares findings about crafting literacy spaces for with students with nonbinary sexual identities. The implications of this chapter speak to literacy programs, materials, and instruction, as well as the decisions that policymakers enact.

This wider conceptualization at the program/school level is then underscored by Amanda Rigell and Arianna Banack's examination of both the theoretical foundation and continued practice of a dialogic classroom for confronting and reconsidering power dynamics in instructional spaces. The affordances of both dialogue and critical conversations serve as a complementary nexus between these two chapters. Mary Roe offers an examination of the adolescent learner, framed through cognitive flexibility theory, in the following chapter. Roe pushes back on reductive approaches to reading development for older readers and includes a more robs consideration of the effects and affordances of the reading process for the middle grades student.

Further illuminating conversation about classroom identities and literacy practices, Matthew Thomas-Reid shares an autoethnographic study of teacher as research participant, with particular focus on queering pedagogy. Thomas-Reid explores texts, practices, and resources in this chapter to facilitate an understanding of the ways in which poststructural, queer, and critical theories take shape in pedagogical spaces. Katie Walker follows this chapter with an exploration of the ways identity is bound up in linguistic practices, troubling the English-centered approach that many regions and districts implement for literacy instruction. Walker provides both a context for this work by moving the conversation from abstraction to personhood and then provides specific strategies that middle grades teachers can use to support the language and literacy development of multilingual early adolescents while providing students with the space to sustain their current cultural, linguistic, and literacy practices.

In "What Do We Believe about Middle Grades Literacy and Race? Interrogating Practices and Pedagogies of Middle Grades Literacy Education through the Lens of Critical Race Theory," Kristie White Smith offers a look at the history and development of Critical Race Theory, as well as the implications for classroom practice for antiracist teaching practices. Fatima van Hattum draws on a visual critical lens for "Dis-Orienting Pedagogy" in the following chapter, challenging notions of Islamophobia and Orientalism. van Hattum constructs a case for critical engagement with depictions of Muslims and people from the Middle East, given the multitude of negative depictions that students at the middle grades level have encountered in media.

As a coda to the book, Jason DeHart offers a chapter on the continued need for reflective and reflexive pedagogy as teachers consider the many time constraints, sudden shifts, and fast pace of their practice. DeHart draws on qualitative data to support the case that reflection is a necessary and yet often neglected component of instructional practice, and highlights an essential bedrock of theory and understanding that undergirds the journey the reader will take throughout this text. In a call back to the subtitle of the volume, this and other chapters offer a glimpse into the inextricable nexus of theory and practice, while suggesting that this is a work that is never completely accomplished.

Through all of these chapters, it is our hope that educators who engage in this work alongside our contributors are both informed and challenged by their content, reminded about the importance of their own theoretical positions, and affirmed in the complicated and living work of co-constructing middle school classrooms where learners are transformed into critical, thoughtful individuals who continue to return to literacy practices as they shape the world that is to come.

## References

Alexander, W. M. (1968). The middle school movement. *Theory into Practice*, 7(3), 114–117.
Alexander, W. M. (1969). From junior high school to middle school. *The High School Journal*, 53(3), 151–163.
Arhar, J. M., Johnston, J. H., & Markle, G. C. (1989). The effects of teaming on students. *Middle School Journal*, 3, 24–27.
Arnold, J. (1985). A responsive curriculum for emerging adolescents. *Middle School Journal*, 16(3), 3–15.
Beane, J. A. (1999). Middle schools under siege: Points of attack. *Middle School Journal*, 30(4), 3–9.
Berliner, D. C. (2013). Effects of inequality and poverty vs teachers and schooling on America's youth. *Teachers College Record*, 115(12), 1–26.
Carnegie Council on Adolescent Development's Task Force on Education of Young Adolescents. (1989). *Turning points: Preparing American youth for the 21st century*. Washington, DC: Carnegie Foundation.
Cochran-Smith, M. & Lytle, S. L. (1999). Chapter 8: Relationships of knowledge and practice: Teacher learning in communities. *Review of Research in Education*, 24(1), 249–305.
Feldman, J., & Ouimette, M. (2004). Examining the Turning Points Comprehensive Middle School Reform Model: The Role of Local Context and Innovation. *Center for Collaborative Education*. Retrieved from http://eric.ed.gov/?id=ED509779
Hall, G. S. (1904). *Adolescence: Its psychology and its relations to physiology, anthropology, sociology, sex, crime, religion, and education*. New York, NY: D. Appleton.
Harrison, L., Hurd, E., & Brinegar, K. (2019). Exploring the convergence of developmentalism and cultural responsiveness. In K. Brinegar, L. Harrison, & E. Hurd (Eds.), *Equity and cultural responsiveness in the middle grades* (pp. 3–21). Information Age Publishing, Inc.
Hatch, J. A. (2015). *Reclaiming the teaching profession: Transforming the dialogue in public education*. Lanham, MD: Rowman & Littlefield Publishers.
Hughes, H. (2012). Always becoming never enough: Middle school girls talk back. In M. Vagle (Ed.), *Not a stage! A critical reconceptualization of young adolescent education* (pp. 93–118). Peter Lang.
Lesko, N. (2001). *Act your age: A cultural construction of adolescence*. New York, NY: Routledge.
Lounsbury, J. H. (1982). *This we believe*. Columbus, OH: National Middle School Association.
Lounsbury, J. H. (2009). Deferred but not deterred: A middle school manifesto. *Middle School Journal*, 40(5), 31–36.
Manning, M. L. (2000). A brief history of the middle school. *The Clearing House: A Journal of Educational Strategies, Issues and Ideas*, 73(4), 192–192.

Moje, E. B. (2010). Re-framing adolescent literacy research for new times: Studying youth as a resource. *Reading Research and Instruction, 41*(3), 211–228.

Schaefer, M. B., Malu, K. F., & Yoon, B. (2016). An Historical Overview of the Middle School Movement, 1963–2015. *RMLE Online, 39*(5), 1–27.

The National Forum to Accelerate Middle-Grades Reform. (2014). *Key initiatives.* Retrieved from http://middlegradesforum.org/key-initiatives/

The National Forum to Accelerate Middle-Grades Reform. (2015a). *Mission & vision statement.* Retrieved from http://middlegradesforum.org/vision-mission/

The National Forum to Accelerate Middle-Grades Reform. (2015b). *Forum funders.* Retrieved from http://middlegradesforum.org/forum-funders/

The National Forum to Accelerate Middle-Grades Reform. (2016). *What is schools to watch.* Retrieved from http://middlegradesforum.org/forum-funders/http://middlegradesforum.org/what-is-school-to-watch/

U. S. Department of Education (2015, December 10). *Every Student Succeeds Act (ESSA).* Retrieved August 8, 2016, from http://www.ed.gov/essa?src=rn

Villegas, A. M., & Lucas, T. (2002). Preparing culturally responsive teachers rethinking the curriculum. *Journal of Teacher Education, 53*(1), 20–32.

# SECTION 1

# TROUBLING NOTIONS OF TEXT

# 1

# USING THEORIES IN THE CLASSROOM TO READ AND CONCEPTUALIZE DIGITAL CHILDREN'S COMICS

*Dani Kachorsky, Alexandria Perez, and Johnathan Hill*

Visual culture, or the way in which images and other visual artifacts are now central to the social, cultural, and meaning-making practices of human beings (Duncum, 2001), has had a powerful influence on the literature designed for youth (Short, 2018). This is demonstrated in the increased publication and popularity of multimodal/illustrated books, wordless texts, and comics/graphic novels (Short, 2018). Multimodal texts, or texts that combine multiple modes of communication (e.g., written language and visual image), such as these, have become a key component in how people understand their social worlds (Rose, 2016).

When individuals engage with multimodal texts, they construct meanings within their individual social, cultural, and historical contexts (Rose, 2016) and enact a wide range of literacy practices (Cope & Kalantzis, 2000; Gee, 1991; Knobel & Lankshear, 2014). Thus, being literate today requires skills beyond reading and writing written language (Kress, 2010; Lankshear & Knobel, 2006; Luke, 1995). It has become increasingly important for educators to address visual culture and visual literacy in school curricula (Reid, this volume). Expanding instruction to include visual and multimodal literacies in classroom spaces is necessary if education is to keep pace with the demands of the 21st century (Bellanca & Brandt, 2010; Hicks, 2009; Serafini, 2012).

The purpose of this chapter is to demonstrate how different theoretical perspectives can be used by teachers and students to engage with and construct meaning with various forms of digital comics. This chapter reflects insights gained from a qualitative content analysis of three digital comics that were available in three variations (e.g., digital immigrant, guided view, and motion book): *My Little Pony: Friendship is Magic* (*MLP*) Issue 1 (Cook, 2013), *Transformers: Autocracy* (*TA*) Issue 1 (Metzen & Dille, 2013), and *Overwatch: McCree Train Hopper* (*OW*) (Brooks, 2016). Most of the variants for each issue are available for free through

DOI: 10.4324/9781003171508-2

various digital applications (e.g., Comixology, Madefire, and IDW). Because we do not have permission to replicate the images here, it is recommended that you access copies of these issues on a tablet, smartphone, or other compatible devices.

## Comics in the Classroom

Historically viewed as low-quality popular reading material (Jiménez & Meyer, 2016), recent years have seen educators acknowledging the literary value and inherent complexity of comics (Short, 2018). Librarians, teachers, and scholars have all made the case for utilizing comics in classroom spaces for a variety of instructional purposes. Comics have proven beneficial for generating reading motivation, interest, and engagement (Gavigan, 2011; Jennings et al., 2014) and useful for teaching traditional literacy skills such as sequencing and predicting (Chase et al., 2014; Martinez-Roldan & Newcomer, 2011). Research has also demonstrated that comics can be used to support content area learning and disciplinary literacy as well as critical literacy (Dallacqua & Sutton, 2014; Hosler & Boomer, 2011; Lin & Lin, 2016; Low, 2015).

While comics can be a valuable instructional tool for a wide range of common classroom practices and learning outcomes, they are an invaluable resource for supporting visual literacy development. Comics are a form of visual text, and therefore visual culture, in which images are essential to understanding the narrative or information (Paligaro, 2014). The medium traditionally combines images with text in the form of panels and arranges these panels in a sequence. Additional conventions, such as speech bubbles and gutters, require readers to apply reading strategies and skills beyond those traditional skills and strategies necessary for reading print-text (Jiménez & Meyer, 2016; Low, 2012; Meyer & Jiménez, 2017; Paligaro, 2014). As readers engage with comics, they develop new, visually oriented reading skills (Brenna, 2013) which better prepare them to be literate in the 21st century.

## Digital Comics

One form of comics that has garnered little attention in classrooms but offers rich visual literacy potential is digital comics. Digital comics is an umbrella term used for a range of digital texts that employ comic book conventions (Kachorsky et al., 2020). While some digital comics are original works, most are digital immigrant (DI) texts (Stichnothe, 2014) which are essentially digitized renderings of their print counterparts. However, moving a text from a print to a digital platform alters the transaction between reader and text in a significant manner (Serafini, 2014, 2015b). While the underlying narrative or information shared is the same, how that narrative or information is presented differs.

Most digital texts are accessed through dedicated software or digital devices (Aguilera et al., 2016; Serafini & Youngs, 2013; Yokota & Teale, 2014) which require readers to have a certain level of familiarity in order to successfully read and navigate the texts. Furthermore, certain digital applications allow the reader to customize the reading experience through a guided-view (GV) which presents individual panels of the comic in sequence (Kachorsky et al., 2020). Still other variants such as motion books (MBs) incorporate additional conventions and modes. Panels, gutters, and speech bubbles are joined by sound effects, musical tracks, animated transition, and within panel motion (Kachorsky et al., 2020). Each additional feature requires additional skills and strategies on the part of the reader in order to construct meaning with the text. As such, educators and readers need theoretical lenses for analyzing these texts and for developing pedagogy around them (Serafini, 2015a).

## Theoretical Framework

In this section, we describe three theoretical lenses that can be used to analyze and understand digital comics. Specifically, we discuss a social semiotic approach to multimodality, film analysis, and game studies. Each lens offers different insights about digital comics but also presents different limitations.

## Social Semiotics

A social semiotic approach to multimodality is a theoretical perspective that helps conceptualize different forms—or modes—of communication. Modes are resources that humans use to communicate and make meaning such as speech, writing, gesture, and image (Kress, 2009). When more than one mode is combined into a single text, the result is a multimodal text. For example, digital comics combine the mode of image with the mode of text and, in some instances, include the modes of sound and music. Within a multimodal ensemble, each mode communicates and represents potential meanings in different ways (Kress, 2009). Readers of multimodal texts must work across the available modes to construct meaning. For a further discussion of multimodality, refer to Chapter 4 in this volume.

Within a social semiotic view of multimodality, scholars have paid particular attention to ways in which readers make sense of images. In particular, Kress and van Leeuwen (2006) developed a visual grammar that offers a starting place for analyzing multimodal ensembles. Adapted from Halliday's (1978) systemic functional linguistic framework, Kress and van Leeuwen (2006) posited that images could be understood according to three metafunctions or systems of choices: the ideational, the interpersonal, and the compositional.

## Ideational System

The ideational system offers choices about the different ways that objects/characters and their relationships with each other are presented (Kress & van

Leeuwen, 2006). In *OW*, for example, the passengers on the train are consistently represented as cowering in fear. Furthermore, the vectors—the "imaginary lines formed between participants, objects, and viewers" (Serafini, 2014, p. 63)—created by the victims looking up connect them with their attackers. Such representation emphasizes the roles of the different characters in the story.

### Interpersonal System

The interpersonal system consists of design choices that create a relationship between the reader and the content of the image (Kress & van Leeuwen, 2006). These include point of view, interpersonal distance, and gaze. Point of review is the perceived angle (i.e., straight on, above, or below) at which a reader views objects and/or participants within an image (Serafini, 2014). Looking up at a participant imbues that participant with power and importance (Serafini, 2014). In *TA*, there are several panels (e.g., pg. 3 panel 3) in which the reader is positioned as looking up at Orion Pax. This point of view emphasizes Orion Pax's authority and power. In contrast, when a reader is positioned as looking down on a participant, the opposite effect is achieved (Serafini, 2014).

Interpersonal distance is the perceived distance between the reader and the objects/characters in an image (Serafini, 2014). According to Serafini (2014), "more intimate relationships are developed by bringing the world in for a closer look; whereas depicting people at a distance makes the viewer feel less connected" (p. 64). For example, on the first page of *TA*, the final panel contains an extreme close up of Orion Pax's face. This close up works to establish a close connection between the reader and the character making us empathize with him.

Gaze is the degree to which the actors or participants represented in an image appear to be looking at the reader (Serafini, 2014). Demands—when characters look at the reader (Kress & van Leeuwen, 2006; Serafini, 2014)—invite the reader into the story and insist that the reader connect with and participate with the character. In contrast, offers—when characters look away from the reader (Kress & van Leeuwen, 2006; Serafini, 2014)—position the reader as an outsider. In *MLP*, the majority of the panels feature offers which makes the few demand gazes—all found on page 9—incredibly impactful. In the first of these, Twilight Sparkle looks directly at the reader while stating that the characters cannot go outside because of the danger presented by the Changelings (i.e., evil copies of other ponies). By demanding the reader's attention in this way, Twilight Sparkle invites the reader to share in the danger and fear the ponies are experiencing. By examining gaze, interpersonal distance, and point of view as part of the interpersonal system, readers are able to consider how digital comics position them to relate to content.

## Compositional System

The compositional system offers choices made in how an image is organized (Kress & van Leeuwen, 2006). This includes where different visual elements are located in an image and how specific visual elements are emphasized. Information values zones—top, bottom, left, right, and center—can indicate a certain value or characteristic of a visual element (Serafini, 2014). Centering an object/character suggests a degree of importance while objects in the periphery are not. For example, Orion Pax is centered 12 times in *TA*. This emphasizes his role as the main character and his importance as a leader. Importance can also be associated with items located at the top of an image. Other associations with the top information zone include idealness and power (Kress & van Leeuwen, 2006; Serafini, 2014).

Left and right information zones offer other potential associations. The left information zone is often associated with things that are old, known, given, or accepted while the right information zones are often associated with things that are new or with new possibilities (Kress & van Leeuwen, 2006; Serafini, 2014). In the second to last panel of *TA*, the Autobots appear on the left side of the panel, unaware of a Decepticon lurking on the right side. At this point, the Autobots are well known, given, and accepted characters. In contrast, the Decepticon represents an unknown/new entity that will presumably play a role in the next issue.

Salience and framing are two other compositional tools that illustrators can use in their design. Salience or the degree to which an object or actor stands out can be used to draw the reader's attention to a specific area of the page (Serafini, 2014). This can be accomplished through the size of an object or the brightness of a color. Salience might suggest that a particular object or character is important to the story—as is the case in *OW* where McCree is made salient through the red scarf he wears—or that a particular moment carries a certain significance. Similarly, framing—the use of borders or white space around an object or character—can either draw a reader's attention to a specific object or actor or separate an object or character from other items in an image (Serafini, 2014). Examining the compositional system in this way allows a reader to consider how the arrangement of and emphasis on certain objects guides their attention and prioritizes what they look at.

## Film Analysis

Film analysis traditionally offers a way of examining how production choices regarding narrative, form, and style are grounded in the traditional, historical, practical, financial, and technical aspects of film-making (Bazalgette & Buckingham, 2013; Geiger & Rutsky, 2013). Digital comics have components and technical aspects that draw from and resemble films, such as sound, editing, and cinematography. While these components are slightly different within the context of a digital comic, they are still necessary for the creators to consider. As such, film analysis lends itself well to analyzing and understanding digital comics.

## Narrative and Form

Narrative, in film analysis, refers to plot, narration, and chronology. Bordwell and Thompson (2013) define narrative as a "chain of events linked by cause and effect and occurring in time and space" (p. 73). The reader's understanding depends upon the patterns of change and stability, cause and effect, as well as time and space, and how these characteristics work together to structure the overall narrative. Causality within a given space and time are pivotal to the narrative (Bordwell & Thompson, 2013). Form, or the ways in which a film's parts "work together to create specific effects" (Bordwell et al., 1993, p. 3), creates a structured experience for the viewer (Bordwell & Thompson, 2013).

Analyzing narrative and form involves looking at various aspects of the plot, narration, pattern, and structure as well as how time progresses within a scene. For example, examining the chronology and the causes/effects that are present in *MLP* helps readers identify instances where creators hope to convey suspense or mystery. When the younger ponies act strangely on page 4, readers know this behavior results from whatever happened to them in the time that elapsed between pages 2 and 3. Similarly, who is narrating the story can create suspense as well as lend or detract from a story's credibility. When the narrator is also a character, as in *OW*, readers gain more insight into the character's perspective which simultaneously limits what they know about the perspectives and experiences of other characters.

## Style

Style plays a particularly important role in film analysis because it serves as the vehicle through which the narrative is conveyed (Bordwell et al., 1993). Style involves the usage of various cinematic techniques such as cinematography, mise-en-scéne, sound, and editing. While not all techniques used by filmmakers translate to the analysis of digital comics, the ones discussed here have proved useful.

In film analysis, cinematography refers to the manipulation of the film strip by the camera as well as choices made by editors in the editing phase (Bordwell & Thompson, 2013). Two characteristics of cinematography—tone and framing—are particularly valuable for analyzing digital comics. Tone refers to the visual contrast (e.g., light vs. dark) between objects/characters. For example, on page 8 of the *TA* MB, the background setting is bathed in cool, blue-gray colors while the Transformers themselves are highlighted in warmer reds. Framing refers to the various viewing angles, distances, and camera movements used in a film (Bordwell & Thompson, 2013). For example, in the MB version of *TA*, cinematography comes into play when introducing Orion Pax. The slow introduction of the character across multiple panels is coupled with zoom-in and drawback effects adding a level of tension and mystery to the scene.

Mise-en-scéne, literally "putting into scene" (p. 113), encompasses a variety of components such as setting, costume, lighting, and staging (Bordwell & Thompson, 2013). Mise-en-scéne draws attention to what is and is not in each scene (Bordwell & Thompson, 2013)—or panel in the case of comics. Setting is the location in which a scene takes place. In film, setting often plays an active role and helps to set the mood for a scene (Bordwell & Thompson, 2013). For example, on page 2 of *TA*, the setting of Tours City is established. The city is run down, with graffiti, trash, and cracked concrete dominating the background. The landscape becomes overwhelming and the buildings appear to loom over the Autobots. Lighting also contributes to this scene. Dark shadows and muted colors add to the depressed mood of the scene. Lighting often plays a large role in setting the mood for a scene through highlights and shadows, quality, direction, source, and color (Bordwell & Thompson, 2013).

Sound plays an important role in film. It engages senses besides sight, helps shape viewers' understanding of images, and directs viewers' attention (Bordwell & Thompson, 2013). For digital comics, only some MBs and GVs have sound components. When analyzing sound, readers look at perceptual properties (i.e., the loudness, pitch, and timbre of the sound), dimension (i.e., the rhythm and alignment of the sound with images), space (i.e., the sounds origin and location), and time (i.e., the synchronicity between sound and image and use of sound to connect panels/pages) (Bordwell & Thompson, 2013). For example, on page 2 of the *TA* MB, the loud sound of revving engines and speeding accompanies the opening scene in which Transformers, in car form, drive through city streets. The sound fades to an idle rumbling as the scene continues.

Editing, or adjustments made to the film after it has been shot, helps to build a film's overall form (Bordwell & Thompson, 2013). In analyzing digital comics, editing focuses on the kind of camera effects and transitions that are used (e.g., fade, wipe, cut, and dissolve) and the variation and angle of the shots. For example, in the GV and MB forms of digital comics, zooms, slides, and fades created emphases that did not exist in the DI forms of the digital comics.

## Game Studies

Game studies is a relatively new academic field of study that is influenced by a variety of disciplines. Debate in the field exists as to what exactly defines *games*. However, interactivity is commonly identified as a feature that distinguishes games from other forms of media (Aguilera et al., 2016). While there are a number of conceptualizations of interactivity, Salen and Zimmerman (2003) describe four types of interactivity that apply to games: cognitive interactivity, functional interactivity, explicit interactivity, and meta-interactivity. Since digital comics borrow many features from games, readers of digital comics can gain insights about the texts by considering these types of interactivity.

## Interactivity

Cognitive interactivity refers to interpretations the player makes of the game (Salen & Zimmerman, 2003). Similarly, when reading a digital comic, readers cognitively process and respond to the media. For example, in the *MLP* MB, when readers encounter arrows along the right edge of the pages, they need to recognize and interpret the purpose of the arrow which is to progress the panels. Explicit interactivity refers to how the player participates with the various design choices made by the game designers (Salen & Zimmerman, 2003). Design choices can include but are not limited to movement of images, links that lead to other pages, the placement of media, and musical composition. The arrows from *MLP* are an example of a design choice. When readers tap the arrows to progress the panels or the screen, they explicitly interact with the digital comic. Functional interactivity includes functional interactions related to the utility of game play (Salen & Zimmerman, 2003). How the participant can use the features present and whether those features function embody the functionality of game play. For instance, glitches in interactive features (such as the arrows in *MLP*) or glitches in sound that change volume, pitch, or tempo alter readers' experiences. Meta-interactivity involves how the player applies game knowledge beyond a specific game (Salen & Zimmerman, 2003). For example, an *MLP* reader might participate in online fan culture.

## Sound

Further, Brian Sutton-Smith (1986) describes specific elements of game experiences which exist within interactivity such as auditory discriminations (i.e., engagement and immersion due to auditory features) as well as motor responses (i.e., psychological connection between what is on screen with player responses). Auditory discrimination can affect readers' immersion in the story. Readers interpret sound through congruence, linearity, effects, instrumentation, tone, and pitch (Collins, 2008, 2013; Kaae, 2008). Congruence refers to the alignment between sounds and what is happening within the story such as a metal scraping sound occurring when a character opens a door in the *OW* MB (Collins, 2013). Readers can ask themselves if the sound makes sense. Congruence can also apply to reader actions that may cause changes in sound such as cutting off music before it is complete progressing the story. The movement of music in time with events on the screen and the real world with relation to the reader is its linearity (Kaae, 2008). Readers can ask themselves if the sounds or music align with events as they happen. Musical and non-musical sounds present in games—and for our purposes, digital comics—serve as symbols and are used to "assist the player in identifying other characters, moods, environments, and objects, to help the game become more comprehensible" (Collins, 2008, p. 130). For example, on page 1 of *OW MB*, there is a sound effect of a train traveling on tracks while a slow western tune begins to play. Then, a whip cracks, which changes the slow tune to one that has a faster tempo. The whip and train track sound effects give hints to the environment at the start of the story while the change in musical tempo adjusts the mood.

Digital comics take varying forms and have design features which can add or detract from the reader experience. According to Gee (1989), what is *learned* and what is *acquired* in the reading process are not synonymous. What is learned through intention as opposed to what is acquired from the subconscious gathering of information is what defines this difference. Therefore, understanding forms of interactivity within the realm of digital literacy is essential if digital comics and other interactive media are to be utilized in educational contexts.

## Case for Multiple Lenses

Ultimately, different theoretical lenses highlight different aspects of digital comics. As such, there is no single theoretical lens that is equal to addressing every digital comics variant. Because of their multimodal nature and the ways in which these texts borrow from other mediums and formats such as games and films, these texts require teachers and readers to borrow from other fields as well.

While a social semiotic analysis of digital comics reveals a great deal about specific images and how their structures work to convey potential meanings to readers, it does not provide readers with a way to conceptualize or understand animations or transitional effects that are used. Similarly, this perspective does not provide tools for analyzing movement or animation within an image or sound. In order to support understanding of transitions, motions, and sounds, both film analysis and game studies prove more capable.

Film analysis is useful for understanding narrative structures and stylistic choices. However, it does not reveal aspects of readers' physical and intellectual interactions with digital comics. Game Studies is able to account for interactivity in a way that neither film analysis nor social semiotics could address.

Other lenses that could be useful in understanding these digital comics that are not addressed here include picturebook studies where scholars have considered the work readers do between images when turning the page (Sipe & Brightman, 2009) and comic book studies wherein scholars have addressed the meaning-making work that readers do in the gutters or white space between panels (Low, 2012).

## Theory into Practice

As educators answer the call to include visual and multimodal literacies in classroom spaces, they need tools and strategies upon which to draw. The theoretical lenses described above can be utilized by teachers and students to analyze and understand digital comics as well as other digital literature and media. In this section, we present two possible lessons that employ one or more of these theoretical lenses to support student reading, understanding, and analysis of one or more forms of digital comics. These lessons can be adapted for use with other comics as well as other media and other lenses and therefore should not be viewed as prescriptive lessons but as starting points for teachers interested in implementing such work in their classrooms.

## Conducting a Single Lens Analysis

Digital comics, and comics in general, provide educators with several opportunities to consider the traditional aspects of reading literature with elements of other mediums such as art and film. In this lesson, the teacher takes a backseat through reciprocal teaching as students work together to improve their understanding of texts as well as their ability to monitor their comprehension through question generation, clarification, summarizing, and making predictions (Slater & Horstman, 2003).

Alongside these traditional literacy strategies, students analyze the digital comic, *Overwatch: McCree Train Hopper*, in the three different variations (i.e., DI, GV, and MB) through a film analysis lens by examining characteristics such as lighting, sound, mise-en-scene, cinematography, and editing. Analysis of the digital comics also allows for comparison between formats. Specifically, examining the static DI alongside the more dynamic and film-like MB, students will be able to compare and contrast the cinematic techniques borrowed from film.

After individual analysis, students will come together as a group to discuss their findings and compare how the various forms of the digital comic impacted the overall meaning and style of the comic. Students analyze digital comics from a film analysis lens.

## Standards

- CCSS.ELA-LITERACY.RL.8.5: Compare and contrast the structure of two or more texts and analyze how the differing structure of each text contributes to its meaning and style (English Language Arts Standards 8th Grade, n.d.).
- CCSS.ELA-LITERACY.RL.8.7: Analyze the extent to which a filmed or live production of a story or drama stays faithful to or departs from the text or script, evaluating the choices made by the director or actors (English Language Arts Standards 8th Grade, n.d.).

## Resources/Preparation

For this lesson, teachers will need:

- tablets/computers
- access to and accounts for the Comixology and Madefire applications
- *Overwatch: McCree's Train Hopper* in DI, GV, and MB forms
- digital or physical copies of the film analysis template (see Appendix A); students will need one template per page in the comic book
- large chart paper and markers

## Instructional Plan

Either prior to or at the beginning of this lesson, introduce students to digital comics. Particular care should be given to describing how the digital comics operate (e.g., how to move from one page or panel to the next, or how to move backward and how to change the mode of the digital comic). At this time, introduce students to the vocabulary for various digital comics features (e.g., gutters, tableau, scene, panel, etc.). This can be accomplished through direct instruction and demonstration. However, we recommend allowing students the opportunity to explore the format on their own to generate discussion about common and unique features.

Since students will need to be familiar with the technical vocabulary found in the film analysis tool, this should also be addressed either prior to or at the beginning of the lesson. We recommend starting this process by watching and applying this vocabulary to popular films or film shorts. The theoretical perspective portion of this chapter will be helpful in defining the necessary vocabulary and providing an example of what this sort of analysis might look like.

For this lesson, it is ideal for each group of students to approach their analysis with fresh eyes. Thus, when introducing the skills needed to navigate digital comics formats, consider using a different digital comic than *OW*. One of the other comics detailed in this chapter can be used for introductory purposes.

Divide the class into three groups. Assign each group a digital comics variant to analyze (e.g., Group 1: DI; Group 2: GV; Group 3: MB). Once groups are assigned, ask students to independently read their respective version of the digital comic. While reading, they should take notes of their thoughts and observations using reciprocal teaching strategies (Table 1.1).

After reading, have students gathered within their groups to analyze their version of the digital comic by using the provided analytical template. Dialogic instruction and practices (Rigell & Banack, this volume) can be leveraged here. If the groups are larger, split the groups into smaller groups, split the digital comic into parts, and allow each group of students to analyze a portion of the comic. After analyzing their digital comics, they will discuss and decide how their version of the comic was impacted by the various forms of film analysis. This information can be recorded on a chart paper (see Table 1.1) to share with the class.

**TABLE 1.1** Group Chart Paper Template for Film Analysis Group Discussions

|  |  |
|---|---|
| *Overwatch: McCree's Train Ride* |  |
| *Digital Immigrant / Guided View / Motion Book* |  |
| *Film Analysis* |  |
| Group predictions: |  |
| Narrative and Form: | How it affected me: |
|  | How it affected the story: |
| Mis-en-scéne: | How it affected me: |
|  | How it affected the story: |
| Cinematography: | How it affected me: |
|  | How it affected the story: |
| Editing: | How it affected me: |
|  | How it affected the story: |
| Sound: | How it affected me: |
|  | How it affected the story: |
| Conclusions: |  |

Finally, each group will then present their findings to the class. Using the group presentations as a jumping off point, the class will discuss how each version of the comic altered the form and style. In guiding the discussion of the class, have the students considered the choices creators made and how those choices are similar to those made by directors in drama/film. Some guiding questions to consider:

- How did mise-en-scéne change the impact of various scenes across the digital comics? Was it more effective for one form than the other?
- In making editing decisions, what were some considerations that were taken across the digital comics? How did the version of the comic impact those decisions?
- Did the use of sound add to or takeaway from the narrative?
- How might the narrative be enacted differently in a film format?

## Final Thoughts

In this lesson, students engage with one analytical lens to aid them in understanding different digital comics formats. This allows them to see the similarities and differences in the formats as well as consider the relationship between films and other media. From here, the teacher and students can explore other analytical lenses to see what they reveal about digital comics. The second lesson demonstrates how to build on this momentum.

### Comparing & Contrasting Digital Forms

In this lesson, students compare and contrast three different comic forms (i.e., DI, GV, and MB) using three different lenses (i.e., social semiotics, film analysis, and game studies). The analysis of these comics using different analytical lenses will lead students to think critically about the features of different media formats, how these affect meaning, and their experience while reading. This is a multiple-part lesson that may span more than one day. The lesson below incorporates cooperative learning strategies (Slavin, 1980).

### Standard

- CCSS.ELA-LITERACY.RL.7.7: Compare and contrast a written story, drama, or poem to its audio, filmed, staged, or multimedia version, analyzing the effects of techniques unique to each medium (e.g., lighting, sound, color, or camera focus and angles in a film) (English Language Arts Standards, n.d.).

### Resources/Preparation

For this lesson, teachers will need:

- tablets/computers
- access to and accounts for the Comixology and Madefire applications
- *Transformers: Autocracy* Issue 1 in DI, GV, and MB forms
- digital or physical copies analytical templates for each lens (see Appendixes A, B, and C); students will need one template per page in the comic book
- large chart paper (2 per group) and markers

### Instructional Plan

Begin the lesson by reviewing the different digital comics types students will analyze including digital immigrant, guided view, and motion book. Use examples in order to demonstrate the varied forms as well as available features. Introduce the vocabulary for each lens that students will need to know in order to conduct their analysis.

Place students in groups of 3-5. Assign each group a different digital comics format (e.g., DI, GV, MB) of *Transformers: Autocracy*. Give each group copies of a different analytical tool so that each group uses a different analytical lens (e.g., social semiotics, game studies, and film studies) in their analysis. Each student should receive multiple copies of the tool—one per page within the comic. Ensure that groups using the same analytical lens are assigned different digital formats to analyze. Ideally, since there are three lenses and three types of digital

**TABLE 1.2** Chart Paper Template for Group Discussions in Compare and Contrast
Lesson

| *Transformers: Autocracy*<br>*(Digital Comics Type)*<br>*(Analytical Lens)* | |
|---|---|
| Group predictions: | |
| Feature 1: | How it affected me: |
| | How it affected the story: |
| Feature 2: | How it affected me: |
| | How it affected the story: |
| Feature 3: | How it affected me: |
| | How it affected the story: |
| Conclusions: | |

comics, there should be nine groups. For example, there should be three groups conducting a film analysis with one group assigned the DI comic, and the others assigned the GV and the MB. This allows every group to look at a different comic through a different lens.

Before starting their analysis, ask groups to briefly discuss and record predictions on chart paper for the comic form they received such as what features will be present in the comic and how those features will affect their reading. Then, have groups read their digital comic, pausing at the end of each page to fill out the analytical tool. Students will fill out one analytical tool per page (Table 1.2).

Once groups have read and analyzed all the pages of their assigned digital comic, ask groups to use chart paper to record noticeable features of the digital comic and how the features, or absence of a feature, affected their reading or interpretation of the story. Students should refer their analytical notes to create this chart. Each group will complete one chart paper together. The sample in Table 1.2 can be adjusted for difficulty or detail based on student needs.

After groups are finished creating their charts, have groups present their charts and findings to the class. Give groups opportunities to show examples from their comics to illustrate their points. Provide time for questions and clarifications as needed.

Finally, to wrap up the lesson, facilitate a class discussion in the manner that best fits your students' needs and class size. Some possible guiding questions include:

- What did other groups notice that you did not?
- How were comics formats similar/different?
- Did different lenses help different groups notice different features?
- What features were most helpful for you as a reader?
- Which features were distracting or hindered you as a reader?
- How do these features apply to the real world?
- Where else have you seen similar features?

*Final Thoughts*

By the end of this lesson, students will have analyzed one comic book form with one analytical tool. They will have learned from their classmates what could be seen in different comic versions using different analytical lenses. This lesson can be replicated and adjusted for other comics and comic forms. This will allow groups to experience these different forms and use varied lenses for new perspectives each time. Further, for a repeated reading strategy, all three comic forms can be read by each group and analyzed by a different version of the analytical tool (Samuels, 1997).

This lesson can also be extended to other forms of media. The digital comics used in this lesson utilize features found in other media that students encounter on a daily basis. Bringing these other texts into the classroom to compare and contrast with digital comics through a similar analytical process allows students to learn how to identify features they encounter and how those features affect their interpretations of media outside of school.

## Conclusion

This chapter has focused on how different theoretical lenses can be applied by students to help them understand digital comics. While this chapter has concentrated on English Language Arts contexts, we see opportunities for educators in other content areas to employ these lenses for analyzing digital and multimodal texts. Social studies teachers might ask students to apply these lenses to the analysis of documentary films, and science teachers might ask students to consider how these lenses help them understand the dissemination of scientific information for public consumption. Outside of schools, students can apply these lenses to the media that they engage with on a daily basis providing them with tools to be more critical consumers and citizens.

Today, communicative and literacy practices and texts are not only multimodal in nature but are also visually dominant relying heavily on visual images to convey possible meanings (Kress, 2003; Serafini, 2012, 2015b). Digital platforms and text, in particular, provide new and different ways of communicating that have the potential to significantly alter the transaction between readers and texts (Serafini, 2014, 2015a). As such, teachers—and readers—need different lenses for analyzing digital texts and developing pedagogy around them (Serafini, 2015a). The theoretical lenses discussed and the lessons outlined in this chapter offer teachers and their students a starting point for analyzing and understanding digital comics and other digital media.

# APPENDIX A: FILM ANALYSIS TOOL

Note: Due to space constraints, we have not organized this tool in handout form. We recommend that for each section of the tool/set of guiding questions students record their notes or observations about a feature in one column and the possible meanings or implications about a feature in another column.

## Text/Source Information

Title:
Page #:

## Narrative & Form Guiding Questions

Story/Plot/Time
*   What is the timeline of the story? Is it chronological or are there flashbacks or flashforwards? Does time change (e.g., speed up, slow down, etc.)? Are there cause and effects present in the story? Do we see the same event happen multiple times?

Narration/POV
*   Who is the narrator or storyteller? What POVs are present? Is there only one or are there multiple POVs? Who knows what when?

Patterns/Structures
*   What patterns occur in the plot or on the page (e.g., parallel events or images, similar events or images, or repetitions?

## Style Analysis—Mise-en-Scéne

Setting
*   What is the setting of the page or panels? How does the setting contribute to mood or tone?

Costume
*   What costumes or clothes do characters wear? What do the costumes or clothes tell you about the time period or the characters?

Lighting
*   What is brightly lit or shadowed? What lighting colors are used? Is the lighting warm or cold?

Staging
*   How are objects and characters arranged on the page or in the panels?

## Style Analysis—Cinematography

Tone
- What is the visual contrast (e.g., dark vs. light) between objects/characters on the page in the panels?

Framing
- What is the shape of the panel? Is the viewer above, below, or to the side? How "far away" is the viewer from the subject of the panel? What affects do these features create?

## Style Analysis—Editing

Edit
- What types of edits (e.g., fade, wipe, cut, dissolve, etc.) are used?

Shot Variation
- What types of shots (e.g., close up, wide shot, medium shot, etc.) are used? Is there a lot or a little variation?

## Style Analysis—Sound

Perception
- How loud are the sounds?

Dimension
- Is there a rhythm to the sound sequence? Does it align with the images?

Space
- Are the sounds part of the action or not? Are the sounds "off-screen" or "on-screen"? Are the sounds linked to a particular character's POV?

Time
- Do the sounds happen at the same time? Does the sound connect one scene to the other?

# APPENDIX B: SOCIAL SEMIOTIC ANALYSIS TOOL

*Note: Due to space constraints, we have not organized this tool in handout form. We recommend that for each section of the tool/set of guiding questions students record their notes or observations about a feature in one column and the possible meanings or implications about a feature in another column.

## Compositional Analysis

Composition/Location/Framing
- Are any design elements framed? How are they framed (e.g., lines, shapes, colors, etc.)? What objects/characters are located at the top, bottom, left, right, center, or periphery of the panel(s)?

Text
- Where is text located in the panel(s)? What size/color is the text? What kind of font is used (e.g., serif/san serif)? Are there multiple fonts?

Salience
- What stands out in the panel(s) or the page? How is it made to standout (e.g., color, size, location, etc.)?

## Ideational Analysis

Setting/Objects
- What is the setting on the page or in the panels? Is the setting realistic (i.e., you can tell what it is) or abstract (i.e., a solid color or pattern)? Do certain objects stand out or play a central role?

Characters/Actions
- Who is included on the page or in the panels? What roles do they play? How are they posed or positioned? What actions are they engaged in?

Vectors
- What vectors (i.e., invisible lines) are on the page or in the panels? What do the vectors connect or divide?

## Interpersonal Analysis

Gaze
- Do the characters look at (i.e., demand gaze) or away from (i.e., offer gaze) the viewer? Are there panels where a particular gaze stands out?

Angle of Interaction
- Is the viewer positioned above, below, or on an equal level with the character(s)? Are there panels where a particular positioning stands out?

Interpersonal Distance
- How close or far is the viewer from the character(s)? Are there panels where this distance stands out?

# APPENDIX C: GAME STUDIES TOOL

*Note: Due to space constraints, we have not organized this tool in handout form. We recommend that for each section of the tool/set of guiding questions students record their notes or observations about a feature in one column and the possible meanings or implications about a feature in another column.

## Music Analysis

Sound Effects/Noises
- What non-musical sound effects are included on the page? Do they align with the movement or motion on the page? Do they sound real?

Instruments
- What instruments or voices are included on the page? Do the instruments align with what is happening on the page?

Tone/Attitude/Mood
- Is the tone happy, sad, scary, or something else? Does the tone change throughout the page or per click? Is the tone impacted by the sounds, the picture, the words, or a combination of these things?

Tempo/Speed
- Is the music fast, slow, or in the middle? Does the speed change? Does the speed align with the actions or the tone?

Believability
- Are the sounds present on the page believable? Do they make sense? Why?

Changes in Sound
- Does the sound loop (i.e., repeat itself over and over again)? Does just the music loop or do sound effects loop also? How often does this happen? Does the reader have control over any of the sounds?

Stop/Start/Change
- How do the music and/or sound effects transition or change as pages or panels are progressed?

## Interaction Analysis

- How do you participate with what is on the page (e.g., do you read, listen, touch, etc.)?
- How well do the features on the page work? Do you understand what the features need you to do or what are they are meant to do? Does anything not work properly?

- Does the comic direct you to interact with the world outside of the story? Does anything link you to another place/website or tell you to go somewhere else? How do you find out additional information?
- How can you participate in fan culture related to the story (e.g., websites, fan art, fanfiction, etc.)?

## References

Aguilera, E., Kachorsky, D., Gee, E., & Serafini, F. (2016). Expanding analytical perspectives on children's picturebook Apps. *Literacy Research: Theory, Method, and Practice*. https://doi.org/10.1177/2381336916661516.

Bazalgette, C., & Buckingham, D. (2013). Literacy, media and multimodality: A critical response. *Literacy Discussion*, *47*(2), 95–102. https://doi.org/10.1111/j.1741-4369.2012.00666.x

Bellanca, J., & Brandt, R. (Eds.). (2010). *21st Century skills: Rethinking how students learn*. Solution Tree Press.

Bordwell, D., & Thompson, K. (2013). *Film art: An introduction* (10th ed.). McGraw Hill Education.

Bordwell, D., Thompson, K., & Smith, J. (1993). *Film art: An introduction* (7th ed.). McGraw-Hill.

Brenna, B. (2013). How graphic novels support reading comprehension strategy development in children. *Literacy*, *47*(2), 88–94.

Brooks, R. (2016). *Overwatch: McCree Train Hopper*. Blizzard Entertainment.

Chase, M., Son, E. H., & Steiner, S. (2014). Sequencing and graphic novels with primary-grade students. *The Reading Teacher*, *67*(6), 435–443. https://doi.org/10.1002/trtr.1242.

Collins, K. (2008). *Game sound: an introduction to the history, theory, and practice of video game music and sound design*. MIT Press.

Collins, K. (2013). *Playing with sound: A theory of interacting with sound and music in video games*. MIT Press.

Cook, K. (2013). *My Little Pony: Friendship is magic* (Vol. 1). IDW Publishing.

Cope, B., & Kalantzis, M. (2000). *Multiliteracies: Literacy learning and the design of social futures*. Routledge.

Dallacqua, A. K., & Sutton, D. (2014). Critical discussion: Using Satrapi's Persepolis with high school language arts students. *ALAN Review*, *41*(3), 33–49. http://scholar.lib.vt.edu/ejournals/ALAN/v41n3/dallacqua.html.

Duncum, P. (2001). Visual culture: Developments, definitions, and directions for art education. *Studies in Art Education*, *42*(2), 101–112. https://doi.org/10.2307/1321027.

English language Arts standards: "Reading: Literature" Grade 7. (n.d.). Retrieved March 31, 2021, from http://www.corestandards.org/ELA-Literacy/RL/7/

English language arts standards: "Reading: Literature" Grade 8. (n.d.). Retrieved March 31, 2021, from http://www.corestandards.org/ELA-Literacy/RL/8/

Gavigan, K. (2011). More powerful than a locomotive: Using graphic novels to motivate struggling male adolescent readers. *Journal of Research on Libraries and Young Adults*, *1*(3), 7–8.

Gee, J. (1991). Socio-cultural approaches to literacy (literacies). *Annual Review of Applied Linguistics*, *12*, 31–48. https://doi.org/10.1017/S0267190500002130.

Gee, J. P. (1989). What is literacy? *Journal of Education*, *171*(1), 18–25.

Geiger, J., & Rutsky, R. L. (Eds.). (2013). *Film analysis: A Norton reader* (2nd ed.). W. W. Norton & Company.

Halliday, M. A. K. (1978). *Language as social semiotic: The social interpretation of language and meaning*. University Park Press.

Hicks, T. (2009). *The digital writing workshop*. Heineman.

Hosler, J., & Boomer, K. B. (2011). Are comic books an effective way to engage nonmajors in learning and appreciating science? *CBE-Life Sciences Education*, *10*(3), 309–317. https://doi.org/10.1187/cbe.10-07-0090

Jennings, K. A., Rule, A. C., & Vander Zanden, S. M. (2014). Fifth graders' enjoyment, interest, and comprehension of graphic novels: Compared to heavily-illustrated and traditional novels. *International Electronic Journal of Elementary Education*, *6*(2), 257–274.

Jiménez, L. M., & Meyer, C. K. (2016). First impressions matter: Navigating graphic novels using linguistic, visual, and spatial resources. *Journal of Literacy Research*, *48*(4), 423–447. https://doi.org/10.1177/1086296X16677955.

Kaae, J. (2008). Theoretical approaches to composing dynamic music for video games. In K. Collins (Ed.), *From Pac-man to pop music interactive audio in games and new media* (pp. 75–91). Routledge.

Kachorsky, D. (in press). Digital children's literature: Current understandings and future directions. In K. Coats, V. Yenika-Agbaw, & D. Stevenson (Eds.), *The Blackwell companion to children's literature*. Blackwell.

Kachorsky, D., Reid, S. F., & Chapman, K. (2020). Education through TIME: Representations of U.S. education on TIME magazine covers. *AERA Open*, *6*(3), 2332858420961110. https://doi.org/10.1177/2332858420961110

Knobel, M., & Lankshear, C. (2014). Studying new literacies. *Journal of Adolescent & Adult Literacy*, *58*(2), 97–101.

Kress, G. (2003). *Literacy in the new media age*. Routledge.

Kress, G. (2009). What is mode? In C. Jewitt (Ed.), *The Routledge handbook of multimodal analysis* (pp. 54–67). Routledge.

Kress, G. (2010). *Multimodality: A social semiotic approach to contemporary communication*, Routledge.

Kress, G., & van Leeuwen, T. (2006). *Reading images: The grammar of visual design* (2nd ed.). Routledge.

Lankshear, C., & Knobel, M. (2006). Sampling "the New" in New Literacies. In M. Knobel & C. Lankshear (Eds.), *A New Literacies sampler* (pp. 1–24). Peter Lang Publishing, Inc.

Lin, S.-F., & Lin, H.-S. (2016). Learning nanotechnology with texts and comics: the impacts on students of different achievement levels. *International Journal of Science Education*, *38*(8), 1373–1391. https://doi.org/10.1080/09500693.2016.1191089.

Low, D. E. (2012). "Spaces invested with content": Crossing the "gaps" in comics with readers in schools. *Children's Literature in Education*, *43*(4), 368–385. https://doi.org/10.1007/s10583-012-9172-5.

Low, D. E. (2015). *Comics as a medium for inquiry: Urban students (re-) designing critical social worlds*. University of Pennsylvania.

Luke, A. (1995). When basic skills and information processing just aren't enough: Rethinking reading in new times. *Teachers College Record*, *97*(1), 95–115.

Martinez-Roldan, C. M., & Newcomer, S. (2011). "Reading between the pictures": Immigrant students' interpretations of *The Arrival*. *Language Arts*, *88*(3), 188–197.

Metzen, C., & Dille, F. (2013). *Transformers: Autocracy: Episode 1* (J. Barber & C. Guzman (Eds.)). IDW Publishing.

Meyer, C. K., & Jiménez, L. M. (2017). Using every word and wmage: Framing graphic novel instruction in the expanded Four Resources Model. *Journal of Adolescent & Adult Literacy*, *61*(2), 153–161. https://doi.org/10.1002/jaal.666.

Paligaro, M. (2014). Is a picture worth a thousand words? Determining the criteria for graphic novels with literary merit. *English Journal*, *103*(4), 31–45.

Rose, G. (2016). *Visual methodologies: An introduction to researching with visual materials* (3rd ed.). Sage Publications.

Salen, K., & Zimmerman, E. (2003). *The rules of play: Game design fundamentals*. MIT Press.

Samuels, S. J. (1997). The method of repeated readings. *The Reading Teacher*, *50*(5), 376–381.

Serafini, F. (2012). Expanding the four resources model: Reading visual and multi-modal texts. *Pedagogies*, *7*(2), 150–164.

Serafini, F. (2014). *Reading the visual: An introduction to teaching multimodal literacy*. Teachers College Press.

Serafini, F. (2015a). Paths to interpretation: Developing students' interpretive repertoires. *Language and Literacy*, *17*(3), 118–133.

Serafini, F. (2015b). *Reading workshop 2.0: Supporting readers in the digital age*. Heinemann.

Serafini, F., & Youngs, S. (2013). Reading workshop 2.0: Children's literature in a digital age. *The Reading Teacher*, *66*(5), 401–404. https://doi.org/10.1002/TRTR.1141

Short, K. G. (2018). What's trending in children's literature and why it matters. *Language Arts*, *95*(5), 287–298.

Sipe, L. R., & Brightman, A. E. (2009). Young children's interpretations of page breaks in contemporary picture storybooks. *Journal of Literacy Research*, *41*(1), 68–103. https://doi.org/10.1080/10862960802695214

Slavin, R. E. (1980). Cooperative learning. *Review of Educational Research*, *50*(2), 315–342.

Slater, W. H., & Horstman, F. R. (2003). Teaching reading and writing to struggling middle school and high school students: the case for reciprocal teaching. *Preventing School Failure: Alternative Education for Children and Youth*, *46*(4), 163–166.

Stichnothe, H. (2014). Engineering stories? A narratological approach to children's book apps. *Barnelitterært forskningstidsskrift/Nordic Journal of ChildLit Aesthetics*, *5*(1), 1–9. https://doi.org/10.3402/blft.v5.23602

Sutton-Smith, B. (1986). *Toys as culture*. Gardner Press, Inc.

Yokota, J., & Teale, W. H. (2014). Picture books and the digital World. *The Reading Teacher*, *67*(8), 577–585. https://doi.org/10.1002/trtr.1262

# 2

# STUDENT VOICE IS POWER

## Incorporating Critical Witness and Testimony in Middle-School Classrooms

*Rachelle S. Savitz and Daniel Stockwell*

Most adults reflect on their middle-school years with a sense of relief. Smiling and shaking their heads that somehow, they made it through those trying years. Of course, middle-school was not a bad time for all. Still, many adults agree that their middle-school years stand out in their minds as particularly difficult. Current middle-school students across the United States are experiencing these typically turbulent times under especially severe circumstances. They have experienced school closures and changing learning environments continuously as the COVID-19 pandemic has taken so many lives here in the United States and globally. These students have lost and grieved loved ones to COVID and learned how to function in new surroundings and situations. Many have experienced difficulties keeping up with their schoolwork because of inequitable and challenging conditions, such as lack of the Internet or electricity. As we know from multiple media sources, including an article published by the New York Times Magazine (Oppel et al., 2020), the pandemic has disproportionately affected Black, indigenous, and Latinx communities because of systemic inequities.

At the same time as the current pandemic, students and teachers across the United States were becoming more aware of systemic racism at the education and institutional level with the brutal murders of Breonna Taylor and George Floyd. This national attention led to many people of all ages protesting police brutality and the then-President of the United States' inappropriate quips and comments related to BIPOC, calling anyone advocating for social justice and racial equity "thugs." During the summer of 2020, racialized middle-school students listened to narratives and tirades on mainstream media networks, talk radio, and Twitter that dehumanized them, their families, and their communities. And then, the assault on the United States Capitol on January 6 demonstrated to so many that bullying and racism were deemed okay and acceptable. On that day,

DOI: 10.4324/9781003171508-3

a mob consisting of primarily White men used violence to try and overturn the election results; the mob's actions communicated to all middle-school students across the nation that a sizable population in the United States does not value or recognize all of humanity.

These are just some of the headline issues that are impacting the lives, minds, and hearts of middle-school students across the nation. Middle-schoolers in the United States are dealing with the loss of a loved one, the imprisonment of a relative, or bullying in school. Many students are experiencing homelessness, poverty, and hunger. Parents and guardians of middle-schools are experiencing unemployment and uncertainty about how to pay next month's rent. Middle-school students often experience stress, heartache, and pain that potentially goes unnoticed. No list of traumas middle-school students in the US experience can be definitive, and more students experience trauma than is often acknowledged. Sadly, trauma is the "norm rather than the exception" for students (Fisher et al., 2020, p. 4).

Traumas that can damage healthy development are called Adverse Childhood Experiences (ACEs; Finkelhor, 2020). ACEs include (a) emotional, physical, or sexual abuse; (b) emotional or physical neglect; and (c) household challenges (e.g., substance abuse, violence, divorce, illegal activity; Centers for Disease Control and Prevention, 2020). According to the 2017–2018 National Survey of Children's Health, one of every three children between birth and age 17 had at least one ACE, and 14.1% had two or more ACEs in the past year. Another alarming fact is how trauma is related to demographics. This same survey reported that 22% of children whose family income falls below the federal poverty level experienced two or more ACEs, whereas only 7.3% of children whose family income is four times the federal poverty level experienced two or more ACEs. Race is also an influence, with a more significant percentage of non-Hispanic Black children experiencing two or more ACEs than non-Hispanic White children (21.3% vs. 12.9%). As Craig (2017) states, "those marginalized by race, sexual orientation, disability, poverty, or immigration status" are especially vulnerable (p. 5).

We know that the most frequent types of trauma reported by 361 school counselors were "major upheaval between parents, including domestic violence, separation, and divorce; the death of a close friend or family member; and emotional abuse," and more of these types of trauma were reported to have occurred in Title I schools (Rumsey et al., 2020). This aligns with what Meyers (2014) found, with the most common trauma experienced by children and adolescents being chronic and/or systemic acts of violence that repeatedly occur within the home or community. Findings like this are important for all educators to understand that, sadly, childhood exposure to trauma is correlated with an increased likelihood of adverse health consequences in adulthood (Fisher et al., 2020). Unfortunately, we must understand that students come to middle-school with hearts, minds, and bodies that have experienced trauma (Dutro, 2019).

These recent issues, and the countless others middle-school students are currently facing, reveal the urgent need for using critical literacy in middle-school English language arts (ELA) classrooms, as ELA classrooms are crucial contexts for dealing with the complexities of trauma (Dutro, 2019). Because teaching critical literacy involves challenging inequitable systems and addressing situations and issues that may relate to traumatic experiences students are facing, this chapter will make clear the connection between critical literacy theory and practice relevant for middle-school educators in the use of teaching "taboo" topics to address trauma with students (Ayers & Ayers, 2014; Dutro, 2019). To do this, teachers must understand that while standards and traditional content, such as classic literature, maybe the preferred route for teaching, instruction also needs to include consideration of students' lived experiences and how they are facing adversity so that they can be better prepared for the challenges and choices they have or will face throughout schooling and beyond (Frey et al., 2019; Fisher et al., 2020).

## Theoretical Framework

Critical literacy instruction in schools today builds on the work of Paulo Freire (1989), who taught adults to read as a means of empowering them (Vasquez et al., 2019). Freire's work demonstrated that critical literacy instruction could be a "way of making visible and examining relations of power in order to change and dismantle inequitable ways of being" (Vasquez et al., 2019, p. 301). For example, critical literacy instruction explores how and why certain political and social groups have more access to power and wealth than others (Bishop, 2014). Critical literacy requires posing challenging questions, like "what is 'truth'? How is it presented and represented, by whom, and in whose interests? Who should have access to which images and words, texts, and discourses? For what purposes?" (Luke, 2012, p. 4). Critical literacy encourages students to ask about the author's position of a text and how it positions the readers (Janks, 2005). Does the author position the text as fact when it is opinion? Does the text position the reader as an active-thinker or simply a passive consumer? Questions like this help students become aware of how texts are "positioned and positioning" (Janks, 2005, p. 97). Students are also encouraged to question how reality is presented in the texts they read and who benefits from such depictions (Bishop, 2014).

Because critical literacy interrogates texts and the systems of power in which the texts were produced, critical literacy involves problem posing. Such instruction also aims to help students see themselves as agents of change who can challenge current injustices and work toward creating a more socially just world (Bishop, 2014; Luke, 2012). Janks (2010) argued engaging students in critical literacy is about helping them gain "access to and facility with the language and literacy tools they need to be both critical and creative, problem posers and problem solvers, social analysts and social agents" (p. 23).

Synthesizing years of work on critical literacy, Bishop (2014) identified five essential aspects of critical literacy instruction:

> (a) mobilizing learners as social actors with knowledge and skills to disrupt the commonplace; (b) conducting research, analysis, and interrogation of multiple viewpoints on an issue; (c) identifying issues focused on socio-political realities in the context of the lives of the learners; (d) designing and undertaking actions focused on social justice outside of the classroom; and (e) reflecting upon actions taken and creating vision(s) for future project(s).
>
> (p. 55)

In other words, critical literacy instruction can create opportunities "to support student healing by providing spaces for students to have a voice and action" (Fisher et al., 2020, p. 113).

In ELA classrooms, through the examination and analysis of texts, students are engaged in questioning author intent and biases, missing perspectives, assessing trustworthiness, and determining how texts marginalize and disempower people (Applebee & Langer, 2013; Bishop, 2014; Vasquez et al., 2019). When engaging students in critical literacy, "students are likely to ask questions that some people prefer they not ask about topics that some people prefer they not address" (Borsheim & Petrone, 2006, p. 82). If middle-school teachers, especially ELA teachers, are to help their students identify injustices and societal problems so they can make this world a better place for themselves, their families, their communities, and, as a result, a better world for all, teachers will need to be prepared to teach the "taboo" (Ayers & Ayers, 2014).

## Teaching The "Taboo"

For students to take action toward social justice, they need to have agency and believe that they can accomplish something. However, students experiencing trauma often lack or have a limited sense of agency (Fisher et al., 2020), needing support from adult role models and peers to recover their sense of agency. Because emotions and stress can negatively impact learning, teachers must teach the whole student and have a "wider view" of learning (Frey et al., 2019, p. 5). "Academic" learning is not enough to prepare students for the inequities and unjust systems they face within and outside of schools (Frey et al., 2019). Many practitioners and researchers have recognized and posited the vast benefits of using literature to not only promote the development of student self-efficacy or their beliefs about their abilities to accomplish a task or goal (Bandura, 1977) but also for students to develop empathy, understand their pre-existing beliefs and assumptions, and learn from others' perspectives (Fisher et al., 2020; Ivey

& Johnston, 2013, 2018; Mirra, 2018; Turner & Reed, 2018). Helping students in this way will impact how they see themselves and their attributes and talents compared to others (i.e., their identities; Frey et al., 2019).

Teaching the "taboo" is about constructing school and classroom experiences "on a base of fearless and relentless inquiry" (Ayers & Ayers, 2014, p. 2). In part, it is about asking *why?* Why is it that the language many Black Americans speak is considered "incorrect" or "non-standard" English (see Baker-Bell, 2020)? Why are migrant children being held in government shelters across the nation? Why is standardized testing culturally biased, and how does it perpetuate myths about personal responsibility and achievement (see Ayers & Ayers, 2014)? Why do people refuse to acknowledge that White privilege exists? Why do people censor books when they go against their political or religious beliefs? Why isn't more done to assist students and families facing hard times or homelessness? Why isn't there a better way for students to talk and share about violence in their communities? How can students influence change related to homelessness and violence? And ultimately, why do we not talk about adversity, hardships, and traumatic experiences in our classrooms?

If teachers encourage their middle-school students to be critical problem posers (Janks, 2010), these students very well might ask these questions (or, deeper, more personal ones). Their questions might bring up "taboo" topics like sex and sexuality, including rape culture and teen pregnancy; the socially constructed nature of race and the racism this engenders (see Delgado & Stefancic, 2017), including White privilege and White supremacy; social injustice and inequities created by classist, sexist, racist systems; and other issues that many parents, administrators, and school board members might wish were left unexamined in classrooms. Teachers and students may also need to discuss what trauma is, how many students are impacted by traumatic experiences such as domestic violence and bullying, and then learn ways to address, deal with, cope, and dismantle the situation. It is only through honest, fearless inquiry, though, that students can disrupt long-lasting injustices so that they can see themselves "as powerful authors of their own narratives" (Ayers & Ayers, 2014, p. 38).

Teaching the "taboo," then, is about engaging students in educational experiences that help them see the value they bring to the classroom and help them realize their agency (Frey et al., 2019). Teaching the "taboo" is a pedagogical practice that involves students in the "struggle toward an education that honors and extends the languages and literacies and practices of our students and communities in the project of social and cultural justice" (Paris, 2012, p. 96). Teaching the "taboo" is about "seeing students as whole human beings with hearts and minds, bodies and spirits" (Ayers & Ayers, 2014, p. 125). Teaching the "taboo" understands that students need authenticity by welcoming their stories and encouraging discussion and questioning (Beckelhimer, 2017; Collins, 2017).

### Testimony and Critical Witness

Unfortunately, as has been mentioned, trauma is the norm and not the exception. Racialized and minoritized students are labeled and tracked and receive inequitable educational services, and they are unfairly referred to the administration for "behavior issues." Bullying happens in the hallways, bathrooms, and classrooms and continues on the Internet between school hours. School shootings and other forms of violence impact students' lived experiences at home and in their communities. Often, and sadly, students do not share their experiences or seek support from adult role models when at school. Many students feel a sense of powerlessness, often accompanied by feelings of shame, humiliation, betrayal, and a "concern that adults will think less of them" if they disclose what happened (Craig, 2017, p. 48). Instead of feeling silenced, these students need to know that the teachers in their lives care about their academic achievement and their well-being. While teachers are not licensed mental health counselors, they can provide means for all students to feel safe, a sense of belonging, and part of the classroom community. Therefore, educators must engage their students in critical literacy instruction that creates space for testimony and critical witness (Dutro, 2019).

Dutro (2019) views testimony as "attesting to an experience" (p. 22) and witnessing as experiencing others' lives. Dutro argued that testimony and critical witness are essential aspects of ELA classrooms because these classrooms' activities allow for sharing and learning about others' experiences. To encourage students to share their testimonies, Dutro recommends that teachers first model vulnerability by sharing their testimonies with students to create a space of reciprocal sharing and witnessing by inviting students to share their testimonies. Witnessing becomes critical, according to Dutro, when the witnesses take steps "to advocate for students and work toward social justice" (p. 24). As will be further developed in Rigell and Banack's chapter on the power of dialogic discussion, this reciprocal process invites students to begin sharing their lived experiences and perspectives.

In addition to sharing their testimonies, teachers can create space for critical witnessing through literature, understanding that literature is a "means to address emotional needs of students" and as a tool for healing (Fisher et al., 2020, p. 46). Pieces of literature can operate as mirrors, allowing readers to see and learn more about themselves, and as windows, allowing readers to see and learn about others (Bishop, 1990). Because literature can enable readers to see themselves and others in what they read, if teachers are intentional about the mentor texts they select and share with students, reading can be part of the testimony and critical witness. Fisher et al. (2020) stated, "confronting traumatic events through literature, both fiction and nonfiction, aids children and adolescents in processing trauma and creating a narrative space where such experiences can be discussed" (p. 59). When teachers intentionally select diverse literature with the potential to offer students mirrors and windows, they create spaces that allow students to share their testimonies and to be critical witnesses.

While some teachers might be uncomfortable with creating space for students to share their experiences with trauma, based on this being a new experience such as is mentioned in Stephanie Reid's chapter documenting a teacher's journey and experiences of guilt and vulnerability when teaching something new, especially if the trauma stems from "taboo" topics, teachers who want to partner with their students in a mission to transform the world with love and courage will find themselves "in the land of the taboo" (Ayers & Ayers, 2014, p. 7). Teachers need to be critical witnesses for their students, but their students can also be critical witnesses for each other. They, too, can take steps to work toward social justice, especially if their teachers engage them in critical literacy pedagogy.

## Theory into Practice

As you read, you may be asking yourself, "How do I begin?" Therefore, we will walk through our steps to begin this much-needed process, providing examples with two different middle-grade appropriate novels. After, we will share an example used by one of the teachers with whom we work, providing her interpretation of inviting students to share their lives with the class read of *Dopesick* (2010) by Walter Dean Myers. It is important to understand that our examples are what either a teacher or we might say to start the reciprocal process. While we share these examples, they are not the only options, and they may not be perfect for you and your classroom, as many factors come into play when incorporating these types of conversations in the classrooms. Importantly, each teacher must consider their student population and the trust built through solid teacher and student and peer relationships (Fisher et al., 2020). We must keep in mind the overarching goal of normalizing conversations and dialogue around trauma, adversity, and student hardships that students are experiencing and *how it* is not for us to judge. When experiencing trauma, there isn't a hierarchy of which experience is more traumatic.

### Choosing Books

The first step is to identify a book used as a whole-class novel or books to be used in student literature circles. While we advocate for the type of collaboration and dialogue that occurs during literature circles over a whole-class novel, we also believe that expectations, norms, and modeling of these discussions are needed before students work only with their peers. Therefore, we advocate for the use of literature circles when the teacher feels confident in students' ability to have respectful, in-depth, and supportive conversations.

Literature circles are helpful as they promote student choice in choosing a book based on their interest or personal connections (Daniels & Steineke, 2004). The teacher may want to use a book pass to encourage students to look at all available options (Beers, 2003; Miller, 2009, 2014). Here, desks are arranged in small pods of between 4 and 6 desks with one copy of each of the 7–10 choice books placed at each pod. Students are given between 3 and 5 minutes to read the covers and skim the book, noting interest after the designated time is up for scanning that book. Depending on the teacher's system, the student can include a number ranking, decide between 1 and 5, allow the student to identify multiple books they would like to read and require the student to provide comments to explain the said notation. The comments will enable the teacher to understand the choice better and get to know the student's interests a little more and determine if the reason was merely that the student already read that particular book or saw the movie version.

An additional benefit to choice is that literature circles promote student accountability and active engagement as all are part of the learning process. Students can be assigned or choose various roles or tasks to accomplish during their designated time (Daniels & Steineke, 2004). Students can read during class so that group members can share, reflect, connect, ask questions, and provide support to one another in-the-moment. Or students can silently read and stop at their group designated spots to engage in conversation. All the options are possible, along with many more. But again, we highly encourage either using a whole-class novel or short story first to allow students to grapple with new expectations, challenges, and types of dialogue. This also promotes space for students to develop a sense of belonging, trust, safety, and support from one another and the classroom environment.

We would be remiss if we did not emphasize that modeling difficult conversations or co-constructing expectations does not mean that conversation will always be on track or helpful, even with established norms. The teacher must constantly be circulating the room and listening in to offer additional advice and suggestions. The class should have already negotiated an "out plan" where students know what to do if they feel uncomfortable, do not want to engage, or need a few moments of space away from the group.

As many excellent middle-grade novels can be used, we suggest that the teacher peruses some favorites and some newly published novels, including staying up to date with current award lists. There are many ways to search for these lists, but a few that we recommend are The International Literacy Association children's choices, teachers' choices, and young adults' choices (literacyworldwide.org/get-resources/reading-lists); the Schneider Family Book Award (ala.org/awards-grants/schneider-family-book-award); Coretta Scott King Book Award (ala.org/rt/emiert/cskbookawards); Award for Excellence in Nonfiction for Young Adults (ala.org/yalsa/); as well as the various *Build Your Stack* blog posts published by the National Council of Teachers of English, to build teacher knowledge and book choices related to different topics, such as race, grief, and compassion (www2.ncte.org/blog/category/booklists/).

### Setting the Stage and Sharing Vulnerability

We use two very different books to share examples from a teacher's perspective of how to share vulnerability and invite students to not only bear critical witness but share their testimonies (See Table 2.1 for additional book information).

### Closer to Nowhere

We know that many students may not fully understand how others deal with and cope with trauma, such as loss. This novel expertly allows the class to consider how assumptions can lead to feelings of isolation and other traumatic experiences. For instance, Hannah only wants her life to go back to normal, not attempting to understand why her cousin Cal is constantly playing pranks on her or using sarcasm to deflect during conversations. Hannah and her father do the opposite of providing needed support and understanding while Cal deals with losing his mother to cancer. Their lack of patience causes Cal to feel like a burden and a charity case. As the teacher, I (Rachelle) may share situations where I felt like Cal and how others were either supportive or not. For instance, I can share how when dealing with my own traumatic experiences in middle-school, the teacher I chose to share details only called my parents, making things worse. I quickly learned to be dependent on myself, feeling that same sense of isolation and encumbering of others. By sharing how I connect with Cal, I model that it is okay to talk about my lived experiences. I can share how I did not have this type of support while I was in school, leading me to become an educator to ensure students' lives were front and center during instruction. Students could be invited to connect with Cal and my situations, or students could be invited to share about a time when they did not understand the severity of someone's loss or hardship.

### Miles Morales: Spider-Man

While many books tell his story, one story that is often said but in a different light is that of Spider-Man. While we know that superheroes help those that need saving, we often do not consider their real lives and experiences. With this novel having a heavy focus on racism experienced by Miles and classmates, before reading the novel, we suggest sharing either a personal connection, either experienced or witnessed. We mention witnessed because while not all may have personal connections with traumatic experiences that they want to discuss with students, we know that secondary trauma occurs when someone is exposed to a traumatic experience through a first-hand account, such as reading disturbing and graphic social media posts related to the many Americans that have died and continue to die, because of the pandemic. The amount of loss and grief is palpable.

**TABLE 2.1** Example Text Descriptions

| Title | Author | Publication Year | Description |
|---|---|---|---|
| *Closer to Nowhere* | Ellen Hopkins | 2020 | A novel in verse that tells Hannah's story, a twelve-year-old who believes her life is perfect, and her cousin Cal, who moves in with her family after his mother's death. The reader follows Hannah as she learns that not everyone has the same experiences as her and begins to understand the need for empathy, even as her father does not hold back in sharing his perceptions of Cal. This novel also expertly touches upon how Cal deals with PTSD, the loss of his mom, an incarcerated father, and homelessness – and how these influence every element of his life – from isolation and being ostracized by his peers and feeling the need to run away from those that love him. |
| *Miles Morales: Spider-Man* | Jason Reynolds | 2017 | It tells the story of Miles, a junior at Brooklyn Visions Academy. While most students at the school are predominantly white, Miles is not. His neighborhood and personal experiences are quite different than most of his peers. In addition to being a Super Hero, he contends with personal, familial, and community trauma such as racism, violence, and poverty. While he believes that his superhero senses are on the fritz, he quickly realizes that something just isn't right at his school. |

While both of us identify as white, as someone that identifies as Jewish (Rachelle), I may share about the time when I was cutting the grass in my front yard, and multiple neighbors came over to comment about how Sunday is the Lord's day. I can also share about the time when I was stopped by a stranger who wanted to share his belief in how Jewish people should not exist after he must have noticed my wearing a Star of David. Another example I could share with students is how most of my mom's family were murdered during the Holocaust. Although she was born shortly after WWII, this horrifying loss and situation impact her to this day. As you can see, there are multiple ways that I could share about my life, inviting students to ask questions and connect with their own experiences.

## During Reading Discussions

While it is important to begin sharing a novel from the start of the reading, it is equally essential to connect during reading as students comprehend the novel and understand how their realities are similar to the characters and others. As has been said, this may occur with the teacher and the whole class, during student-teacher reading conferences, or among students in literature circles.

### Closer to Nowhere

The first page introduces the reader to Cal and how he lost his mom three years ago and now feels lost in life. He believes that his current situation living with family will last, but he also believes that there is nothing he can do about it. This first page unpacks quite a few ways to invite students to share their similarities. As the teacher and wanting first to share my vulnerability, I may talk about various losses of my own – from my dad's unexpected death eight years ago or losing a beloved pet after a vicious neighborhood dog attack. Or I may want to focus on when I had felt that my decisions and life were out of my control, such as when my family required my brother and myself to leave the house every day after school to be outdoors. There wasn't a discussion with me regarding having friends in the neighborhood or if there were things to do, just the requirement to be outside without any form of my input.

Another seemingly innocuous situation is when Hannah and Cal's teacher assigns a cross-curricular unit on heredity. While Hannah can ask her family about her past, name, and other important information, Cal faced not being able to ask his mother or father, as he is in prison. Through this assignment, Hannah begins to question her attitude and treatment of Cal, learning about her privilege and his experiences. On the other hand, Cal has to make up most of his family story, using creativity, critical thinking, and humor to deflect away from his life. Yet, this project that retraumatized Cal brought understanding and empathy to Hannah. As the teacher, I may want to share similar experiences related to assignments that made me uncomfortable, such as when we are asked to write about the most influential person in our lives. Or I may want to tell my students of a time where something else, like the project, made me better understand a friend, such as when I was in middle-school and learned about a friend's father taking his own life.

## Miles Morales: Spider-Man

Throughout the book, Miles shares positive and negative influences that surround him and his community. One major factor that Miles must contend with is drugs and criminal activity – witnessed on the streets and among family members. This is such an integral element of Miles's life that when he struggles with the buzzing from his spidey-senses, he compares himself to people going through withdrawal and the need to just hang in there.

Throughout the book, Miles and his classmates face a history teacher who believes that slavery is a needed part of American life, even sharing how prisons are established to keep people enslaved. They are forced to listen to multiple lectures on this, including when the teacher states how "Slavery was the building block of our great country" (p. 60). He states how students should consider how the enslaved wanted and appreciated being enslaved. Miles grapples with what to do when facing an authority figure sharing sentiment that is not only morally wrong but catastrophic for others to hear, attempting to problem-solve how to navigate the situation. As a teacher, I could share connections related to the school to prison pipeline or other inequalities related to systemic racism, like tracking and overrepresentation of disciplinary referrals of Black and Brown students (Nieto & Bode, 2018). Or I could connect with not knowing how to navigate a difficult situation with an authority figure, sharing a personal experience where I had to speak up to an administrator when they told me that students could not read based on the identification of disabilities.

Similarly, throughout the book, there is a heavy emphasis on Miles' strict structure and discipline so that he does not turn out like his Uncle, who died after many years of criminal activity. There is little belief that Miles is a good student who takes on extra responsibilities to support his parents' need to pay for him attending this particular school. As a teacher, I may want to share about times when I was constantly compared to my brother by my teachers and how this did not allow them to see and understand me as an individual, requiring me to work even harder or give up. I could also share my parents' strictness based on my mother's childhood with parental Holocaust survivors.

## Protective Factors

It is important to note that each of these novels also provides ways to share testimonies related to protective factors, which negate or lessen the likelihood of long-term issues and adverse outcomes from traumatic experiences. Promoting opportunities for students to share and validate their experiences, building strong, supportive peer-to-peer and teacher-to-student relationships, and supporting the development of prosocial skills are ways to provide protective factors that improve academic and personal outcomes (Fisher et al., 2020; Holmes et al. 2018). For instance, Miles has a great relationship with his best friend, Ganke, and others who are not okay with their history teacher. Miles also has strong parental support, especially from his mother. Cal's Aunt represents support and understanding in the beginning, along with a couple of his teachers. But by the end, Hannah is his prominent supporter.

## Putting this Together – One Example with Dopesick

One crucial understanding when implementing the reciprocal process of bearing witness and sharing testimony is that this type of discussion does not occur overnight. It takes time, especially building a trusting and supportive classroom environment centered on strong and positive teacher-student and student-student relationships. Lisa Evans, a middle-school teacher at Hannah Pamplico Elementary/Middle-School in Florence County School District 2 in South Carolina, emphasizes this with her instruction when reading *Dopesick* (2010) by Walter Dean Myers with her eighth-grade students. In a modern-day version of The Christmas Carol, Lil J is forced to reflect on his past, present, and future when hiding out in an abandoned building after being sought for potentially shooting and killing an undercover police officer during a drug bust. Lisa shared many themes that she introduces to her students, including issues of not telling the whole truth, the idea presented that males are not supposed to talk about their feelings or trauma, and the neglect of parental figures.

At the beginning of the unit, Lisa guides her students to discuss what is considered "right" and what is considered "wrong." As part of the discussion, she engages them with a few questions to lead the discussion. Here are a few examples:

1. Based on the title *Dopesick*, what do you think the book will be about?
2. Does money make people confident? Why or why not?
3. Have you ever misjudged someone? Why or why not?
4. Can people blame behavior on location?
5. What is something you like about being at home?

One can see that these questions guide students not only thinking about the main themes of the upcoming read but also about their own lives. This gets them ready to make pertinent connections as they read together, with the characters and one another. Another scaffold that Lisa includes in her classroom to support students' ability and comfort in sharing their own experiences is through a reflection journal that they respond in at the beginning of each chapter. Lisa asks that her students reflect on their own lives in their writing.

Lisa acknowledges how some of the topics and questions can get quite personal, so she first shares her vulnerability by responding to the same prompts asked of her students and sharing with the class. She emphasizes the need to share her personal stories as she has witnessed this created more comfort and trust with students for them to not only share their writing with her when she meets with them during one-on-one conferences but also with the class as they read the book. Lisa stresses that it is vital to be aware that some students may not be comfortable talking about their writing, and if what is written by the student is too personal, then she asks them to fold the page closed and write "private" on the outside so that she knows not to read that response. For her and her students, this builds trust and respect and the relationship between her and her students. In return, often, even after a student folds the page to signal private, they end up sharing with her what they wrote when they are ready. Table 2.2 provides a few example reflection questions given to students to respond to as they read.

At the end of the read, students choose one reflection question to expand upon while responding to the question posed by Lil J in the book, "Who do you see when you look in the mirror?"

Because of these supportive relationships built among her students and herself, they often share the good and bad about their lives, even asking for advice and seeking options. For instance, when reading about Lil J describing his mother's alcohol issues and how he did not want anyone to see her like that, one of Lisa's students connected with Lil J, sharing that they had a similar situation with their mother and that is why they do not get to see their mother anymore. This student further related to Lil J's feelings and anger when someone brought up their mother's problem with alcohol. Another student shared how they got into a lot of trouble hanging out with someone who lied to a cop about what they were doing and how the cop seemed to believe the lie merely because the other person told their side first. Sadly, the student ended the discussion with his statement of how he felt "no one would believe him anyway, so why try to argue."

**TABLE 2.2** Student Reflection Prompts

| Chapter | Question |
| --- | --- |
| 1 | Write about a time you felt trapped. |
| 2 | Write about a mistake you wish you could change. |
| 3 | Write about a time the truth made you angry. |
| 4 | Write about a time someone misjudged you. |
| 5 | Write about a time you wanted to be someone else. |
| 6 | Write about a time you felt like you were in Quicksand. No matter what you do, you continue to sink. |
| 7 | Write about a time you felt like you let someone important to you down. |

## Application across Contexts

While this chapter uses middle-grade novels related to an English language arts classroom, the concept of critical literacy and the reciprocal process of bearing critical witness are applicable for all disciplines. In a social studies classroom, middle-grade novels related to the required content would provide the connection. For instance, the novel by Jason Reynolds promotes the opportunity not only to discuss perspectives related to racism, familial and community relations, bullying, and violence, but also the Civil War. There are also middle-grade novels that relate to science and math, such as *The Someday Birds* by Sally J. Pla (2018), *Saving Wonder* by Mary Knight (2016), *Seven Clues to Home* by Polisner and Baskin (2020), the Miscalculations of Lightning Girl by Stacy McAnulty (2019), or *Solving for M* by Jennifer Swender (2019). To not only discuss these traumatic experiences through the characters' eyes and actions, but we can also invite our students to investigate further, research, and potentially create ways to advocate for others through service-learning.

## References

Applebee, A. N., & Langer, J. A. (2013). *Writing instruction that works: Proven methods for middle and high school classrooms.* Teachers College Press.

Ayers, R., & Ayers, W. (2014). *Teaching the taboo: Courage and imagination in the classroom* (2nd ed.) [eBook edition]. Teachers College Press.

Baker-Bell, A. (2020). *Linguist justice: Black Language, literacy, identity, and pedagogy.* Routledge.

Bandura, A. (1977). Self-efficacy: Toward a unifying theory of behavioral change. *Psychological Review,* 84(2), 191–215.

Beckelhimer, L. (2017). One teacher's experiences: Responding to death through language. *English Journal,* 107(2), 41–46.

Beers, K. (2003). *When kid's can't read: What teachers can do.* Heinemann.

Bishop, E. (2014). Critical literacy: Bringing theory to praxis. *Journal of Curriculum Theorizing,* 30(1), 51–63.

Bishop, R. S. (1990). Mirrors, windows, and sliding glass doors. *Perspectives,* 6(3), ix–xi.

Borsheim, C., & Petrone, R. (2006). Teaching the research paper for local action. *The English Journal,* 95(4), 78–83.

Centers for Disease Control and Prevention. (2020, April 13). About the CDC-Kaiser ACE study. https://www.cdc.gov/violenceprevention/aces/about.html?CDC_AA_refVal=https%3A2F%2Fwww.cdc.gov%2Fviolenceprevention%2Facestudy%2Fabout.html

Collins, B. R. (2017). Associative mourning: Learning to lose through literature. *English Journal,* 107(2), 47–52.

Craig, S. E. (2017). *Trauma-sensitive schools for the adolescent years: Promoting resiliency and healing.* Teachers College Press.

Daniels, H., & Steineke, N. (2004). *Mini-lessons for literature circle.* Heinemann.

Delgado, R., & Stefancic, J. (2017). *Critical race theory: An introduction* (3rd ed.). NYU Press.

Dutro, E. (2019). *The vulnerable heart of literacy: Centering trauma as powerful pedagogy [eBook edition].* Teachers College Press.

Finkelhor, D. (2020). Trends in adverse childhood experiences (ACEs) in the United States. *Child Abuse & Neglect*, 108, 1–8, 104641.

Fisher, D., Frey, N., & Savitz, R. S. (2020). *Teaching hope and resilience for students experiencing trauma: Creating safe and nurturing classrooms for learning [eBook edition]*. Teachers College Press.

Freire, P. (1989). *Pedagogy of the oppressed* (31st ed.). Bloomsbury.

Frey, N., Fisher, D., & Smith, D. (2019). *All learning is social and emotional: Helping students develop essential skills for the classroom and beyond [eBook edition]*. ASCD.

Holmes, M. R., Yoon, S., Berg, K. A., Cage, J. L., & Perzynski, A. T. (2018). Promoting the development of resilient academic functioning in maltreated children. *Child Abuse & Neglect*, 75, 92–103.

Ivey, G., & Johnston, P. (2013). Engagement with young adult literature: Outcomes and processes. *Reading Research Quarterly*, 48(3), 255–275.

Ivey, G., & Johnston, P. (2018). Engaging disturbing books. *Journal of Adolescent & Adult Literacy*, 62(2), 143–150.

Janks, H. (2005). Language and the design of texts. *English Teaching Practice and Critique*, 4(3), 97–110.

Janks, H. (2010). *Literacy and power*. Taylor & Francis Group.

Luke, A. (2012). Critical literacy: Foundational notes. *Theory into Practice*, 51, 4–11.

Meyers, L. (2014). The toll of childhood trauma. *Counseling Today*, 57, 28–36.

Miller, D. (2009). *The book whisperer: Awakening the inner reading in every child*. Jossey-Bass.

Miller, D. (2014). *Reading in the wild: The book whisperer's keys to cultivating lifelong reading habits*. Jossey-Bass.

Mirra, N. (2018). *Educating for empathy: Literacy learning and civic engagement*. Teachers College Press.

Nieto, S., & Bode, P. (2018). *Affirming diversity: The sociopolitical context of multicultural education* (7th ed.). Pearson.

Oppel, R. A., Gebeloff, R., Lai, K. K. R., Wright, W., & Smith, M. (2020, July 05). The fullest look yet at the racial inequity of Coronavirus. *New York Times Magazine*. https://www.nytimes.com/interactive/2020/07/05/us/coronavirus-latinos-african-americas-cdc-data.html?referringSource=articleShare

Paris, D. (2012). Culturally sustaining pedagogy: A needed change in stance, terminology, and practice. *Educational Researcher*, 41(3), 93–97.

Rumsey, A. D., McCullough, R., & Chang, C. Y. (2020). Understanding the secondary exposure to trauma and professional quality of life of school counselors. *Professional School Counseling*, 24(1), 1–11.

Turner, K. H. & Reed, D. (2018). Responding to young adult literature through civic engagement. In J. S. Dail, S. Witte, & S. T. Bickmore (Eds.), *Toward a more visual literacy: Shifting the paradigm with digital tools and young adult literature* (pp. 41–52). Lanham, MD: Rowman & Littlefield.

Vasquez, V. M., Jankes, H., & Comber, B. (2019). Critical literacy as a way of being and doing. *Language Arts*, 96(5), 300–311.

## Literature Cited

Hopkins, E. (2020). *Closer to nowhere*. Putnam.

Knight, M. (2016). *Saving wonder*. Scholastic Press.

McAnulty, S. (2019). *The miscalculations of lightning girl*. Yearling.

Myers, W. D. (2010). *Dopesick*. Amistad.

Pla, S. J. (2018). *The someday birds*. Harper Collins.

Polisner, G., & Baskin, N. R. (2020). *Seven clues to home*. Knopf Books for Young Readers.

Reynolds, J. (2017). *Miles Morales: Spider-man*. Marvel.

Swender, J. (2019). *Solving for M*. Crown Books for Young Readers.

# 3

# EXPLORING WHAT COUNTS AS TEXT

## The Possibilities of Picture Books and Graphica with Early Adolescents

*Stephanie F. Reid*

This chapter details what happened when a seventh-grade English teacher incorporated a unit on multimodal texts and theoretical concepts into his curriculum for the first time. The multimodal texts he used included picturebooks, multimodal novels, and graphic novels. Mr. Bergeron (all names are pseudonyms) considered himself a novice regarding multimodal literacies pedagogy but was committed to expanding what counted as reading and writing in his classroom. Students interpreted a wide range of multimodal texts during the unit and created their multimodal compositions. Mr. Bergeron wanted to prepare students for encounters with multimodal texts in their everyday lives and ensure that students had a school-sanctioned opportunity to construct texts with both images and words.

In this chapter, I first provide a call to action that explains why I believe that students benefit when teachers and other educational stakeholders adopt a multimodal approach to literacy pedagogy across the disciplines. Second, I expand upon the theoretical framework that underpins multimodal approaches to literacy education and share further details regarding the context of the study reported herein and the data I collected as part of the study. I then detail what happened as Mr. Bergeron introduced theoretical concepts and multimodal texts into his classroom community. I conclude by considering implications beyond Mr. Bergeron's classroom.

## A Call to Action

When teachers assume an explicitly multimodal approach to pedagogy (Archer, 2017), they support students in developing an expanded understanding of what counts as reading and writing. In classrooms that embrace multimodality, written

DOI: 10.4324/9781003171508-4

and spoken language are still considered necessary. However, other modes of representation and communication are deemed significant to meaning-making (Jewitt, 2017). For example, students might make meaning with images, movement, facial expressions, music, and sound effects. In such classrooms, students read and compose multimodal texts that are made material through different modal combinations. An animated short offers its narrative through moving image, music, sound effects, and maybe language. A comic incorporates visual resources and often language across its image sequences and panels. Lewis (2001) also acknowledged the integration of words and images in picturebooks and chose to represent this relationship through the compound noun, *picturebook* (as opposed to *picture book* or *picture-book*).

Restricting students' interpretive experiences to predominantly language yields two potential consequences. First, students' meaning-making capabilities may be limited because they do not attend to other modes when they read and write (Reid, 2020). Second, schools may continue to privilege readers and writers who excel at standardized ways of reading and writing (O'Brien, 2012) when the goal should be to recognize the brilliance and genius of all meaning-makers (Muhammad, 2020). Indeed, Cowan and Kress (2017) argued that taking a multimodal stance to teaching and learning is a democratic enterprise focused on recognizing every student's meaning-making work as valuable and significant. When teachers make space for multimodal texts in their curriculum, they also expand students' opportunities to represent and communicate their ideas (Reid & Moses, 2021).

Calls for educators to expand what counts as text in schools are not new. For example, over two decades ago, The New London Group (1996/2000) acknowledged that traditional literacy pedagogy is "a carefully restricted project—restricted to formal, monolingual, monocultural, and rule-governed forms of language" (p. 60). According to Cope and Kalantzis (2000), members of the New London Group, gone were "the days when learning a single, standard version of the language [English] was sufficient" (p. 6). In addition to advocating for schools to embrace multiple languages, the New London group proposed a pedagogical framework that acknowledged multimodality. They argued that people use multiple modes to represent their ideas and communicate with each other; they stated that students should have opportunities in school to build their communicative repertoires. As the world told became the world shown (Kress, 2003, p.1) through advances in digital and media technologies, scholars in new literacies argued that education needed to keep up (Lankshear & Knobel, 2003) with the proliferation of visual and multimodal texts that inundate the lives of our students. National literacy organizations like the National Council of Teachers of English (NCTE) released position statements (NCTE, 2005) and constructed standards (International Literacy Association, 2018) that also advocated for students to read and compose multimodal texts in school.

However, the institution of school continues to recognize written and spoken language as the most significant meaning-making resources and often adheres to old paradigms of literacy (O'Brien, 2012) that favor essayist and assessment-oriented approaches to literacy education (Gee & Hayes, 2011). Although the National Assessment Governing Board is currently reviewing updates to the National Assessment of Educational Progress (NAEP) Reading assessment that addresses students' multimodal and visual literacy capabilities, many standardized forms of assessment continue to privilege written English. With high-stakes assessments remaining focused on students' skills in reading and writing English, it is not surprising that the state and national standards also prioritize written and spoken language (Mills & Exley, 2014) and use mostly linguistic measures to determine text complexity and grade-level suitability (Cappello, 2017). Indeed, test-centric instructional procedures have pervaded and shaped school literacy practices so that school reading and writing look less and less like the kind of literacies students value in their lives beyond school (Davis & Willson, 2015). Siegel (2012) stated that literacy educators might find it challenging to make time "for multimodality in schools shaped by the accountability culture" (p. 675).

At the time of writing this chapter, American schooling remains disrupted by the coronavirus pandemic. Some students are experiencing in-person learning (although much altered in format), while other students are learning via online or hybrid platforms. Teachers across the country are adjusting their curriculum, redesigning resources, and designing adapted and new teaching practices. In 2020, many states canceled their annual tests. The pandemic has challenged the dominance of standardized assessment and the "single standard of language, literacy, and modes or sign-making" these tests advance (Siegel, 2012, p. 675). As Harris (2020) stated, "if we want students to make gains that outlast a single assessment and lead to a lifetime of learning, we can't sacrifice the kind of meaningful learning experiences that we know children need." It may be that the time for a shift away from traditional conceptions of reading and writing is now.

## Theoretical Framework

This study was informed by social semiotic perspectives on multimodality, teaching, and learning (Kress, 2010; Bezemer & Kress, 2016). Scholarship on reading visual and multimodal text—particularly in school contexts—also guided this work.

## Social Semiotic Perspectives on Multimodality

I understand multimodality through the theoretical lens of social semiotics (Kress, 2010). Social semiotics offers a way to understand how humans represent their ideas through material forms to communicate those ideas to other people. Kress (2010) understands each person as a motivated sign-maker who draws upon available semiotic resources to fashion a message for an addressee to receive and interpret. It is important to note that the semiotic resources include—but are not limited to—language. Sign-makers can make their thinking visible through movement, facial expression, music, numerical notation, and image. Sign-makers consider the affordances of the semiotic resources available to them in any given context, choosing resources that are most apt for both the ideas they wish to represent and the audience with whom they are communicating. It is equally important to note that the addressee will interpret each sign-complex (or text) differently. Meaning is always made anew—messages are not transmitted precisely from one person to the other. For greater insight into how this theoretical lens might influence text interpretations, see Kachorsky, Perez, and Hill (this volume).

Assuming a social semiotic approach to multimodality also impacts how I understand teaching and learning. As Bezemer and Kress (2016) observed, the teacher represents and communicates their content using the materials and tools available to them in their instructional context. How one teacher represents and communicates disciplinary concepts will not mirror exactly how another teacher represents that same knowledge. Additionally, interpretation of the content will differ from student to student. Teachers can direct students' attention to criterial aspects of content, but they cannot ensure a precise transmission of information or ideas (Bezemer & Kress, 2016). In this way, teachers set the frame for learning while students interact with the teacher's curriculum designs (Kress & Selander, 2012). How the teacher or students enact a planned curricular experience cannot be wholly predicted.

As shaping agents, it is essential for teachers to "name the practices they want to improve" (Garcia & O'Donnell-Allen, 2014, p. 67). Teachers must assume a position before inevitably experiencing *wobble* as they work toward experiencing *flow*, those moments when teachers achieve the desired improvement in practice (Garcia & O'Donnell-Allen, 2014, 2016). Mr. Bergeron assumed a new pose when he decided to adopt an explicitly multimodal approach to pedagogy and demonstrated wobble as he reflected on lessons and lesson segments that had not gone according to plan. As shaping agents, teachers can remake their curriculum over time as they craft improvements to their instructional designs.

## Reading Visual and Multimodal Texts

Although critics have positioned comics as less-literary than other formats such as the novel (Low, 2012; Jiménez & Meyer, 2016), a range of scholarship has demonstrated the complexity of visual and multimodal texts. For example, with regards to the comics medium, Jiménez and Meyer (2016) investigated how expert readers encountered and navigated graphic novels, showing the complex array of comprehension moves made by the readers in their study. Low (2012) discussed the significance of the gutters—those spaces between panels—as crucial to making meaning. McCloud (1993) described how the comics medium brings together sequential art and literature to create artistic works that merit attention and appreciation. Words and images carry different semiotic loads (Kress, 2010). Paying attention to both words and images expands the interpretive options available to readers.

Children's literature scholars have also provided us with various means of understanding how images and words work together in visual and multimodal texts. Nikolajeva and Scott (2000) studied picturebooks and constructed metalanguage that recognizes different kinds of word-image relationships. They suggested that images either (1) attempted to mirror the information provided by the written text, (2) offered additional but complementary and connected information, or (3) showed a counterpointing or conflicting story to the one presented in the text. Building on this work, Reid and Serafini (2018) analyzed a data corpus of multimodal novels. Multimodal novels are chapter books that incorporate visuals or image sequences into the narrative space taken up by the story (front covers and endpapers, therefore, were not a part of this analysis). In most multimodal novels included in the study, images sometimes offered supplementary information that would not impact a reader's comprehension of the story if deleted from the text. In other novels, images played a more critical role, either sharing or dominating the reading/viewing of the story being told.

## Reading Visual and Multimodal Texts in Classroom Contexts

Research conducted in both elementary and middle-school contexts has shown how young readers can read and respond to complex visual and multimodal texts (Pantaleo, 2012a, 2012b). Particularly when preceded by close analysis of multimodal texts, young authors have also shown themselves to be adept composers of multimodal narratives and nonfiction texts (Chase, Son, & Steiner, 2014; Dallacqua & Peralta, 2019; Pantaleo, 2011, 2013a, 2013b, 2017b). Pantaleo (2013a, 2013b, 2015, 2017b, 2019) showed how explicit instruction that directly addressed how images and words work within picturebooks and graphic novels impacted students' multimodal composing work. The elementary and middle-school students featured in Pantaleo's studies were able to speak to their multimodal design decisions, naming the different design features they used and providing a rationale for their use.

To offer explicitly multimodal instruction, classroom teachers must have developed a comprehensive knowledge of how visual and multimodal texts work. Callow (2008, 2018) and Connors (2012) observed that teachers need to know important metalanguage foundational to discussions of picturebooks and comics. Yet, as Meixner et al. (2019) argued, English teachers may not have experienced the opportunity to learn this knowledge. Teachers may not be as comfortable with multimodal composing as they are with written language texts. It may be that "students sometimes know as much, if not more," than their teachers about how multimodal texts work (Hassett & Curwood, 2009, p. 280). Teachers might need to position themselves as learners in their classrooms (Moses & Reid, 2021; Reid & Moses, 2021) or assume the perhaps unfamiliar role of knowledge co-constructor (Hassett & Curwood, 2009). Thus, an explicitly multimodal approach to pedagogy may result in disruptions to traditional classroom hierarchies (Moses & Reid, 2021; Reid & Moses, 2021). In this volume, Rigell and Bannack describe how dialogic pedagogy can disrupt expected classroom power structures that position the teacher as the most significant knowledge-broker. Multimodal approaches to pedagogy also have the potential to render classrooms as more democratic and accessible spaces.

## Introducing Mr. Bergeron's Classroom

At the time of the study, Mr. Bergeron (33, white, male) had taught middle-schoolers English Language Arts for eight years. He was approaching the end of his second-year teaching at the school site, a K-8 charter school near a large southwestern city. Mr. Bergeron was also working toward his doctorate in English Education in addition to teaching full-time. When asked to describe his teaching philosophy, he explained that he prioritized creating a classroom environment where students felt safe, welcomed, and comfortable. Mr. Bergeron also emphasized student autonomy, offering students time each block period for choice independent reading and creating open-ended assignments that encouraged student creativity. His expertise was written communication, and he considered himself a novice with regards to multimodal texts and visual literacy pedagogy.

Although multimodal texts were present in Mr. Bergeron's classroom (Figure 3.1 shows Mr. Bergeron's meme wall) and curriculum, Mr. Bergeron felt he could "do a much better job incorporating and leveraging more modes and media" in his classes. His students had created infographics and explored data visualizations during the argumentative writing unit, and they had also experimented with visual poem formats during a poetry unit. However, Mr. Bergeron felt that he had not directly and explicitly studied multimodal texts with his students. When asked why he was interested in participating in a research study centered on incorporating multimodal texts into the curriculum, Mr. Bergeron stated:

> We're always trying to predict what these kids might need by the time they graduate. And visual literacy is not in the standards. They have art once a week here…No one's teaching them how to read those kinds of messages. I care that they'll graduate and have the things that I think they need.

He wanted his students to read and compose multimodal texts because their social worlds are saturated with such texts.

Mr. Bergeron designed the eight-week multimodal literacies curriculum unit for all four English Language Arts classes each day (three sixth-grade classes and

**Unit Overview**

Notions around literacy—what it is, what "counts," what can/should be taught in schools, what can/should be tested, what might need to be prioritized, etc.—have direct impact on language arts classrooms, and therefore, importantly, on students lives.

In the current climate of standardization and high-stakes testing, writing and reading of writing are the given central attention. While those are crucial skills for students to learn, they alone do not prepare students for the many and varied ways of making meaning in the world.

Why visual literacy? Because we communicate visually! It can easily be argued that visuals are a form of writing: Is the inclusion of a chart, graph, map, illustration, or photograph in a written text not "writing?" Is the author not considering purpose and audience in the decision to include visual elements? Is the author not using a writing-like process—brainstorming, drafting, revising—in working with visuals?

Regardless of how the use of visuals is defined, they are clearly ubiquitous as a means of communication. From billboards and commercials to memes and photographs, architecture and landscaping to road signs and company logos, students are bombarded with visual messages. In such a context, even the most advanced users of textual writing will be at a serious disadvantage to those who can "read" and "write" with visuals.

**Essential Questions**

This unit is the beginning of a broader multimodal curriculum. With a focus on visuals, students will consider the following essential questions:

- What is reading and writing? What "counts?" What is a "text?"
- How are textual writing and visuals similar? Different? What are the affordances and limitations of different modes?
- How do authors and illustrators shape meaning?
- Why do we sometimes arrive at different interpretations of meaning?
- What does a critical perspective reveal about texts?

**Objectives**

This unit will be guided by the following objectives:

- Students will use academic vocabulary when discussing visual texts.
- Students will analyze visuals, explaining how visual elements work together to shape meaning.
- Students will analyze the interaction of visual and textual modes.
- Students will use visual elements to aeate visual texts and explain/justify their use of visual elements.
- Students will discuss oonnections (compare, contrast, etc.) among texts studied.
- Students will use critical lenses to consider representation (including the absence of representation) in texts studied.

**FIGURE 3.1**  The cover page to Mr. Bergeron's multimodal literacies curriculum unit.

one seventh-grade class). I collected data in one of these classes—his seventh-grade class. This class comprised 31 students. School records indicated that 65% of the students were white, 23% of students were Hispanic or Latino/a/x, 6% of students were Black, and 6% of the students were American Indian. I invited all 31 students to participate in the study. I received parental consent and student assent for 29 students. I did not collect data from the two students who did not wish to participate.

With Mr. Bergeron's help, I invited four students to be focal contributors to this research study. Blue (13, Male, Latino) was a vocal contributor to discussions and often related curriculum content to sociopolitical issues. He loved performing but did not always enjoy reading. Norman (13, Male, white) learned to read in fifth-grade and associated images with books for young children. He voraciously consumed and created texts with words. Pinon (13, Female, American Indian) was a talented artist who often combined images with words in her class-work. Regina (13, Female, white) excelled at school literacy tasks and was an enthusiastic participant in this classroom community. I hoped that each student would share their unique perspective on the curriculum unit.

Throughout this study, I acted as a consultant and researcher. As a consultant, I shared scholarly resources with Mr. Bergeron and supplied the picturebooks and multimodal novels that students read during the unit. Please see Table 3.1 for a list of key resources and texts I shared. I also listened to Mr. Bergeron's instructional ideas, responded to questions he had regarding multimodality theoretical concepts, and provided pedagogical recommendations when Mr. Bergeron asked for my input. Ultimately, as the classroom community expert, Mr. Bergeron made all final curricular decisions. As a researcher, I documented how the curriculum unfolded, collecting and managing a variety of data.

## Multimodal Data Collection

My data collection strategies honored the study's visual focus. Therefore, I collected visual, verbal, and multimodal data. I photographed the classroom environment daily, and I photographed students transacting with picturebooks, multimodal novels, and various tools and materials. Although I used writing to construct daily fieldnotes (Emerson, Fretz, & Shaw, 2011), I embedded photographs of the classroom context, student work, and class activity in my fieldnotes. When it felt salient to do so, I also included audio-clips I had recorded with my cell phone. Image, sound, and written language offer different representational information (Kress, 2010). Furthermore, I collected all student- and teacher-created artifacts, including their multimodal compositions. Mr. Bergeron also audio-recorded his reflections after each lesson.

Additionally, I video-recorded whole-class discussions and peer interactions, reflecting on my role in constructing visual data through theoretical memos (Pink, 2007). I also video-recorded semi-structured and informal student interviews (Olson, 2011). The video cameras recorded what was said and by whom. The video cameras also made it possible to see the visuals under discussion and how the students physically interacted with the visual texts. Video data was beneficial when interviewing Pinon because she would transition from speech to drawing and back again while making her point. Insisting on spoken language alone for the interviews would have limited the ideas and thoughts Pinon wished to communicate to me.

I conducted a first-cycle analysis (Saldaña, 2016) of my field notes and the data I constructed. I coded line-by-line as I read through the entire data corpus (Emerson, Fretz, & Shaw, 2011), tagging, when appropriate, text segments with in

**TABLE 3.1** List of visual and multimodal resources shared with Mr. Bergeron

| Picturebooks/Graphic Novels | Copies |
| --- | --- |
| Cordell, M. (2017). *Wolf in the snow*. Feiwel and Friends. | 1 |
| Fleming, C. *Giant squid*. Roaring Brook Press. | 1 |
| Gravett, E. (2006). *Wolves*. Simon & Schuster Books for Young Readers. | 1 |
| Morales, Y. (2018). *Dreamers*. Neal Porter Books/Holiday House. | 1 |
| Myers, W. D. (1997). *Amiri and Odette*: A love story. Scholastic Press. | 1 |
| Staake, B. (2013). *Bluebird*. Schwartz & Wade Books. | 20 |
| Steptoe, J. (2016). *Radiant child: The story of young artist Jean-Michel Basquiat*. Little, Brown, and Company. | 1 |
| Tan, S. (2007). *The arrival*. Arthur A. Levine Books. | 20 |
| Tan, S. (2019). *Cicada*. Arthur A. Levine Books. | 1 |
| Tan, S. (2015). *The singing bones*. Arthur A. Levine Books. | 1 |
| Tan, S. (2011). *Lost and found*. Arthur A. Levine Books. | 20 |
| *Multimodal Novels* | |
| Almond, D. (2008). *The savage*. Candlewick Press. | 5 |
| Harrold, A. F. (2014). *The imaginary*. Bloomsbury Children's Books. | 5 |
| Ness, P. (2011). *A monster calls*. Candlewick Press. | 5 |
| Said, S. F. (2016). *Phoenix*. Candlewick Press. | 5 |
| Selznick, B. (2007). *The invention of Hugo Cabret*. Scholastic. | 5 |
| Selznick, B. (2011). *Wonderstruck*. Scholastic. | 5 |
| Selznick, B. (2015). *The Marvels*. Scholastic. | 35 |
| Smy, P. (2017). *Thornhill*. Roaring Brook Press. | 5 |
| Walter, V. (1998). *Making up Megaboy*. DK Children. | 5 |
| Wiles, D. (2010). *Countdown*. Scholastic. | 5 |
| Wiles, D. (2017). *Revolution*. Scholastic. | 5 |
| Yelchin, E. (2015). *Breaking Stalin's nose*. Square Fish. | 5 |

vivo codes (Saldaña, 2016) to ensure I attended to Mr. Bergeron's words. I wrote coding memos to document the codes and patterns I constructed. During my second-cycle focused coding, I established three conceptual bins (Tracy, 2013) inspired by Garcia and O'Donnell-Allen's (2014) notions of (1) pose, (2) wobble, and (3) flow as aspects of teachers' professional growth. I used these conceptual bins to group together data excerpts that showed his multimodal pose, data points that showed when Mr. Bergeron wobbled and revealed the gap between theory and practice, and data sequences that suggested Mr. Bergeron had achieved flow.

## Theory into Practice

Three categories comprised my findings: (1) visible evidence of a multimodal approach to pedagogy, (2) practices that flow, and (3) moments of pedagogical wobble.

## Visible Evidence of a Multimodal Approach to Pedagogy

Over eight weeks, Mr. Bergeron constructed a 49-page curriculum document that recorded his instructional moves. The opening page contained his rationale for the curriculum, a list of essential questions (inspired by the work of Wiggins & McTighe, 2005), and a series of learning objectives (see Figure 3.1). The influence of theory on his curriculum designing was apparent. Through his essential questions, Mr. Bergeron sought to expand what counted as text and composition in his classroom, and he purposefully drew attention to illustrators in addition to authors. Mr. Bergeron also positioned students as users of academic metalanguage and as analysts of images and multimodal texts through his learning objectives. These objectives were a significant departure from previous learning objectives that focused predominantly on written and spoken language (Table 3.1).

The curriculum unit contained three significant phases. Influenced by Serafini's (2014) recommendations, Mr. Bergeron began the unit by exposing students to a wide range of multimodal texts: magazine covers, wordless picture-books (e.g., Staake, 2014), picturebooks (e.g., Marsden & Tan, 1998/2011), and a graphic novel (Tan, 2007). To support students' wide reading of multimodal texts, Mr. Bergeron incorporated lessons on reading images. During one key lesson within this first phase, Mr. Bergeron used Bang's (2000) *Picture This* to support students in talking and thinking about the art they were seeing. Students learned to think about line, shape, color, perspective, and scale. After viewing Bang's representation of Little Red Riding Hood, students used this knowledge to construct their own single-image representations of fairy tales or other well-known stories. This lesson also supplied students with analytical tools to apply to the images they encountered in other texts. Students in his class were used to mentor texts as guides to quality written language. This lesson marked the first time that Mr. Bergeron used a visual text to mentor students in image-making and visual composition.

Mr. Bergeron found that the initial exposure phase took longer than expected. During one reflection, he commented:

> I don't know how many stories we need to go through before I feel like they're ready to take on the whole class novel. But my inclination is to go slow…I want the students to really understand you can keep looking at an image and making meaning for a long time.

Mr. Bergeron realized that students needed time to read images carefully. The temporal nature of writing (Kress, 2010) is easily observed because we can see the number of lines in a page and count pages as we turn them. Readers understand that reading one paragraph will likely take less time than one page. Because images are often understood as spatial representations (Kress, 2010), teachers might underestimate the time readers need to navigate through a single image. When Mr. Bergeron dedicated significant classroom time to reading visuals and discussing single images, he demonstrated to his students that he valued this work and was willing to commit precious classroom time to this undertaking. Newkirk (2011) suggested that verbal texts should be read carefully and slowly. Mr. Bergeron showed that visual and multimodal texts should be considered in a similarly mindful fashion.

During the second phase of the curriculum unit, students explored single texts in more depth. Mr. Bergeron allocated time for independent reading at the start of each of the lessons in this phase. Students chose a multimodal novel to read during this time and recorded a response to their reading in their reading journals at the end of these class segments. Students could read as many novels as they wished. They met in book clubs weekly, although the book clubs' membership shifted according to students' reading decisions and pace. Mr. Bergeron used this time to model being a reader of visual and multimodal texts. He sat at the front of the classroom, reading multimodal novels while they read and sharing his reactions as they occurred. Before groups gathered in their book clubs during one lesson, he asked the class if there was a group reading Harrold's *The Imaginary* (2015). Four students raised their hands. "I'll be joining you," he told them. "This is way different than I expected, and I'm loving it." Mr. Bergeron modeled investment in the multimodal texts he asked his students to read.

Alongside their independent reading, Mr. Bergeron's class studied Selznick's *The Marvels* (2015) together. This novel is uniquely structured. The first 400 pages depict the Marvel family's stories across five generations. The double-spread images move the reader rapidly through time. The novel then switches mode, and the next 200 pages of the story are told through writing. The reader is presented with new characters who are living in a different era. Mr. Bergeron designed several visual tasks that encouraged students to connect the visual and verbal sections as they read. The connections between the images and the words are not immediately visible. Students needed to read the images and the words carefully. If students did not heed one modal portion of the novel, the narrative does not make sense. Students often found themselves flipping back through the pages to secure their understanding of what happened. They tended to turn the pages too fast and often backtracked to re-establish comprehension of the story and its characters.

The final phase of the curriculum unit allowed students to work on creating their multimodal compositions. Mr. Bergeron allowed students to choose their genre and medium. Students also chose how they balanced the different modes from which they drew while constructing their texts. Norman, for example, in keeping with his modal preference for words, focused more on writing. Pinon, in contrast, focused on creating a sequence of visuals that represented. Her image sequence included very few words. Despite feeling more confidence in her writing capabilities than her image-making skills, Regina appreciated the opportunity to experiment and take risks. She decided to create a wordless comic following the movements of a paper airplane. When I asked Regina about her most meaningful learnings from the unit, she replied, "Being able to write a story with images and being able to understand it without words." Just as he modeled reading multimodal texts during the independent reading phase, Mr. Bergeron modeled multimodal composition for students. He showed how he transformed a story he had written into a comic with panels, images, narrative boxes, and speech and thought bubbles.

## Practices that Flow

As the curriculum unit progressed, Mr. Bergeron adapted existing literacy practices to fit his multimodal stance and established new literacy practices (Barton, Hamilton, & Ivanič, 2000). I understand literacy practices to be social routines—ways of being, knowing, and doing—that are deemed valuable within different social contexts and communities. Knowing, understanding, and participating in such social routines means that individuals can be recognized and identified as members of given communities. Literacy practices, then, differ from classroom activities. I deem classroom activities to be stand-alone tasks that students complete on distinct occasions. They are not enacted frequently nor valued enough to be repeated.

A new practice that developed in Mr. Bergeron's classroom across this study was the act of noticing and naming (Serafini & Ladd, 2008). Students paid attention to tiny details in images, noted the importance of sound effects, and discussed the impact of music choice. Blue and his partner, Gabrielle, for example, spent a lesson focused on analyzing the images, symbols, and diagrams that appeared in the borders and background outside the panels dedicated to the story of *The Lost Thing* (Tan, 2011a). Similarly, Regina and Pinon searched for and tracked the red leaf depicted on each page of Tan's (2011b) *The Red Tree*, deliberating its potential meanings and building several interpretations. This practice was also an embodied practice: pointing to and touching aspects of the images under discussion were a part of this work.

However, even when experiencing flow, Mr. Bergeron was intent on working toward improving his pedagogy. In his exit interview, he commented: "In the future, I'd like to make sure that everyone is getting to the point of analysis." He saw the benefit of the noticing and naming practice but wanted to evolve it further to include thinking about why each noticing might matter. Future iterations of this unit would involve helping students connect their minute noticings to the page, the story, and the story's connections to sociopolitical issues in the world. Thus, even though deemed a valuable literacy practice, noticing and naming will not stay statically bound to its initial rendering in this classroom community. The hallmark, perhaps, of a valued literacy practice is its continued evolution.

## Moments of Pedagogical Wobble

Before the unit's official start, when only his plans were articulated, Mr. Bergeron stated that he thought the unit would be "smooth-sailing" and fun for everyone throughout. However, as he progressed through the unit, he realized that certain aspects of the unit were more challenging than he thought. Not everything proceeded smoothly. Mr. Bergeron found that some theoretical concepts were more accessible and more easily explained to students than other concepts. He also learned that some of the multimodal tasks he designed were experienced as drudgery (Dewey, 1915) by some students and did not rise to the level of valued literacy practices.

### Issues Introducing New Metalanguage

The multimodal curriculum unit required Mr. Bergeron to become familiar with new theoretical concepts and analytical language. He then needed to teach this new metalanguage to students to equip them for multimodal text analysis and critique. However, his approach to students' use of the metalanguage (or not) seemed to reflect his approach to grammar instruction. When he teaches grammar, he uses correct grammatical terms but does not insist on students using them. Students' abilities to strategically use any given language device are more important to Mr. Bergeron than their ability to name a particular grammatical term. Within this study, the consequences of this approach were twofold. First, Mr. Bergeron's students did not take-up the new metalanguage in their conversations or analysis. Second, they tended to focus on the aspects of visual analysis most familiar and comfortable to them. For example, students mentioned line, color, shape, and size frequently during their conversations. Thus, metalanguage such as *salience* or *framing* remained at the level of academic vocabulary instead of being viewed as analytical tools that can help readers interrogate and analyze texts.

Furthermore, while Mr. Bergeron felt comfortable introducing some multimodality concepts and the accompanying terminology, he avoided others. For example, he decided not to use the term *affordances*. In our conversations about multimodality, Mr. Bergeron expressed that he was interested in helping students think about the affordances of different modes. He initially believed this knowledge would help them expand their options when composing texts of their own. He made sure that students knew that there were different modes (e.g., still images, moving images, music, sound effects, gestures) but resisted talking about affordances when teachable moments occurred. In one lesson, Regina commented that the sound effects in the animated rendering of Tan's (2011a) picturebook, *The Lost Thing*, made a new interpretation and connection possible. Another student mentioned that the animation could feature a television commercial, something that a book with pages could not.

When we conversed after the lesson, Mr. Bergeron revealed that he had wanted to talk about affordances. He knew that this concept is essential to social semiotic perspectives on multimodality (Kress, 2010). However, Mr. Bergeron felt that this was a concept he understood, but he worried that its import would not be apparent to students. He felt similarly about the concept of *representation*, which is trickier to explain to students because *represent* and its variations are used so frequently by students in everyday conversations about images. Mr. Bergeron talked to students about *modes of communication* but rarely used the extended version, *mode of representation and communication*. He stated that he was "all for metalanguage" but, ultimately, felt that discussing representation would be too confusing.

### Literacy Activities—Not Practices

There were consequences to Mr. Bergeron's decisions not to introduce certain concepts that may have resulted in additional moments of curricular wobble. For example, he designed three multimodal progress that students were to complete as they progressed through their reading of Selznick's (2015) multimodal novel: (1) a visual depiction of a moment from the written language section of the novel, (2) a series of baseball cards connecting the visual parts of the story to the written sections, and (3) a videoed reaction to the novel. Mr. Bergeron did not think that most students found these three activities meaningful. Students' unit evaluations tended to confirm Mr. Bergeron's thoughts. Students had not understood why they were meaningful.

If Mr. Bergeron had linked these tasks to key multimodality concepts such as *transduction* (Kress, 2010), the act of remaking meaning across different modes, or linked students' work on the baseball cards to word-image scholarship (e.g., Nikolajeva & Scott, 2000), the work might have become more purposeful for students. Without these vital theoretical linkages, the tasks stayed at the level of a one-time classroom activity instead of rising to the level of a repeated and valued literacy practice. More explicit theoretical instruction might have clarified for students Mr. Bergeron's purpose in designing some of the key tasks and may, in turn, have helped students see the value in undertaking this work.

## Significance Beyond Mr. Bergeron's Classroom

I conclude by identifying three key implications for teachers looking to work with new theories for the first time. The first implication highlights the idea that teaching is also always learning. Mr. Bergeron self-identified as a "novice" when it came to assuming an explicitly multimodal approach to pedagogy. He was in the process of constructing knowledge about teaching with multimodal concepts as he was teaching; he understood that this approach was "moving away from very traditional understandings of what should be in a language arts class" (exit interview). This curriculum unit represented Mr. Bergeron's first moves away from a logocentric English Language Arts curriculum. His pedagogical journey will be marked by new curricular decisions and instructional decisions, each building on what has happened before. In his concluding interview, he stated his plans for future iterations of this work. One plan included incorporating multi-modality across his curriculum units to scaffold students' work with visuals and other modes. He realized that "there's a lot more to [teaching with multimodal-ity] than just do it…There's so much more to get into—moving past the surface level." Working to connect theory with practice takes place over time, and curriculum units will undergo multiple redesigns. There will always be moments of both flow and wobble (Garcia & O'Donnell-Allen, 2014).

Secondly, this research highlights the role of reflection in the instructional design process. Mr. Bergeron constantly moved between theory and practice throughout the unit. His knowledge of students and teaching shaped his approach to incorporating multimodal concepts and texts in his class. However, Mr. Bergeron's understanding of theory helped him draw students' attention to the criterial aspects of visual and multimodal texts. Theory is powerful because it offers a way of explaining how things in our world—or texts—work. When classroom tasks are informed by multimodal theories, those tasks become practice for making sense of a broad range of texts. When tasks were not grounded in theory, students did not see the relevance of the activity beyond curricular, school-bound instances. Thus, Mr. Bergeron's consideration of theory and practice also enabled him to differentiate between classroom tasks that became valuable and repeated practices and those tasks that stayed at the level of one-time classroom activities. This movement between theory and practice helped him identify which curricular components he should keep and which aspects could be let go.

Through this kind of reflection, Mr. Bergeron also saw ways to develop these new practices further. Even aspects of pedagogical flow can be redesigned to have a more significant impact on students' learning experiences. When asked to explain what he felt were the most beneficial practices students developed, Mr. Bergeron stated that all his students now practiced noticing and naming different aspects of multimodal texts. However, he was determined to develop this practice further during future academic years: "In the future I'd like to make sure that everyone is getting to the point of analysis." He planned to still make time for naming and noticing but would ensure that students connect their noticings to the text and the world beyond the text.

Third, this study indicated that conversations around multimodality should be extended across grade-levels and content areas. Mr. Bergeron's motivation for teaching with visual and multimodal texts was that "no one is teaching [students] how to read those kinds of [visual] messages." My initial interviews with the four focal students supported that they are not learning about visual and multimodal texts in other subjects. One student even worried that she would never have the opportunity to do this kind of work in a school context again. Additionally, students like Pinon develop their expertise through choice reading and composition outside of school but may experience few chances to demonstrate their thinking and knowledge in school if representation and communication practices are limited to a few key school genres and spoken and written language. If multimodal and visual literacies instruction is left to an individual teacher within a specific discipline, students' interpretive repertoires may not be as expansive as might be possible. I believe that stakeholders in education should map multimodality across the entire K-12 curriculum. Conversations about multimodal meaning-making should be extended to teams of teachers, schools, districts, and beyond.

## References

Archer, A. (2017). Power, social justice and multimodal pedagogies. In C. Jewitt (Ed.), *The Routledge handbook of multimodal analysis* (pp. 189–199). Routledge.

Bang, M. (2000). *Picture this: How pictures work*. Chronicle Books.

Barton, D., Hamilton, M., & Ivanič, R. (2000). *Situated literacies: Reading and writing in context*. Psychology Press.

Bezemer, J., & Kress, G. (2016). *Multimodality, learning and communication: A social semiotic frame*. Routledge.

Callow, J. (2008). Show me: Principles for assessing students' visual literacy. *The Reading Teacher, 61*(8), 616–626.

Callow, J. (2018). Classroom assessment and picture books: Strategies for assessing how students interpret multimodal texts. *Australian Journal of Language & Literacy, 41*(1), 5–20.

Cappello, M. (2017). Considering visual text complexity: A guide for teachers. *The Reading Teacher, 70*(6), 733–739.

Chase, M., Son, E. H., & Steiner, S. (2014). Sequencing and graphic novels with primary-grade students. *The Reading Teacher, 67*(6), 435–443.

Connors, S. P. (2012). Toward a Shared Vocabulary for Visual Analysis: An Analytic Toolkit for Deconstructing the Visual Design of Graphic Novels. *Journal of Visual Literacy, 31*(1), 71–92.

Cope, B., & Kalantzis, M. (2000). Introduction: Multiliteracies: The beginnings of an idea. In B. Cope & M. Kalantzis (Eds.), *Multiliteracies: Literacy learning and the design of social futures* (pp. 3–9). Routledge.

Cowan, K., & Kress, G. (2017). Documenting and transferring meaning in the multimodal world: Reconsidering transcription. In F. Serafini & E. Gee (Eds.), *Remixing multiliteracies: Theory and practice from New London to new times* (pp. 50–62). Teachers College Press.

Dallacqua, A. K., & Peralta, L. R. (2019). Reading and (re)writing science comics: A study of informational texts. *The Reading Teacher, 73*(1), 111–118.

Davis, D. S., & Willson, A. (2015). Practices and commitments of test-centric literacy instruction: Lessons from a testing transition. *Reading Research Quarterly, 50*(3), 357–379.

Dewey, J. (1915/2015). Democracy and education. In D. Reed (Ed.), *The collected works of John Dewey: The complete works (Kindle edition)* (pp. 331–6137). PergamonMedia.

Emerson, R. M., Fretz, R. I., & Shaw, L. L. (2011). *Writing ethnographic fieldnotes*. University of Chicago Press.

Garcia, A., & O'Donnell-Allen, C. (2014). Wobbling in public: Supporting new and experienced teachers. *English Journal, 103*(6), 65–70.

Garcia, A., & O'Donnell-Allen, C. (2016). Wobbling with writing: Challenging existing paradigms of secondary writing instruction and finding new possibilities. *Literacy Research: Theory, Method, and Practice, 65*(1), 348–364.

Gee, J. P., & Hayes, E. R. (2011). *Language and learning in the digital age*. Routledge.

Harris, T. (2020, October 27). *Meaningful learning experiences: Teaching the student and not the content (blog post)*. Colorado Council: International Reading Association. https://ccira.blog/2020/10/27/meaningful-learning-experiences-teaching-the-student-and-not-the-content/

Harrold, A. F. (2015). *The imaginary*. (E. Grevatt, Illus.). Bloomsbury Publishing.

Hassett, D. D., & Curwood, J. S. (2009). Theories and Practices of Multimodal Education: The Instructional Dynamics of Picture Books and Primary Classrooms. *The Reading Teacher, 63*(4), 270–282.

International Literacy Association. (2018). *Standards for the preparation of literacy professionals 2017*. Author.

Jewitt, C. (2017). An introduction to multimodality. In C. Jewitt (Ed.), *The Routledge handbook of multimodal analysis* (pp. 15–30). Routledge.

Jiménez, L. M., & Meyer, C. K. (2016). First impressions matter: Navigating graphic novels utilizing linguistic, visual, and spatial resources. *Journal of Literacy Research: JLR, 48*(4), 423–447.

Kress, G. (2003). *Literacy in the new media age*. Routledge.

Kress, G. (2010). *Multimodality: A social semiotic approach to contemporary communication*. Routledge.

Kress, G., & Selander, S. (2012). Multimodal design, learning and cultures of recognition. *The Internet and Higher Education, 15*(4), 265–268.

Lankshear, C., & Knobel, M. (2003). *New literacies: Changing knowledge and classroom learning*. Open University Press.

Lewis, D. (2001). *Reading contemporary picturebooks: Picturing text*. Routledge.

Low, D. E. (2012). "Spaces invested with content": Crossing the "gaps" in comics with readers in schools. *Children's Literature in Education, 43*(4), 368–385.

Marsden, J., & Tan, S. (1998/2011). The rabbits. (S. Tan, Illus.). In S. Tan (Author & Illustrator) *Lost & Found: Three by Shaun Tan* (Reprint edition). Arthur A. Levine Books.

McCloud, S. (1993). *Understanding comics: The invisible art*. Harper Collins.

Meixner, E., Peel, A., Hendrickson, R., Szczeck, L., & Bousum, K. (2019). Storied lives: Teaching memoir writing through multimodal mentor texts. *Journal of Adolescent & Adult Literacy, 62*(5), 495–508.

Mills, K. A., & Exley, B. (2014). Narrative and multimodality in English language arts curricula: A tale of two nations. *Language Arts, 92*(2), 136–143.

Moses, L., & Reid, S. (2021). Supporting literacy and positive identity negotiations with multimodal comic composing. *Language and Literacy, 23*(1), 1–24.

Muhammad, G. (2020). *Cultivating genius: An equity framework for culturally and historically responsive literacy*. Scholastic.

National Council of Teachers of English (NCTE). (2005, November 17). *Multimodal literacies: Position statement*. National Council of Teachers of English. https://ncte.org/statement/multimodalliteracies/

Newkirk, T. (2011). *The art of slow reading: Six time-honored practices for engagement*. Heinemann.

Nikolajeva, M., & Scott, C. (2000). The dynamics of picturebook communication. *Children's Literature in Education, 31*(4), 225–239.

O'Brien, D. (2012). "Struggling" adolescents' engagement in multimediating: Countering the institutional construction of incompetence. In D. E. Alvermann & K. A. Hinchman (Eds.), *Reconceptualizing the literacies in adolescents' lives: Bridging the everyday/academic divide* (pp. 71–92). Routledge.

Olson, K. (2011). *Essentials of qualitative interviewing*. Left Coast Press.

Pantaleo, S. (2011). Warning: A grade 7 student disrupts narrative boundaries. *Journal of Literacy Research: JLR, 43*(1), 39–67.

Pantaleo, S. (2012a). Exploring grade 7 students' responses to Shaun Tan's The Red Tree. *Children's Literature in Education, 43*(1), 51–71.

Pantaleo, S. (2012b). Middle-school students reading and creating multimodal texts: A case study. *Education 3–13, 40*(3), 295–314.

Pantaleo, S. (2013a). Matters of design and visual literacy: One middle years student's multimodal artifact. *Journal of Research in Childhood Education, 27*(3), 351–376.

Pantaleo, S. (2013b). Paneling "matters" in elementary students' graphic narratives. *Literacy Research and Instruction, 52*(2), 150–171.

Pantaleo, S. (2015). Exploring the intentionality of design in the graphic narrative of one middle-years student. *Journal of Graphic Novels and Comics, 6*(4), 398–418.

Pantaleo, S. (2017a). Exploring the artwork of young students' multimodal compositions. *International Journal of Primary, Elementary and Early Years Education, 45*(1), 17–35.

Pantaleo, S. (2017b). The semantic and syntactic qualities of paneling in students' graphic narratives. *Visual Communication,* 1470357217740393.

Pantaleo, S. (2019). Metalepsis in elementary students' multimodal narrative representations. *Research in the Teaching of English, 54*(1), 8–30.

Pink, S. (2007). *Doing visual ethnography: Images, media and representation in research* (2nd Ed.). SAGE Publications.

Reid, S. F. (2020). Playful images and truthful words: Eighth-graders respond to Shaun tan's "Stick Figures". *Journal of Language and Literacy Education, 16*(1).

Reid, S. F., & Moses, L. (2021). Rewriting deficit storylines: The positioning of one fourth-grader as comics expert. In *English Teaching: Practice & Critique.* (First available online).

Reid, S. F., & Serafini, F. (2018). More than words: An investigation of the young adult and middle-grade multimodal novel. *Journal of Children's Literature, 44*(2), 32–44.

Saldaña, J. (2016). *The coding manual for qualitative researchers*. SAGE.

Selznick, B. (2015). *The Marvels*. Scholastic.

Serafini, F. (2014). *Reading the visual: An introduction to teaching multimodal literacy*. Teachers College Press.

Serafini, F., & Ladd, S. M. (2008). The challenge of moving beyond the literal in literature discussions. *Journal of Language and Literacy Education, 4*(2), 6–20.

Siegel, M. (2012). New times for multimodality? Confronting the accountability culture. *Journal of Adult and Adolescent Literacy, 55*(8), 671–681.

Staake, B. (2014). *Bluebird*. Random House.

Tan, S. (2007). *The arrival*. Arthur A. Levine Books.

Tan, S. (2011a). The lost thing. In S. Tan (Author & Illustrator) *Lost & found: Three by Shaun Tan* (Reprint edition). Arthur A. Levine Books.

Tan, S. (2011b). The red tree. In S. Tan (Author & Illustrator) *Lost & found: Three by Shaun Tan* (Reprint edition). Arthur A. Levine Books.

The New London Group. (1996/2000). A pedagogy of multiliteracies: Designing social futures. In B. Cope & M. Kalantzis (Eds.), *Multiliteracies: Literacy Learning and the Design of Social Futures* (pp. 9–39). Routledge.

Tracy, S. J. (2013). *Qualitative research methods: Collecting evidence, crafting analysis, communicating impact*. John Wiley & Sons.

Wiggins, G. P., & McTighe, J. (2005). *Understanding by design*. ASCD.

# SECTION 2

# Troubling Notions of Situating Practice

# 4

# A CALL TO ACTION

## Setting the Stage for Equity in the Classroom

*Kim O'Donnell*

Literacy teachers of middle school students are in a unique position to engage students who are transgender or non-binary. Strategic shifts in materials, thinking and planning are key, along with administrative understanding and district level guidance that recognizes and protects all students, creating a more equitable and meaningful school environment. In providing safe spaces, intentional instruction and materials gives our students a chance to not only see the world, but likely themselves in a place of value not shame.

Valuing diversity in school today is simply not optional; classrooms are filled with students of varied backgrounds, beliefs, and identities. Student engagement is more important than ever, and to respect the varied tapestry within a classroom, students should see and hear themselves within the context and curriculum of their classes. Although race is often at the forefront of recognizing diversity, educators must be cognizant of other marginalized groups within the classroom setting. By doing so, not only will engagement be promoted, but a statement is made regarding the acceptance of the breadth of diversity within our own culture.

In a 2014 *Scientific American* article, Katherine Phillips suggested that socially diverse groups tend to be more creative and innovative as well as more successful at solving challenging problems. Any educator will recognize the value in that statement, and it makes sense to leverage diversity to better instruct and develop students.

Within this chapter, I will explore the call to recognize and support transgender and non-binary identities in the context of the classroom. First, understanding the ramifications of not recognizing this potential subgroup will be discussed along with influential policies at both the federal and state levels to develop a deeper understanding of why this work is so relevant. Second, I will offer a framework for teachers to support equity when planning lessons and considering content.

DOI: 10.4324/9781003171508-6

Middle school students are at a crossroads in their social, emotional, and physical development. Although still child-like in many ways, the level of physical and mental change between the ages of 10 and 15 is remarkable. Perhaps, one of the most important considerations we, as educators, must keep in mind is that our middle level students are existing in a place where they are developing their own sense of personal identity, morality, and perception. With growing maturity comes the ability to see the world through many different lenses; our curricula and practice must feed this growing nuance if we are to help our students develop into productive and democratic citizens (National Middle School Association, 2003).

Youth today are also developing an awareness of their orientation, sexual attraction, and gender identity at younger ages, 12 to 13 years old (Grossman, et al., 2009). Literacy teachers of middle school students are in a unique position to engage students who are transgender or non-binary. Strategic shifts in materials, thinking and planning are key, along with administrative understanding and district level guidance that recognizes and protects all students, creating a more equitable and meaningful school environment.

## Setting the Context: Key Issues in LGBTQI+ Education

In schools today, it is highly evident that minorities are visible more so than ever before, adding a rich and often complicated diversity to the school community. One minority, often not considered and marginalized within the school context, is LGBT and non-binary youth. Schools are sites for students to develop socially, emotionally, and academically, but often issues like bullying and harassment mar the culture for students, even more for students who identify as LGBT or non-conforming gender. These issues lead to complications for students, including risky behaviors, absenteeism, substance abuse, and even suicide for this population. LGBT students come to school with unique needs that cannot be overlooked or ignored due to inherent bias, externally or internally. Transgender students deal with higher levels of bullying and harassment (Rands, 2009) and research in school climate and culture shows that safety is always a significant concern (Kosciw et al., 2016). This lack of safety impacts engagement and success in the school setting; it is time to recognize the lack of equity in access between cisgender and those who are transgender and non-binary students.

The results of the Gay Lesbian Straight Educators' Network 2015 Safe Schools (GLSEN, 2015) survey of LGBT students regarding the challenges and successes of the LGBT population in school are concerning. At school, 85.2% of LGBT students report being verbally harassed or threatened based on gender identity or personal attributes, usually sexual orientation (71%) or gender expression (55%). Students also report physical assault for similar reasons, 13% for sexual orientation and 9% for gender expression. In addition to physical and verbal harassment, 47% of students reported cyber harassment through texting and social media like Facebook.

Of significant concern, 58% of LGBT students who experienced these issues in school did not report to school personnel. The students perceived the interventions as being ineffective and expressed concern that reporting the issues would make them worse. In addition to being subjected to negative comments and harassment by school staff and their peers, 63% of respondents indicated that, despite awareness, nothing was done by staff or administration to mitigate the harassment (GLSEN, 2015). Considering this statistic, concern should be very elevated, and every student should feel safe, physically and mentally within our schools.

A further marginalized subgroup under the LGBT umbrella, transgender students encounter numerous obstacles within the school setting (Goodenow et al., 2006). Transgender students indicated that they experienced discriminating school policies. Over 42% of transgender students reported they were prevented from using their preferred name/pronouns and nearly 60% reported being required to use locker rooms and bathrooms of their birth sex designation. Roughly 32% of transgender students questioned indicated they were also prevented from wearing clothes that were representative of their preferred gender identity (GLSEN, 2015).

As a result, the report suggested LGBT students in general are likely to have increased depression, earn lower grades, and have increased absenteeism. The situation for transgender students is even more concerning. Transgender students, specifically, are three times more likely to miss school, have even lower grade point averages, have even higher rates of depression, and are twice as likely not to pursue post-secondary education (GLSEN, 2015).

Schools today, at all levels, are faced with addressing these issues specific to lesbian, gay, bisexual, transgender, and non-binary students. Leaders, from the Central Office to the building leadership are in a unique position to support the LGBT population. This responsibility is translated back to the classroom and with staff overall as culture and climate have a true impact on students within these marginalized subgroups (O'Donnell, 2020).

Literacy leaders, principals or otherwise, have an opportunity to create gender inclusive and aware classrooms and curriculum. What is concerning about this? The significant lack of practical knowledge about gender and inclusivity. Without a base of knowledge to build upon, the concept of a widely inclusive curriculum is daunting at best. Leading a school is a complicated responsibility and leadership preparation is varied. School administrator preparation focuses on a wide breadth of diversity which unfortunately offers definite limits when dealing with certain marginalized groups such as LGBT/TGNC youth. What matters is that principals can make a positive difference, even if their preparation for administrative positions is lacking (Boyland, 2016), and they are responsible for supporting vulnerable or marginalized students (Mugisha, 2015).

In their managerial role, principals need to develop an understanding of social justice, fostering an equitable experience for all including marginalized groups.

Administrative preparation programs, to date, lack this concept of social justice and the LGBTQ experience is almost entirely missing from the literature on principal preparation (Boyland, 2016). In a detailed review of literature by O'Malley and Capper (2015), limited empirical data exists on how programs across the country support administrators in developing a skill set to work with the LGBTQ population, be it staff, students, or families.

As much as principals have a marginal or absent base of understanding, teachers are in the same quandary, if not deeper. Teacher pre-service programs prepare new educators to face the many challenges of today's youth through curriculum and instruction. One area found consistently lacking in teacher preparation is understanding sexual minorities, be it gay, lesbian, transgender, or other sexual identities. The attitudes and perceptions of teachers are critical in how these students interact and function in the school setting. Although some mention of LGBT students may be made in a class dealing with minorities in general, pre-service teachers would benefit from a more in-depth exploration of the issues and attitudes that specifically impact LGBTQ students. Along with principals, who in many instances are responsible for professional development, teachers must be very intentional and precise in acquiring deeper knowledge of the LGBTQ and gender expansive student group.

Institutionally, teachers face curriculum demands, increased workloads, varied professional training, and the actual written policies of the district. Coupled with a commonly shared teachers' theme of not trusting administration to respond when they do report, teachers often attempt to address issues within the microcosm of their classroom instead of a broader attempt institutionally (Meyer, 2008). Further, teachers pointed out that professional development in managing LGBT issues was sorely lacking as they were most often channeled into development related to their content area or instruction (Meyer, 2008).

Beyond the formal institutional issues within schools and districts, teachers also face social influences (Meyer, 2008), in administration perception, community values, and interpersonal relationships. Teachers indicated that administrators demonstrated their personal beliefs and values in how they handled situations around sexual and homophobic/transphobic harassment. Clearly, the impact of leadership response will have a trickle-down effect on staff. "By choosing to not address these issues, administrators teach their staff that these behaviors are not considered problematic…" (Meyer, 2008, p. 562). This statement is worrisome, especially considering how much impact an administrator's action or non-action has on the school setting and climate.

Although not always a major influence, teachers indicated that parents have an impact on how issues are handled within the school community, from insufficient support of administrator and teacher decisions to actual verbal harassment of staff when in disagreement with their consequences for inappropriate behavior (Meyer, 2008). Coupling this with the fact that peer influence within any school community is also a strong variable; one can see how the culture of response within a school or district can be impacted. Finally, teachers have to manage their own internal beliefs and values. These are built upon experiences both within family and their own education (Meyer, 2008).

Where should educators begin, in giving consideration to trans and non-binary equity within the classroom? The inclusivity of students who are transgender or non-binary goes beyond a single classroom as the culture and climate of a school or arguably a district have due influence on pedagogy and practice. By developing an understanding of policy, both current and historical, as well as understanding the positions of influential national educational organizations and affiliates, both teachers and leaders can take steps to adopt a framework to apply to literacy instruction, and overall instruction that supports an equitable and inclusive classroom experience for all students.

## More than One Place

Teachers, well intended in how they may create an inclusive classroom, are one part of a larger microcosm. As previously stated, the climate and culture of the school begins with leaders. In typical hierarchical fashion, the dictates of the school board to the superintendent trickle down to other stakeholders, including building principals and teachers. However, it is critical to realize that student differences are not a hierarchy but need to be viewed in an equitable manner, accepting that an individual is an intersection of many identities including intellect, race, gender, language, sexuality, gender identity, and many more (Lugg, 2003).

To truly embrace a sustaining change for students, policy and practice must merge. The efforts of a singular teacher or principal will have an impact, but with the ever-increasing numbers of students who are transgender or gender expansive, we have a responsibility to start from the top. To best understand where policy lies, it is important to have both a federal and state/local perspective.

## Policy: A Historical Perspective for Understanding Gender Issues

In order to have context for why, as educators, it is absolutely critical to make appropriate adjustments to pedagogy and curriculum, one must develop a sense of how the legal and policy landscape has shifted over the years at both the federal and state level. Interestingly enough, laws have evolved yet classroom practice, for the most part, has lagged behind.

Protections for LGBT students start at the federal level and funnel through the states and local school districts. Beginning at the federal level, Title VII and Title IX have been applied to issues involving transgender students and employees. Both laws, in different applications, went beyond binary gender to gender identity and in some cases specifically applied to transgender students.

Other protections include the First Amendment to the Constitution, with the seminal case *Tinker vs. Des Moines* (Tinker v. Des Moines Independent

Community School, 393 U.S., 503), that protects free speech, allowing for students to be "out" or to protest peacefully. This also includes the right to take a same sex date to the prom and allows for students to dress based on their preferred gender identity (GSAFE, n.d.). The Equal Protection Clause of the 14th Amendment to the Constitution states that all citizens have a federal and constitutional right to equal protection. This protection is afforded to all citizens and indicates that schools have a duty to protect LGBT students from harassment on an equal basis as with other students (DeGarmo, 2017; Title VII of the Civil Rights Act of 1964, § 7, 42 u.s.c. § 2000e et seq 1964).

Title VII is applicable to employment law, clearly outside of the school realm. However, the law, much as Title IX, has been applied to individuals who are transgender outlining that discrimination can take place on the presumption of how individuals of a specific gender should act or present themselves. The concept of nonconformity is important, despite the fact that it is an employment law, because from a legal standpoint the law recognizes that transgender individuals do have rights. Taylor (2007) suggested that the law is no longer based on external genitalia but also in gender identity.

Title IX was originally passed in 1972 during the Nixon years and has undergone multiple revisions to date, most recently to students who identify as transgender or non-conforming gender. The law encompasses gender equity for boys and girls in every educational program that receives federal monies. In its entirety, the law states that no person in the United States shall, on the basis of sex, be denied the benefits of, or be subjected to discrimination under any education program or activity receiving Federal financial assistance (Title IX, 1972). Title IX is applicable to both state and federally based programs, including 16,500 school districts, 7,000 post-secondary institutions, charter schools, libraries, for-profit schools, and museums.

Most often, when people refer to Title IX, they are operating under the presumption that it is about women's sports. This is true, but the law also covers multiple areas including access to higher education, education for pregnant or parenting students, employment, learning environment, math and science, sexual harassment, and standardized testing and technology.

From 1972 when it was enacted, to 1975 when Title IX became a law, Title IX has undergone multiple attempts, and often failures, for revision in the area of discrimination, mainly in the area of sports. The Office of Civil Rights (OCR) began oversight in 1980 and continues to address complaints and provide support and supervision to date (Title IX of 1972). Until very recently, the law has been applied to binary genders; however, in 2013, complaints surrounding students that identify as transgender or non-conforming gender appeared and were reviewed.

Title IX has been applied a number of times beyond its original intent. For the purpose of this discussion, the most significant application is the recognition that harassment against transgender students constitutes a violation of rights. The OCR (U.S. Department of Education's Office for Civil Rights) is focused on the concept that genitalia are not the only basis of gender identification (Darden, 2014). This recent application posed significant challenges for school districts, which are largely unprepared to create and manage safe and non-discriminatory settings for both transgender students and staff.

In February of 2017, President Trump rolled back guidance for transgender students that had been established by the Obama administration. Attorney General Jeff Sessions felt that the Obama administration's legal analysis was weak, and evidence was limited. Sessions recommended that the guidance be pulled back despite strong reactions from human rights and other advocacy groups. Former President Trump added that the treatment of students who are transgender is a state issue and should be handled in that manner. Betsy DeVos, the former Secretary of Education, was initially reluctant to have the guidance letter pulled back, stressing that schools must protect all students. Her position was later reiterated by the Justice Department under the label of bullying, indicating that all students, including LGBTQ students, should be protected. The rollback had implications for high-profile cases, such as Gavin Grimm, a transgender student from Virginia who sued his school in order to use the restrooms aligned to his gender identity. A local judge issued an injunction, but the Supreme Court, who agreed to hear his case, blocked that injunction at the request of the school board. At the time, this was a breakthrough case, because of the Supreme Court's action (*Grimm v. Gloucester Cnty. Sch. Bd.*, 972 F.3d 586 (4th Cir. 2020). However, once the Trump Administration rolled back the guidance letter, the Supreme Court returned the case to the US Court of Appeals, Fourth Circuit who in turn returned the case to the state level courts. Gavin's quest to use the restroom of his choice for his senior year was now a moot point as he had graduated. The behavior of the current administration and courts was deemed to have a significant negative impact.

Despite the rollback, Title IX, by court rule, has been applied to transgender issues but the U.S. Department of Education is not likely to investigate or respond to these issues—leaving the states to handle issues if they are so inclined. To date, only 16 states have legislation specifically related to transgender individuals.

## State and Local Level Policies

Coupled with federal protections, numerous states and municipalities have put protections in place for both transgender students and employees. Twenty-two states have hate crime laws that cover sexual orientation. However, the inclusiveness of protection for transgender individuals is not nearly as broad. These protections vary in consistency and application, so in a broad sense, it is reasonable to seek specific understanding of these available protections relative to one's geographic location.

In some states, policies exist to protect the rights of transgender/nonconforming gender students. California, in January of 2014, became the first state to legally require schools to allow transgender students to use the bathroom, locker room, and participate in sports based on their identified gender (Darden, 2014). In February of 2014, the Virginia High School league enacted a policy that supported transgender students having undergone sex reassignment surgery or hormonal treatment being able to join the athletic team that fits their identity (Darden, 2014).

In addition to policies, cases ruled upon at the state level indicate shifting support for transgender students. Two recent examples include the case of Coy Mathis, a happy six-year-old from Colorado born biologically male but identifying as female, and the case of Nicole Maines, from the state of Maine. Coy, who dressed and identified as female, was forbidden to use the girl's restroom in her school by officials. Coy's parents, Katherine and Jeremy, learned that their son struggled with what was referred to as gender dysphoria. The school, not considering the well-being of the child, held fast to their refusal of bathroom access based on self-identified gender (Whitelocks, 2013). The parents of Mathis filed a complaint and the Colorado Division of Civil Rights found that her rights had been violated based on her gender identity (Katherine Mathis and Jeremy Mathis, On Behalf of Coy Mathis, Minor v. Fountain-Fort Carson School District #8, 2012). In Maine, Nicole Maines, born Wyatt Maines, won a significant victory against RSU 26, with the Maine Supreme Judicial Court voting five-one that the Maine Human Rights Act was correct in ruling that the school district discriminated against Nicole's rights under the application of gender identity (Doe, et al. v. Clenchy, 2011).

Although the rulings of these cases are isolated to their respective states, they demonstrate a changing view of the law in that both Maines and Mathis' self-identified gender was recognized as opposed to their birth gender. In thinking of federal policy, this is not unlike the cases of Macy v. Holder (2012) or Price Waterhouse v. Hopkins (1989).

Clearly, discomfort still exists amongst parents, teachers, and community members in large and religious organizations in regard to transgender rights. However, those in positions to make decisions need to put away their discomfort and opinions and focus on what is in the best interest of students, ultimately and hopefully limiting the legal issues that may arise (Darden, 2014). It is clear that some foundational legal actions lend themselves to supporting trans and gender expansive students, the question remains how to do so.

## Professional Organization Supports: In the Right Direction

A number of professional organizations have lent their voice and influence toward supporting trans and non-binary students. The National Association of Secondary School Principals (NASSP) has a position statement specific to transgender students, encouraging school leaders to create equitable and safe schools, and has suggested several actions that federal, state, and local policy makers should follow to support this work. NASSP also provides professional standards and stresses the importance of school administrators understanding how laws, most specifically Title IX, intersect with gender in the school setting. As principals are most often at the forefront of professional development, NASSP stresses the importance of principals providing professional development that develops a healthy culture around gender and gender identity (NASSP, 2021). In similar fashion, the National Association of Elementary Principals has offered similar guidance and direction (NAESP, 2021).

Although district leaders and school principals have due influence on the development and sustaining safe school culture, the true change agents are those who stand in front of students every single day, the teachers. A number of professional organizations have taken positions on gender/transgender issues, offering members support and guidance.

The National Council of English Teachers (NCTE) responded swiftly to the 2016 Trump rollback, reaching out to members with a call to activism. NCTE advocated for making gender ordinary, not exceptional across multiple media, including books, film, plays, poems, and other modes of expression. NCTE stressed that through instruction, an affirming and expansive view of gender is achievable (NCTE, 2021).

The International Literacy Association (ILA) has posited that diversity in literature is essential and "reflects a dynamic intersection of race, ethnicity, gender, sexual orientation, ability, economic condition, religion and more …" (p.2).

The National Educational Association (NEA) and the American Federation of Teachers (AFT) both lend great support to students who are LGBTQI, from providing member training to supporting policies that affirm the identities our students choose.

The AFT has adopted resolutions that lend strong support to LGBT/TGNC students in both matters of safety and instructional practice at the district and school level. Politically, the AFT has urged states to adopt policies that support and protect this marginalized student group. This resolution followed the political actions of former President Trump in 2016 and has remained active since that time. It should be noted that the American Federation of Teachers boasts well over one million members and has historically supported equity and civil rights (American Federation of Teachers, n.d.)

Similarly, the National Educational Association (NEA) has multiple references available that both illustrate the actions that educators are taking to support LGBT/TGNC youth. NEA members also have access to a number of resources specifically related to TGNC support in schools and have also given a very clear message that education is a civil right, for all students (National Educators Association, 2021) (LGBTQ Nation, 2021).

For teachers, having the support of their local and national organizations is critical as this work challenges the status quo, or heteronormativity that is largely prevalent within our schools. Given that I have already identified that research indicates principals have limited background knowledge regarding LGBT/TGNC youth and may not have the depth of knowledge to support teachers, it is important that these resources are broadly shared as the impact will be significant on students, especially from a social justice perspective.

While these organizations champion gender expansive and transgender students, the onus of the support will fall into the school and classroom. In such, it will be important for teachers to have a practical framework to build upon, especially within their content area. Literacy instructors are in a position to access and utilize multiple resources that mirror the existence of students who are trans or non-binary. Doing so allows for opportunity to not only build relationships but also provides desperately needed validation to marginalized students.

## Beyond the Binary: A Gender Expansive Learning Experience

As teachers, we all enter our classrooms with a breadth of different experiences and backgrounds. Taking inventory of that and understanding one's limits and capacities is a strong first step when breaking down the binary or heteronormative barrier. Consider how familiar you are with terminology relevant to gender or gender identities. What biases do you have? How has your environment impacted your beliefs about gender expansive youth? In understanding self, the intentionality in setting up a classroom, preparing lessons, and selecting curriculum can be done with a lens of equity. Coupled with understanding of the complexities of middle school age growth and development, a truly inclusive and accessible setting that supports students in seeing gender expansiveness is in reach.

Content aside, basic parameters exist for both classroom setting and planning. Intentionally creating accessible learning spaces has the additional benefit of not only recognizing all students but likely will create an environment that nurtures creativity, encourages problem solving, and improves overall decision making (Levine & Stark, 2015; Phillips, 2014). To develop and nurture those spaces, as suggested by Dana Stachowiak, teachers can utilize four practices to support a gender inclusive classroom:

- acknowledge gender as fluid;
- identify gender category oppression, where male is privileged over female;
- recognize transgender category oppression, where the same woman oppressed by men and male privilege is privileged over a transgender woman because she conforms to gender category norms;
- challenge gender and transgender category oppression.

(Stachowiak, 2018)

Not only do teachers need to embody these actions within the confines of their classroom, they must encourage students to as well. By acknowledging chosen names/pronouns and respecting the confidentiality of the transgender or non-binary student, the teacher by default has already committed to a vested interest in that student. Setting a tone of respect and not making assumptions about the student is also key in creating a welcoming environment. Ideally, the creation of a classroom where multiple perspectives and views are recognized and acknowledged, the better the opportunity for all students to feel included.

As previously discussed, students that present with alternative gender or expression struggle to stay in school. By creating a curriculum that is inclusive, research has shown that a positive correlation exists between that curricula construct and LGBT/TGNC students remaining and succeeding in school (Kosciw, Greytak, Giga, Villenas, & Danischewski, 2016). In the words of Rudine Sims Bishop (1990):

> Books are sometimes windows, offering views of worlds that may be real or imagined, familiar or strange. These windows are also sliding glass doors, and readers have only to walk through in imagination to become part of whatever world has been created or recreated by the author. When lighting conditions are just right, however, a window can also be a mirror.
>
> (p. 10)

Literacy instructors are particularly well positioned to support a gender expansive experience for their students. The inclusion of gender creative or LGBTQ+ literature in the classroom is not a standalone event but should be a through-line, especially when considering equity. This intentional inclusion also removes the stigma of gender fluidity or preference as abnormal, or separate from themes traditionally found within the ELA classroom or curriculum (Clark & Blackburn, 2009). Largely, our schools are heteronormative and by challenging this norm, teachers are able to present our students who are LGBTQ/gender expansive as part of the school community, not outsiders. By disrupting this norm, it is quite possible that teachers can impact the issue of intolerance and even bullying as they reduce the purported "difference" and embrace gender in an expansive manner.

The practice, or pedagogy of teaching using literature with LGBTQ themes, must go further than simply offering or introducing the material to students. In such, dismantling the prevalent standard of heteronormativity and embracing other identities sets the stage for social action, as Clark and Blackburn (2009) offered, creating a disruption of the assumption that all students are straight and potentially homophobic. Classrooms and libraries should have materials and books that represent gender expansiveness and LGBT identities, first normalizing it, and second to provide students an opportunity to choose books that may very well represent themselves.

Much as we ask students to view content through the lens of race and racism, a similar practice, or reading "queerly," can be employed with text that does not necessarily include LGBTQ or gender fluid content. Rich critical conversation can be had regarding the absence of character or in concept, pending the material being used. Much as critical race theory encompasses systemic racism and marginalization of people of color, approaching text from a queer perspective allows for examination and discussion around the omission, or inclusion of LGBT and gender expansive individuals. The point is to have students develop the capacity to have conversations that look beyond the print, recognizing missing perspectives, challenging those absences and discussing how that impacts the text as a whole.

We have established that students who are LGBTQ/gender expansive experience higher levels of bullying and intolerance in school. Wood, Kissel and Miller (2016) suggested that teachers should "intentionally position their classroom community as a safe space." The lack of safety in school is a prevalent marker for LGBT/TGNC students, creating a safe space or as Wood, et al. (2016) posits, a safe-enough space, the teacher opens pathways to both academic engagement and student well-being. Blackburn and Schey (2017) also suggested that by incorporating intersectionality in the study of LGBTQ centered literature, the teacher sets the stage for all students to find elements of themselves within the content. In doing so, the teacher broadens the conversation about civil rights and equity for numerous marginalized groups, furthering the inclusivity of the classroom and, one would believe, creating a more open and tolerant environment for broad discussion.

Perhaps the most functional approach to supporting LGBT/TGNC students within the literacy classroom is best outlined by the National Council of Teachers of English. NCTE has maintained a steadfast commitment to supporting marginalized students and their suggestions have room for broad application to content as well as a more focused approach for a literacy classroom (NCTE, 2021). It is critically important for teachers to reflect upon their own beliefs and understandings, taking into consideration their own experiences with gender/gender expansiveness. This reflective practice, an intentional awareness of how gender is represented within literature directly, or possibly indirectly, sets a stage for preparing to assist students in having discussions that center around gender within the classroom context. Multiple resources are at the ready, identifying books of varied genres and topics for middle grade students. Organizations like the Human Rights Campaign Foundation Welcoming Schools (HRC, 2021), Learning for Justice (Learning for Justice, n.d.) and Teach for America (Teach for America, 2021) have specific resources to support educators as they take steps to broaden the classroom experience. These resources vary from professional reading, professional development, and even suggestions for curriculum materials. By no means is this an exhaustive list, but several of many examples widely available to support teachers as they build their classrooms, seek content, and plan for inclusive and equitable learning for all students.

With an established and intentional mindset, the educator must turn to the more tangible, the actual curriculum materials within their classrooms and perhaps beyond, for example, the school library. If educators are truly attempting to set equity in front, students should have access to materials that reflect not only the LGBT/TGNC group but also other intersecting identities. Earlier, I discussed that this work needs to be a consistent part of the instructional landscape, the practice of examining the presence or absence of gender within literature should be an ingrained practice amongst literacy practitioners.

What is important to consider is that much like race, it is never too early (or late for that matter) to call attention to what has been established as a societal norm that, with the shifts in our society, is overdue to be challenged. The delineation of boys and girls, men and women, is not the absolute of our larger population; research is clear in showing that more than ever, previously marginalized groups and subgroups are emerging from the background, no longer wishing to be silenced. It is our duty, and as the NCTE so succinctly states, the correct ethical teaching approach to help students view the world beyond the binary, recognizing that gender is far more than the male/female ideal. Middle school students are developmentally unique and at a stage where their ability to think about the world around them, the potential conflicts and situations of others (and very possibly themselves) can facilitate an engaging and thought-provoking learning experience that constructs meaning and context (Georgiady & Romano, 1977). For many students, this will be an opportunity to affirm their own feelings or reflect on situations that are directly or indirectly related to their existence (Lewis & Sembiante, 2019). Much as our political and policy landscape has evolved, classroom practice has lagged behind the current context of society. By opening up to new perspectives and perceptions, we allow students the opportunity to engage in thoughtful discourse and analysis without inflicting or assuming the overbearing belief that heteronormativity is the only norm, within our own schools or larger society.

Providing safe spaces, intentional instruction and materials gives our students a chance to not only see the world, but likely themselves in a place of value not shame. Literature opens a window to rich discussion when a practitioner is willing to challenge the norm of school, the heteronormative stance that has largely dictated the perspective of our content. Earlier in this chapter, I pointed out that we cannot look at marginalized groups in hierarchy, one is not more important than the other. As educators we have a responsibility and ability to open up the opportunity to help students see the world in a broader perspective, to question the norms that have long dictated our practices within school. More so, the safety and well-being of students is at risk, our classrooms need to be safe spaces for critical thinking and discourse and we need to support students in finding out about their own identities, intersections, and beliefs. With all of this in mind, the remainder of Rudine Sims Bishop's (1990) quote is most appropriate in closing this chapter.

> Literature transforms human experience and reflects it back to us, and in that reflection we can see our own lives and experiences as part of a larger

human experience. Reading, then, becomes a means of self-affirmation, and readers often seek their mirrors in books.

(p. 10)

Now more than ever, our students need to develop skills to look at the world through a lens of equity and feel confident in their ability to ask hard questions, demand answers, and formulate creative solutions to the current issues our world faces. They will be the change, our duty as educators is to ensure they are ready.

## References

American Federation of Teachers. (n.d.). About us. Retrieved from http://www.aft.org/about

Bishop, R. S. (1990). Mirrors, Windows and Sliding Glass Doors. *Perspectives: Choosing and Using Books for the Classroom*, *6*(3), ix–xi.

Boyland, L. G., Swensson, J., Ellis, J. G., Coleman, L. L., & Boyland, M. I. (2016). Principals Can and Should Make a Positive Difference for LGBTQ Students. *Journal of Leadership Education*, *15*(4), 117–131.

Clark, C. T., & Blackburn, M.V. (2009). Reading LGBT-Themed Literature with Young People: What's Possible? *English Journal*, *98*(4), 25–32.

Blackburn, M.V., & Schey, R. (2017). Adolescent literacies beyond heterosexual hegemony. *Adolescent Literacy: A Handbook of Practice-Based Research*, 38–60.

Darden, E. C. (2014). ED LAW: The law trends toward transgender students. *Phi Delta Kappan*, *96*(2), 76–77. https://doi.org/10.1177/0031721714553415

DeGarmo, A. (2017, April 12). The 14th Amendment's Equal Protection Clause and Transgender Students: Gavin Grimm's Plight [Web log post]. Retrieved April 9, 2018, from https://www.concordlawschool.edu/blog/equal-protection-clause-transgender-students/

Doe v. Regional School Unit 26, 86 A.3d 600, 2014 M.E. 11 (Me. 2014). Retrieved from https://casetext.com/case/doe-v-regl-sch-unitG.G V. Gloucester County School Board 822 F.3d 709 (4th Cir. 2016).Retrieved May 3, 2021 from https://www.supremecourt.gov/docket/docketfiles/html/public/20-1163.html

Georgiady, N. P. & Romano, L. C. (1977) Growth Characteristics of Middle School Children: Curriculum Implications, *Middle School Journal*, *8*(1), 12–23. DOI: 10.1080/00940771.1977.11494804

Goodenow, C., Szalacha, L., & Westheimer, K. (2006). School support groups, other school factors, and the safety of sexual minority adolescents. *Psychology in the Schools*, *43*(5), 573–589.

Grossman, A. H., Haney, A. P., Edwards, P., Alessi, E. J., Ardon, M., & Howell, T. J. (2009). Lesbian, gay, bisexual and transgender youth talk about experiencing and coping with school violence: A qualitative study. *Journal of LGBT Youth*, *6*(1), 24–46.

*GSAFE Creating Just Schools for LGBTQ+ Youth*. GSAFE. (2021, May 5). Retrieved from https://gsafewi.org/.

Guidelines for Affirming Gender Diversity through ELA Curriculum and Pedagogy. NCTE. (2021, March 24). Retrieved from https://ncte.org/statement/guidelines-for-affirming-gender-diversity-through-ela-curriculum-and-pedagogy/.

Human Rights Campaign. (2021, May 5). *Welcoming Schools: Welcoming Schools*. Human Rights Campaign. Retrieved from https://www.welcomingschools.org/.

Kosciw, J. G., Greytak, E. A., Giga, N. M., Villenas, C. & Danischewski, D. J. (2016). *The 2015 National School Climate Survey: The experiences of lesbian, gay, bisexual, transgender, and queer youth in our nation's schools*. GLSEN.

Learning for Justice. (n.d.) Retrieved from https://www.learningforjustice.org/.

Levine, S. S., and Stark, D. 2015. "Diversity Makes You Brighter." *The New York Times*. Retrieved from http://www.nytimes.com/2015/12/09/opinion/diversity-makes-you-brighter.html (April 11, 2016).

Lewis, R. K. and Sembiante, S. F. 2019. "Research and Practice in Transition: Improving Support and Advocacy of Transgender Middle School Students," *Middle Grades Review*, 5(1), Article 2. Retrieved from https://scholarworks.uvm.edu/mgreview/vol5/iss1/2

LGBTQ Nation. (2021, May 4). Teachers union pledges full support for transgender students. *News*. Retrieved from https://www.lgbtqnation.com/2016/07/teachers-union-pledges-full-support-transgender-students/

Lugg, C. A. (2003). Our straitlaced administrators: The law, lesbian, gay, bisexual, and transgendered educational administrators, and the assimilationist imperative. *Journal of School Leadership*, 3(2), 51–86.

Macy v. Holder, 2012 W.L. 1435995 (2012). Retrieved from https://harvardlawreview.org/wpcontent/uploads/pdfs/vol126_macy_v_holder.pdf

Mathis v. Fountain-Fort Carson Sch. Dist., 8 Charge. (2021, April 12) Retrieved from https://archive.org/stream/716966-pdf-of-coy-mathis-ruling/716966-pdf-of-coy-mathis-ruling_djvu.txt

Meyer, E. J. (2008). Gendered harassment in secondary schools: Understanding teachers' (non) interventions. *Gender and Education*, 20(6), 555–570.

Mugisha, V. M. (2015). Fostering tolerance through curricular initiatives: International students contending with LGBT-affirming campus cultures in the US. In J. Aiken, L. Flash, W. Heading-Grant, & F. Miller, (Eds.), *Theory to practice: Fostering diverse and inclusive campus environments*, (192–203). Ypsilanti, MI: National Council of Professors of Educational Administration.

National Association of Elementary School Principals. NAESP. (2021, April 16). Retrieved from http://www.naesp.org/.

National Association of Secondary School Principals. NASSP. (2021, April 16) Retrieved from http://www.nassp.org/

National Council of Teachers of English. (2021, March 24). Guidelines for affirming gender diversity through ELA curriculum and pedagogy. Retrieved from https://ncte.org/statement/guidelines-for-affirming-gender-diversity-through-ela-curriculum-and-pedagogy/

National Educators Association. (2021, May 4). Advocating for a change. *Racial & Social Justice*. Retrieved from https://www.nea.org/advocating-for-change/racial-social-justice

National Middle School Association. (2003). *This we believe: successful schools for young adolescents: a position paper of the National Middle School Association*.

O'Malley, M. P., & Capper, C. A. (2015). A measure of the quality of educational leadership programs for social justice: Integrating LGBTIQ identities into principal preparation. *Educational Administration Quarterly*, 51(2), 290–330.

O'Donnell, K. J. (2020). *Examining School Administrators' Beliefs & Perceptions regarding Transgender Students* (Doctoral dissertation, University of Southern Maine).

Phillips, K. W. (2014, October 1). *How Diversity Makes Us Smarter*. Scientific American. Retrieved from https://www.scientificamerican.com/article/how-diversity-makes-us-smarter/.

Price Waterhouse v. Hopkins, 490 U.S. 228, 109 S. Ct. 1775, 104 L. Ed. 2d 268 (1989). Retrieved from https://www.law.cornell.edu/supremecourt/text/490/228

Rands, Kathleen E. "Considering Transgender People in Education." *Journal of Teacher Education*, vol. 60, no. 4, 2009, pp. 419–431., doi:10.1177/0022487109341475.

Stachowiak, D. (2018, August 9). Creating a Gender Inclusive Classroom [web log]. Retrieved from https://www.literacyworldwide.org/blog/literacy-now/2018/08/09/part-5-creating-a-gender-inclusive-curriculum.

Taylor, J. K. (2007). Transgender identities and public policy in the United States: The relevance for public administration. *Administration & Society*, *39*(7), 833–856.

Teach For America. (2021, April 14). Retrieved from http://www.teachforamerica.org/.

Tinker v. Des Moines Independent Community School District. (Retrieved April 14, 2018, from https://www.oyez.org/cases/1968/21

Title IX of the Education Amendments Act of 1972, 20 U.S.C. §§1681 - 1688 et seq. (1972). Retrieved from https://www.justice.gov/crt/fcs/TitleIX-SexDiscrimination #:~:text=%C2%A71681%20et%20seq.%2C%20into,funded%20education%20 program%20or%20activity.

Title VII of the Civil Rights Act of 1964, § 7, 42 u.s.c. § 2000e et seq (1964). Retrieved from https://www.eeoc.gov/statutes/title-vii-civil-rights-act-1964#:~:text=EDITOR'S %20NOTE%3A%20The%20following%20is,religion%2C%20sex%20and%20 national%20origin.

Whitelocks, S. (2013, June 24). Coy Mathis: Transgender child, 6, in Colorado wins civil rights case to use girls bathroom at school. Retrieved from https://www.dailymail.co.uk/news/article-2347149/Coy-Mathis-Transgender-child-6-Colorado-wins-civil-rights-case-use-girls-bathroom-school.html

Wood, K., Kissel, B., & Miller, E. (2016). Safe zones: Supporting LGBTQ youth through literature. *Voices from the Middle*, *23*(4), 46–54.

# 5

# DIALOGUE AS DISRUPTION

## The Power of Middle Grades Classroom Talk

*Amanda Rigell and Arianna Banack*

In an increasingly polarized political climate (Pew Research Center, 2014), shifting our focus from argumentative prowess to dialogic problem-solving will be essential in helping prepare our students to live successful, fulfilled lives and contribute to our democratic society (Juzwik et al., 2013). Gardoqui (2018) suggested that the current laser focus on argument in classroom instruction makes students "susceptible to an epidemic of our time: the tendency to select facts that support a certain perception of reality" (n.p.). Foregrounded in a scene of national ideological discord is the reality that teachers and students meet in the classroom with varied ethnic, cultural, and racial backgrounds. A workforce of teachers who are predominantly (nearly 80 percent) white and female (Will, 2020) must design instruction that serves an increasingly diverse student body (de Brey et al., 2019). Dialogic classroom structures can help create inclusive environments within diverse classrooms by prioritizing respectful discourse and empathy for one another's perspectives and experiences.

Beyond building inclusive classroom communities, dialogic instruction has potential as a language scaffold for culturally and linguistically diverse learners. Piazza et al. (2015) identified dialogue as one of five key areas of culturally responsive teaching across a review of the literature and reported that "when students engage in dialogue, particularly around texts and life experiences, they use new language, connect the known to the unknown, and expand their worldviews" (p. 8). Dialogic classrooms not only provide opportunities for students to engage with each other, but also with texts and the world around them.

From a literacy perspective, dialogic classroom spaces offer hope for a dire reality middle grades teachers face. Thirty-four percent of eighth grade students who completed the 2019 NAEP assessment demonstrated proficiency in reading, and disaggregated data reveals disparities based on socioeconomic status,

DOI: 10.4324/9781003171508-7

race, and disability (National Center for Education Statistics, 2019). Low reading achievement scores must also be contextualized within decades of research indicating that motivation to read declines from elementary school to the middle grades (Biancarosa & Snow, 2006; Gottfried, 1985; Troyer, 2017). However, literacy research also arms us with information about what kinds of instructional moves support reading motivation, engagement, and achievement. This research emphasizes the significance for adolescents of social interactions around reading (Ivey & Johnston, 2013; Kim et al., 2017; Moje et al., 2008; Piazza & Duncan, 2012), as well as the significance of teacher-student relationships (Bergman, 2017; Kim et al., 2017; Ivey & Johnston, 2013; Piazza & Duncan, 2012; Troyer, 2017). Dialogic teaching, teaching that is designed to give students opportunities to engage in learning talk (Juzwik et al., 2013), opens the door for social interaction around texts as well as more intentional, compassionate teacher-student relationships. Engaging in learning talk with our students positions us to disrupt not only narrow definitions of knowledge or meaning (Bakhtin, 1984; Nystrand, 1997; Rosenblatt, 1993), but also disparities in achievement (Nystrand, 2006) and power dynamics (Kay, 2018).

## Theoretical Framework

This chapter is grounded in social constructivist theory (Vygotsky, 1978), a theory of learning which holds that students experience and understand what they learn through frameworks of language and culture. Our advocacy for dialogic instruction is grounded in the social constructivist tenets that learning is collaborative and that knowledge is co-constructed. Dialogic classrooms allow students to help shape conversations and understand the texts they read and the world they live in through different perspectives.

Dialogic pedagogy, or dialogic teaching, is a pedagogical framework. It has theoretical roots in the work of Bakhtin (1984), who believed meaning is constructed through conversation between people as well as between readers and texts. When our students are in classrooms centering dialogic discussion, they are able to co-construct knowledge in a variety of ways through their interactions with their teacher, peers, and the texts they read.

A dialogic pedagogical framework disrupts the notion of the "right answers." Bakhtin (1984) explained that

> "the dialogic means of seeing truth is conterposed to *official* monologism which pretends to *possess a ready-made truth*... truth is not born nor is it found inside the head of an individual person, it is born *between people* collectively searching for truth, in the process of their dialogic interaction".
>
> (p. 110)

In dialogic discussions, teachers do not begin discussions looking for preconceived answers, or "a ready-made truth." Instead they respond to students and ask them to elaborate on their opinions in order to collectively search for meaning in their dialogic interactions.

Rosenblatt's (1993) transactional theory of reading also aimed to reject "the notion of the autonomous text embodying a single determinate meaning…the wish for a single 'correct' or absolute meaning' for each text" (p. 382). Dialogic pedagogy echoes Rosenblatt's assertion that there is not an "absolute meaning" to be found in the text. When a reader interprets a text written by an author outside their culture, language, peer group, value system, or temporal context, they have to constantly decide whether their interpretation of the text is valid. We suggest that teachers should also provide support for students to engage in dialogue "with the author" of the texts they read through background research and bring this reader-author "dialogue" into class discussions as well. The understandings from such reader-author transactions also contribute to the many "correct" interpretations of a text.

Nystrand (1997) wrote about dialogic pedagogy as instruction that enables students to deeply understand a text, relate to it on a personal level, and move beyond literal comprehension tasks of recall. Dialogic pedagogy goes beyond asking students to recite plot points or remember important dates but seeks to have teachers and students engage in meaningful discussion to co-construct an understanding of literature as it relates to themselves and the present day.

Research literature suggests that dialogic teaching positively impacts learning and growth (Kim & Wilkinson, 2019). Applebee et al. (2003) found that students whose classroom experiences emphasized discussion-based approaches were more prepared to then independently complete challenging literacy tasks. Nystrand (2006) found that dialogic classrooms sparked greater understanding of texts and reduced achievement differences across race, ethnicity, and socioeconomic status. Lysaker et al. (2011) found that the use of dialogic instruction helped increase students' reading comprehension and understandings of others. They explained:

> [D]ialogic pedagogy provides children with demonstrations of the teachers' authentic responses to text… and it invites children to make similar personal connections to the text world. These connections are accepted, valued, and reflected upon by others through discussion, providing a rich context for the development of understanding as well as each reader's contribution to those understandings.
>
> (p. 535)

This *invitation* to students is of the utmost importance as it makes space for student voice(s) in the classroom and "provides teachers opportunities to know their students and cultivate learning activities that connect to their lived experiences" (Gordon, 2019, p. 13). In his brilliant book about dialogic classrooms where participants have meaningful conversations about race, Kay (2018) wrote: "dialogic pedagogy disrupts the traditional classroom power dynamic, positioning school as a place where students have an equal share in their education" (p. 5). In ongoing classroom dialogues, students' contributions are valued as the teacher and students share responsibility in co-constructing knowledge through discussion.

## Models of Dialogic Pedagogy

Scholars have defined and redefined dialogic pedagogy and dialogic teaching, delineating and outlining its principles over decades (see Kim & Wilkinson, 2019). We provide overviews of two commonly cited models here, Alexander (2017) and Nystrand (1997), along with suggestions for the role of each model in thinking about dialogic pedagogy.

Alexander (2017) outlined a dialogic teaching model which consists of five principles. In this model, dialogic teaching is:

- *collective*: teachers and children address learning tasks together, whether as a group or as a class, rather than in isolation;
- *reciprocal*: teachers and children listen to each other, share ideas, and consider alternative viewpoints;
- *supportive*: children articulate their ideas freely, without fear of embarrassment over "wrong" answers; and they help each other to reach common understandings;
- *cumulative*: teachers and children build on their own and each other's ideas and chain them into coherent lines of thinking and enquiry;
- *purposeful*: teachers plan and facilitate dialogic teaching with particular educational goals in view.

(p. 28)

The model also enumerates dozens of indicators that describe contexts for and features of dialogic teaching (Kim & Wilkinson, 2019). We suggest that the five principles above are of great value in setting intentions for a dialogic teaching practice and in guiding ongoing reflection within one's teaching praxis.

Christoph and Nystrand (2001) described a compact model of dialogic teaching moves based on Nystrand's (1997) *dialogically organized instruction* model. These teaching moves may be more easily operationalized than those of other models as teachers work within restrictive curricular mandates or district-level expectations about classroom instruction. They include:

a) asking authentic questions, which value and elicit student ideas and not just mastery of information; b) practicing uptake, in which teachers ask students follow-up questions to pursue points and lines of inquiry introduced by students; and c) using high-level evaluation, which valorizes students' responses and allows their ideas and responses to influence the direction of classroom discourse.

(p. 251)

By asking authentic questions, which incorporate both informational requests and open-ended questions, students are given the opportunity to contribute to discussions in ways that determine the course of dialogue (Nystrand, 1997). Students also take a more active role in the discussion as the conversation moves in the direction the students take it. Authentic questioning asks about students' personal experiences as a way to spark discussion and engage students (Nystrand 1997).

After using authentic questions to spark discussion, practicing uptake is dependent on participants listening to one another during discussion as the conversation builds upon each other's responses. Uptake builds on the thoughts of everyone involved by creating links between each participant and helps create cohesion in the discussion through connection making (Nystrand et al., 2003). Incorporating uptake into a conversation makes student responses a new topic of discussion, therefore giving students a more active role in contributing to the dialogue. It also requires students to stay engaged during discussion as the topic is dependent on the dialogue happening. Nystrand (1997) noted "uptake plays a prominent role in discussion as conversants listen and respond appropriately to each other" (p. 39). When a teacher fails to use uptake to ask for additional opinions, the opportunity to make connections, and meaning, can be lost. Asking students to elaborate on each other's answers, or provide a counterpoint to their response, can be ways of encouraging uptake in dialogic discussion.

To encourage further dialogue, teachers must use high-level evaluation in response to student talk. Christoph and Nystrand (2001) helped explain criteria to determine if a teacher's comments move beyond simply validating (e.g. "that's right") by noticing if the teacher's response both validated the student's answer *and* moved the discussion forward (p. 282). Christoph and Nystrand (2001) operationalized high-level evaluation using two criteria:

> a) the teacher's certification of response ("Good," "Interesting," etc.) and b) the teacher's incorporation of the response usually in the form of either an elaboration (or commentary) or a followup question (e.g., "Can you say more about that?" or "Why do you say that?").
>
> (p. 282)

High-level evaluation during discussion incorporates both aspects of the above criteria so students feel both validated and are given the opportunity to further contribute and shape the discussion. Teacher responses that stop at "correct" or "good point" fail to promote critical thinking and can stall discussion rather than enable it to flourish.

By utilizing the three discourse moves, authentic questioning, uptake, and high-level evaluation, outlined by Christoph and Nystrand (2001), teachers can help their classrooms become places where dialogic discussion is the norm, student ideas are valued, and students are placed at the center of their own learning. While Christoph and Nystrand (2001) emphasized the role of the teacher in the structure above, we believe students can also participate in driving uptake and high-level evaluation. As teachers model the above strategies, they can then encourage students to take on more responsibility during discussions by using uptake and high-level evaluation to respond to their peers. This allows students to disrupt the power dynamics of the classroom even further and take stake in their own learning as they become the driving forces behind discussion.

## Theory into Practice

Co-constructing a dialogic classroom with our middle grades students isn't easily facilitated by reading one book, one chapter, or the notes we've scribbled after one professional development session. It is ongoing work predicated on intention. Christoph and Nystrand (2001) noted that the effect of instructional moves intended to spark discussion is cumulative and thus requires patience and deliberateness. Fecho et al. (2015) wrote "the work done in classrooms is an ongoing and reflective process that remains in a perpetual state of flux, refinement, and challenge" (p. 96). Other advocates for dialogic pedagogy define it as an overall teaching stance rather than a set of instructional tools (Boyd & Markarian, 2015; Juzwik et al., 2013). Across the literature, dialogic teaching is framed as an engaged, reflective, purposeful, and transformative approach to instruction.

We examine five dialogic activities here, along with a discussion of which component of Christoph and Nystrand's (2001) model (i.e., asking authentic questions, practicing uptake, or using high-level feedback) each activity is most useful in scaffolding. We emphasize writing in each of these activities, in addition to talk, as writing about texts and accompanying discussions "externalizes the reading process, making assistance, modeling, and scaffolding easier for teachers to design" (Katz, 2019, p. 549). We also offer ways for students to practice the dialogic strategies from Christoph and Nystrand (2001) in writing, which may be especially helpful for students who do not feel comfortable sharing their opinions with the whole class. Writing also provides opportunities for all students to practice these skills, especially uptake and high-level evaluation.

## Asking Authentic Questions: Reader-Author Dialogue

Prior to reading any type of fiction or nonfiction text, we suggest asking students the questions below to scaffold their dialogue with the "author persona" (Rosenblatt, 2019, p. 466) of all texts, using background research and collaborative discussion.

- Who is the author?
- Where and when was this text written? What else was happening there at the time?
- For what purpose was this text written? For what audience?

- What is known about the author's political stance(s)? What power or privilege do/did they have or want to maintain?
- How do I perceive this author's persona? Would they be my friend, foe, or neither? Why?

After seeing their teacher model this process of investigating the author's identity and context, students might address these questions in small groups about subsequent texts, and eventually as a larger whole class group when such a discussion is beneficial. This exercise places students in conversation with the author and each other, seeks critical evaluation of the author's context, and recognizes the student's political or cultural identity as well.

## Asking Authentic Questions: Two-Voice Poetry Workshops

Two-voice poetry provides a space for perspective-taking for students. This structure may be used collaboratively or individually and may serve as a scaffold for engaging in dialogue with both their peers and provided texts. A two-voice poem is written to be read by two voices. As laid out on the page, each voice reads its half of the poem from top to bottom. Same-line phrases are spoken simultaneously. Two-voice poems are of particular value in units of study connecting historical events or perspectives, or units exploring polarizing concepts or events because they encourage students to consider both sides of one story. Two Voice Poetry scaffolds asking authentic questions like: *How do I feel about this issue? What has happened over time and what are the different perspectives about this event/issue/etc.?*

The example below was written by an eighth grade student during a unit of study centered around NFL protests during the national anthem. The format of the two-voice poem allowed this student to powerfully and succinctly portray two diametrically opposed perspectives in just 13 lines (Figure 5.1).

During this unit, students read an article from an NFL player's perspective about his decision to kneel during the protests, informed by his faith. They also read an article from a commentator's perspective about the perceived damage the protests would have on the NFL at large. They annotated these articles before drafting their two-voice poems, which could be from any two perspectives relevant to the protests (e.g., player-fan, Trump-Kaepernick, angry fan-neutral observer, player-player).

The question at hand was an authentic one: *how do I feel about NFL players kneeling during the national anthem?* Not only does this question "value and elicit student ideas" (Christoph & Nystrand, 2001), it was also being discussed by nearly every adult in their community and across every media platform they encountered.

The potential for perspective-taking in the two-voice poetry exercise makes it perhaps best suited for students to use as they grapple with authentic questions.

| Kaepernick | Trump |
|---|---|
| I was just kneeling | |
| | He was just ... *kneeling* |
| I have my freedom of speech | |
| | You always stand during the anthem |
| I was | |
| | He wasn't |
| respectful | respectful |
| If the army doesn't fight for | If the army doesn't fight for |
| freedom | |
| | the flag |
| What do they fight for? | What do they fight for? |

FIGURE 5.1  An eighth grader's two-voice poem.

However, it might also offer an opportunity for teachers to engage in high-level evaluation with students as they continue to write and revise. Students' use of layout and word choice offer countless entry points for teachers to affirm powerful or resonant craft decisions and to raise questions that lead to sustained inquiry. In the student example above, a handful of word choices by the young poet might lead to questions about freedom of speech as defined in our Constitution, questions about systemic racism, or questions about patriotism that could lead to meaningful revision or further reading and reflection.

Two-voice poetry might find applications across content areas in middle grades as students discuss bioethics and biotechnology, parallel injustices (e.g., codified disenfranchisement and contemporary gerrymandering), parallel social movements (e.g., the Civil Rights Movement and the Black Lives Matter movement), literary foils, or polarizing topics like gun control or legalization of marijuana.

## Practicing Uptake: Cooperative Learning Debates

Amanda used this cooperative learning debate activity in her middle school classroom to create structured discussions for students. Time allotments are flexible, but below we have provided a timing structure that has been successful in middle grades debates about literary texts. Debates about broad concepts or controversial issues necessitate a longer allotment of time.

This tool may work best with debate teams of two. One team agrees with a simple statement, like "People can always change their lives if they really want to" – taken from an anticipation guide for *The Outsiders* in Amanda's eighth grade classroom. The other team of two disagrees with the statement. The debate is structured as follows:

## Moderator reads 1st statement

Agree – 1-minute opening statement (prepared)

Disagree – 1-minute opening statement (prepared)

2 minutes for regrouping

Agree – 1-minute rebuttal

Disagree – 1-minute rebuttal

Everyone completes a written reflection about the debate

1. Repeat #1 for each statement being debated today
2. Each team starts with 25/25 points

   -1 for every interruption

   -1 for disruptions when you are in the audience

   -1 for exceeding allotted time

   +1 for every citation from the text to support your stance

In the case of literary debates, students are all working from the same text for evidence and support for their stance. In debates about controversial topics, or about informational texts in social studies, science, or STEM classes, scaffolding students' background knowledge about the authors of their sources is important for bolstering their citational authority and their credibility as stance-takers in the debate. This structure centers students' dialogue with one another and with the texts they are using for support.

Students' engagement in practicing uptake is implicit in this debate structure because they have to respond to the other team's opening in their rebuttal. The debate structure also provides a space for practicing uptake by asking further questions of students in their written reflections about the debate. Students must be paying attention to their peers' comments throughout the debate in order to reflect and reply to their peers in writing. Some reflection questions that have worked to extend discussion in Amanda's classrooms include:

• What arguments surprised you today? Did you change your mind about any of the statements after the debate? Which ones and why?
• Which statement, argument, or rebuttal was most important to you? Why?
• What strategies did you notice your classmates using when they debated? Which ones were not effective as an audience member? Which were interesting and influenced you as a listener?

These reflections may drive whole-class or small group discussions or lend themselves to more extensive writing projects, depending on context.

This set of post-debate questions also allows students to practice providing high-level evaluation to peers. Debate scaffolds high-level evaluation because they practice noticing what was effective (or not) and adding elaboration or substantive commentary in response. Teachers may use the same reflection questions to provide their own high-level feedback to students engaged in debates, or they may synthesize their own evaluation with key comments from peers.

## Practicing Uptake: Conversation Playing Board

The conversation playing board (adapted from Serravallo, 2015, p. 336) offers an opportunity for student-facilitated discussion. After students read the assigned material, they answer two assigned questions on two separate sticky notes. Example questions for varying genres of text and purposes of discussion are suggested in Table 5.1 below.

After students have answered the questions assigned by their teacher, they write down *four brilliant thoughts* about the text on four separate sticky notes. A list for students to consider:

- A word, sentence, or longer quote that stood out to you and why you chose it
- Questions about why something happened or why a character acted a certain way
- Your emotional reaction to a claim, fact, scene, or event in the passage
- Your takeaways as a writer, reader, or thinker
- A connection you made to the text (e.g., text-self, text-text, text-world)
- Any other brilliant insight you might have!

**TABLE 5.1** Example Questions using Specific Reading Lenses

| *Critical Lens* | *Rhetorical Lens* | *Literary Craft and Structure Lens* | *Informational Craft and Structure Lens* |
|---|---|---|---|
| Who holds power in this text, and how do you know? | What rhetorical strategies did the author use in this passage? | How did this passage drive the plot forward? | What text structure did the author use? |
| Whose voices are missing from this text and why? | How effective were these strategies for you as a reader and why? | How did this passage convey conflict/ character development/ theme/moral? | Who is the intended audience for this piece, and how do you know? |

When students have completed their independent responses to the questions and recorded their four brilliant thoughts, they should be divided into small groups (Arianna used groups of four in her classroom). Each member stacks their sticky notes in a pile on an individual square of the playing board. When the discussion begins, one member selects an idea and places it in the center square of the board making that idea the topic of discussion. All group members discuss the idea in the center for as long as possible. When the group members feel the topic has been fully discussed, a different student takes an idea from their pile, reads it, and moves that one to the center to discuss. This process continues throughout the time allotted.

Conversation playing boards scaffold practicing uptake because students begin the activity with prepared discussion topics, but they then direct the flow of conversation moving from one idea to the next supported by their notes and questions they ask their peers. Students have their notes to rely on but must engage in listening to their peers to drive conversation and can practice high-level evaluation by validating their peer's responses and asking them to elaborate. High-level evaluation can be furthered by students in each group selecting the "best idea" from their conversation and presenting it to the whole class for extended discussion. This validates the student's response and presents it to the class to drive deeper discussion around a common topic. The conversation playing board offers a balance of teacher-selected questions and student-selected ideas as the foundation for the discussions taking place, placing power and responsibility in student's hands throughout the activity.

## Using High-Level Feedback: Writers' Carousels

Another flexible dialogic structure centered around writing is a Writers' Carousel. It is a version of a commonly used discussion activity often referred to as Concentric Circles or Speed Dating. In a writer's carousel model, students sit in two concentric circles, with each student facing another. This activity is particularly useful during the drafting phase of a writing project, during a novel study threaded with short written responses, or during a unit that asks students to take a stance about big concepts, themes, or events and write about it.

Over a brief period of time (five minutes may be plenty), students read short pieces of writing (one typed page or less may be plenty) and use post-it notes to record their responses and feedback for one another as they read. The discussions in the carousel may be conducted solely through sticky note feedback, or teachers may allot time for students to write down their feedback as well as to take turns discussing each writing sample. This structure allows students to receive peer feedback on their writing from as many as four classmates in 20 minutes.

Teachers will have to gradually release responsibility to students in seeking and providing peer feedback beyond the questions of "Did you like it?" or "Is it good?" In this sense, using a carousel or concentric circles model may require long-term scaffolding or extensive modeling.

Providing high-level evaluation during a carousel discussion is most rewarding for the teacher and students when the teacher acts as a discussion participant during iterations of this structure over time. Students benefit from one-on-one high-level evaluation (e.g., "I appreciated the writing you shared, and it caused me to reconsider my own craft decision about [x] because…"). Having the teacher participate in this process provides personalized expert modeling of the practice of high-level evaluation through writing.

Writers' carousels may be useful as students develop argumentative or claim-evidence-elaboration pieces of writing; the structure allows them to focus their own piece while dialogically taking up counterpoints or alternate perspectives their peers may offer. They also facilitate real-world reader-author interactions, as peer readers help peer authors construct, rewrite, or refine their writing and thinking.

## Conclusion

We are writing this chapter after a calendar year of life in a pandemic. Many of us are in the midst of four pandemics: COVID-19, anti-Black racism, the impending economic collapse trailing COVID-19, and climate catastrophe (Ladson-Billings, 2020). A lack of co-constructive, collaborative discourse is a problem writ large across the American society in which our students are coming of age. Many of the adults who are shepherding them into full citizenship don't even agree on how facts or truth are constituted (Mitchell et al., 2021). While we are not suggesting that dialogic teaching practices are a panacea for healing the divides of a society, we wish to point to a dialogic teaching stance as a part of educators' sphere of influence. Dialogic teaching's potential to disrupt dynamics of power (Kay, 2018), disparities in academic success (Applebee et al., 2003; Nystrand, 2006; Lysaker et al., 2011), and monologic concepts of knowledge (Bakhtin, 1984; Rosenblatt, 1993; Nystrand, 1997) offers teachers a powerful entry point for alleviating disconnection and discord. Co-constructing classroom communities built on learning talk positions students to engage dialogically with texts, with others, and with the world around them.

### For Further Reading

For a quick read:

Gonzalez, J. (2015, October 15). *The big list of class discussion strategies*. Cult of Pedagogy. https://www.cultofpedagogy.com/speaking-listening-techniques/
Juzwik, M. M., Dunn, M., & Johnson, A. (2016, April 14). From dialogic tools to a dialogic stance. *International Literacy Association*. https://literacyworldwide. org/blog/literacy-now/2016/04/14/from-dialogic-tools-to-a-dialogic-stance

For sustained talk and reflection:

Alexander, R. J. (2017). *Towards dialogic teaching: Rethinking classroom talk.* (5th edition). Dialogos.

Fecho, B., Falter, M., & Hong, X. (Eds.) (2015). *Teaching outside the box but inside the standards: Making room for dialogue.* Teachers College Press.

Johnston, P. H. (2012). *Opening minds: Using language to change lives.* Portland, ME: Stenhouse. Juzwik, M. M., Borsheim-Black, C., Caughlan, S., & Heintz, A. (2013). *Inspiring dialogue: Talking to learn in the English classroom.* Teachers College Press.

Kay, M. (2018). *Not light but fire: How to lead meaningful race conversations in the classroom.* Stenhouse.

## References

Alexander, R. J. (2017). *Towards dialogic teaching: Rethinking classroom talk.* (5th edition). Dialogos.

Applebee, A., Langer, J., Nystrand, M., & Gamoran, A. (2003). Discussion-based approaches to developing understanding: Classroom instruction and student performance in middle and high school English. *American Educational Research Journal, 40*(3), 685–730.

Bakhtin, M.M. (1984). *Problems of Dostoevsky's poetics.* (C. Emerson, Ed. & Trans.). University of Michigan Press.

Bergman, D. (2017). "It's easier when it's personal": What made reading real for twotweens with learning disabilities. *Language Arts, 94*(3), 180–189.

Biancarosa, G., & Snow, C. (2006). *Reading next--A vision for action and research in middle and high school literacy: A report to Carnegie Corporation of New York* (2nd ed.). Alliance for Excellent Education. https://www.carnegie.org/media/filer_public/b7/5f/b75fba81-16cb-422d-ab59-373a6a07eb74/ccny_report_2004_reading.pdf

Boyd, M., & Markarian, W. (2015). Dialogic teaching and dialogic stance: Moving beyond interactional form. *Research in the Teaching of English, 49*(3), 272–296.

Christoph, J. & Nystrand, M. (2001). Taking risks, negotiating relationships: One teacher's transition toward a dialogic classroom. *Research in the Teaching of English, 36*(2), 249–286.

de Brey, C., Musu, L., McFarland, J., Wilkinson-Flicker, S., Diliberti, M., Zhang, A., Branstetter, C., & Wang, X. (2019). *Status and trends in the education of racial and ethnic groups 2018 (NCES 2019-038).* National Center for Education Statistics. https://nces.ed.gov/pubs2019/2019038.pdf

Fecho, B., Falter, M., & Hong, X. (Eds.) (2015). *Teaching outside the box but inside the standards: Making room for dialogue.* Teachers College Press.

Gardoqui, K. (2018, October 1). We spend too much time teaching students to argue. *Education Week.* https://www.edweek.org/teaching-learning/opinion-we-spend-too-much-time-teaching-students-to-argue/2018/10

Gordon, C. T. (2019). Trusting students' voices in critical English education. *Journal of Language and Literacy Education, 15*(1), 1–32.

Gottfried, A. E. (1985). Academic intrinsic motivation in elementary and junior high school students. *Journal of Educational Psychology, 77*(6), 631–645. https://doi.org/10.1037/0022-0663.77.6.631.

Ivey, G., & Johnston, P. H. (2013). Engagement with young adult literature: Outcomes and processes. *Reading Research Quarterly*, *48*(3), 255–275. https://doi.org/10.1002/rrq.46.

Juzwik, M.M., Borsheim-Black, C., Caughlan, S., & Heintz, A. (2013). *Inspiring dialogue: Talking to learn in the English classroom.* Teachers College Press.

Katz, M.-L. (2019). Enacting rhetorical literacies: The expository reading and writing curriculum in theory and practice. In D.E. Alvermann, N. J. Unrau, & R. B. Ruddell (Eds.), *Theoretical models and processes of literacy* (pp. 533–562). Routledge.

Kay, M. R. (2018). *Not light but fire: How to lead meaningful race conversations in the classroom.* Stenhouse.

Kim, J. S., Hemphill, L., Troyer, M., Thomson, J. M., Jones, S. M., LaRusso, M. D., & Donovan, S. J. (2017). Engaging struggling adolescent readers to improve reading skills. *Reading Research Quarterly*, *52*(3), 357–382. https://doi.org/10.1002/rrq.171

Kim, M.-Y. & Wilkinson, I.A.G. (2019). What is dialogic teaching? Constructing, deconstructing, and reconstructing a pedagogy of classroom talk. *Learning, Culture, and Social Interaction*, *21*, 70–86.

Ladson-Billings, G. (2020, October 19-23). *StillBlack@Stanford.edu: Confronting the Anti-Black Racism Pandemic with a Hard Re-set.* [Conference presentation]. *2020 RILE Conference, Stanford Graduate School of Education. (Virtual).*

Lysaker, J., Tonge, C., Gauson, D., & Miller, A. (2011). Reading and social imagination: What relationally oriented reading instruction can do for children. *Reading Psychology*, *32*(6), 520–566. https://doi.org/10.1080/02702711.2010.507589

Mitchell, A., Jurkowitz, M., Oliphant, J. B., & Shearer, E. (2021). *How Americans navigated the news in 2020: A tumultuous year in review.* Pew Research Center. https://www.journalism.org/2021/02/22/how-americans-navigated-the-news-in-2020-a-tumultuous-year-in-review/

Moje, E. B., Overby, M., Tysvaer, N., & Morris, K. (2008). The complex world of adolescent literacy: Myths, motivations, and mysteries. *Harvard Educational Review*, *78*(1), 107–154. https://doi.org/10.17763/haer.78.1.54468j6204x24157

National Center for Education Statistics. (2019). *NAEP report card: Reading.* U.S. Department of Education. https://www.nationsreportcard.gov/reading/nation/groups/?grade=8

Nystrand, M. (1997). *Opening dialogue: Understanding the dynamics of language and learning in the English classroom.* Teachers College Press.

Nystrand, M. (2006). Research on the role of classroom discourse as it affects reading comprehension. *Research in the Teaching of English*, 40(4), 392–412.

Nystrand, M., Wu, L., Gamoran, A., Zeiser, S., & Long, D. (2003) Questions in time: Investigating the structure and dynamics of unfolding classroom discourse, *Discourse Processes*, 35(2), 135–198.

Pew Research Center. (2014). *Political polarization in the American public.* Author. https://www.pewresearch.org/politics/2014/06/12/political-polarization-in-the-american-public/

Piazza, S.V., & Duncan, L. E. (2012). After-school literacy engagements with struggling readers. *Reading & Writing Quarterly*, *28*(3), 229–254. https://doi.org/10.1080/10573569.2012.676363

Piazza, S. V., Rao, S., & Protacio, M. S. (2015). Converging recommendations for culturally responsive literacy practices: Students with learning disabilities, English language learners, and socioculturally diverse learners. *International Journal of Multicultural Education*. *17*(3), 1–8.

Rosenblatt, L. M. (1993). The transactional theory: Against dualisms. *College English*, *55*(4), 377–386.

Rosenblatt, L. M. (2019). The transactional theory of reading and writing. In D. E. Alvermann, N. J. Unrau, & R. B. Ruddell (Eds.), *Theoretical Models and Processes of Literacy* (pp. 451–479). Routledge.

Serravallo, J. (2015). *The reading strategies book: Your everything guide to developing skilled readers*. Heinemann.

Troyer, M. (2017). A Mixed-methods study of adolescents' motivation to read. *Teachers College Record, 119*(5), 1–48.

Vygotsky, L.S. (1978). *Mind in society: The development of higher psychological processes* (M. Cole, V. John-Steiner, S. Scribner, & E. Souberman, Trans.). Harvard University Press.

Will, M. (2020, May 14). Still mostly white and female: New federal data on the teaching profession. *Education Week*. https://www.edweek.org/leadership/still-mostly-white-and-female-new-federal-data-on-the-teaching-profession/2020/04

# 6

# LITERACY FOR THE MIDDLE GRADES

## Its Antecedent Necessities, Subsequent Needs, and Future Aspirations

*Mary Roe*

"I can tell you really like kids," the principal interviewing me said. His impression, along with my Latin minor which qualified me to teach first year Latin, landed me my first job as a middle school (then called a junior high) English and Latin teacher in Lansing, Michigan. I left the interview happy, employed, but perplexed. Wouldn't anyone who sought a teaching job really like kids? I had a lot to learn.

One of my first of many eye-opening moments came with realizing that once being 12 did not equate to understanding 12-to-14-year-old students as their teacher. I addressed this gap by getting a Master's degree in educational psychology with an emphasis on growth and behavior. The many things I learned helped me understand students like Dale Miller (all names are pseudonyms) who told me on the first day of class, "I hate you. I hate all teachers. The only teacher I ever liked was Mrs. Smith." Unfortunately, Mrs. Smith was not amenable to a second year with Dale. Dale, and other very troubled middle grade students I encountered across the years, provided me many growth points.

A second realization, and more concerning, involved too many students' low literacy achievement, lack of interest, or both. My English major and the education courses related to my secondary certification did not suffice. In my view, this plight has not changed. English teachers should not be expected to be reading teachers. Their educational backgrounds, like other teachers of content areas, may include an applicable course here or there that offers general and helpful tips, but these courses do not offer an in-depth grasp of reading as a process. I initially addressed this gap by getting a second master's degree in reading education and later, after many years of teaching, a Ph.D. This ongoing concern about the literacy achievement of primarily middle level students and the teachers with whom they interact has remained the focus of my professional career as a teacher, reading specialist, teacher educator, and researcher. My learning continues.

DOI: 10.4324/9781003171508-8

The many twists and turns that middle level literacy entails compel my embracing three guiding principles: (1) cognitive flexibility theory, (2) principled eclecticism, and (3) wickedity. I begin by explaining these three foundational beliefs before turning directly to middle level literacy and its connections to them.

## Cognitive Flexibility Theory

Many middle level literacy stakeholders hold strong opinions about things to do and how to do them. These staunch positions, often diametrically opposed, too often lead to loggerheads or in-fights rather than progress. Cognitive flexibility, defined as "the ability to simultaneously consider multiple aspects of a single situation or observation" (Homer & Hayward, 2008, p. 20), offers a road forward. Cognitive Flexibility Theory (CFT) (Spiro et al., 2019) sanctions a way to accommodate the ongoing mental agility that the presence of abundant and at times contradictory information entails. Cognitive flexibility addresses complexity while abandoning a forced, singular choice. Instead of seeking a program, a right way, or a silver bullet, CFT advocates for a consideration of multiple alternatives and perhaps even a crisscrossing use of them (Spiro et al., 1987).

A call for cognitive flexibility is not new. Cartwright (2018) edited a volume devoted to cognitive flexibility in learning and teaching. Chapter by chapter and topic by topic, this text builds the case for its importance. Epstein (2019) concurs and attests that "knowledge with enduring utility must be very flexible, composed of mental schemes that can be matched to new problems" (p. 98).

## Principled Eclecticism

Cognitive flexibility depends on a flexible mindset and a willingness to change course. Cohen (2013) cautions against "beliefs [that]calcify into unconsidered doctrine" (p. 105). Displaying principled eclecticism can strengthen an avoidance of this harmful possibility. Principled eclecticism points to the appropriateness and sometimes necessity of joining theoretical frameworks as well as teaching practices that initially seem ill-suited for co-existence. Within principled eclecticism, frameworks and practices can zig and zag in a way that remains thoughtful and warranted for the context of use (Kander & Roe, 2018). In keeping with cognitive flexibility, it steps away from an exclusive choice accompanied by complete allegiance to either a specified literacy practice or a singular explanatory framework.

## Wickedity

Wickedity (Rittel & Webber, 1973) was applied to indicate the differences between relatively tame problems and those more entangled. The problems categorized as wicked remain immune to a definitive solution. Attending to comparable educational opportunities and the many pieces linked to it offers one example of ongoing, wicked, problems. Progress is possible and expected, but a definitive ending remains elusive.

Wickedity, too, demands an avoidance of cognitive entrenchment. Nash (2019) explains that "the challenges schools face are multifaceted, have numerous potential solutions, and with almost no exceptions, impact people" (p. 1). Nash views wicked problems as tricky, thorny, problematic, and not clearly formulated. Along with colleagues, I quickly became convinced that "dispositions and approaches that honor wickedity's complexity eschew once and for all problem solving that seeks agreed upon single-pronged solutions" (Jordan, Kleinsasser, & Roe, 2014, p. 422).

The following sections of my consideration of middle level literacy indicate my acceptance of CFT as a metatheory and principled eclecticism and wickedity as important partners to it. Their common threads of complexity, adaptivity, and multiplicity directly apply to education in general and especially literacy learning at the middle grades.

## *The Progression of Middle Level Literacy Achievement*

In the Newbery Medal Winner text, *Flora and Ulysses* (DiCamillo, 2013), one of the central characters, William Spiver, states this: "The truth is a slippery thing. I doubt that you will ever get to *The* Truth. You may get to a version of the truth. But *The* truth? I doubt it very seriously" (p. 221). The same cautionary reminder applies to the following sections where I address middle level literacy. I do not proffer these ideas as either definitive or inclusive of other, and perhaps equally important, options. The limitations of time and space required a narrowing of ideas to present and examples to provide. I begin with influences that occur before students enter the middle grades. I then turn to ideas that continue to hold importance during the middle grades before turning to hopes for the future. This progressive orientation reflects O'Day and Smith (2019) who encourage an attention to transition points. Each section reflects what I have thought, adjusted, and learned during my decades considering middle grade literacy. They remain, however, a moment in time – this moment. I encourage the readers to hold this caveat in mind.

## Antecedent Demands

I believe in the value of education and especially literacy competence. I also believe that some students need teachers more than others. I primarily focus on that subsection of middle level students for whom teachers hold central significance and consequence.

Reading, defined as comprehending text, involves a complex process that has multiple components and innumerable paths for success. Spiro and Myers

(1984) compare it to a "reading pie" that includes "a broad and irregularly over-lapping family of activities'" (p. 471). Durkin (1993) notes several contributors to comprehension: word identification (saying words quickly and accurately and attaching meaning to them), vocabulary (understanding a word's meaning in a given context), and understanding connected text (not grasping a text's meaning even when a student correctly and fluently pronounces the words and attaches an appropriate meaning to them). Not all readers need the same attention to these attributes.

Middle level students' literacy challenges do not commence at age 12. Their early years and literacy experiences mold their future achievements and dispositions and warrant attention. I do not intend to offer an in-depth account of the multitudinous research and recommendations that guide early reading instruction. I instead insert an important ingredient that is often overlooked and extremely important for setting the stage for middle level success: instruction that empowers readers to *flexibly* use any strategy available to them. An initial inclusion of flexible thinking and flexible strategy use in the pursuit of understanding a text gets readers off to a good start and continues to serve them well into their later years. As the following comments and examples indicate, the important and far-reaching importance of flexibility does not always occur.

When I started school in Detroit, Michigan, I could already read. I don't remember how I learned to read. I just read. I am not alone in this ease of becoming a reader. A nephew of a former student framed his experience this way: "Poof! I could read." I did not have instruction in the ways and around the topics we currently deem important. Neither did he. We just read. Then, in grade 3, my family moved to East Detroit and then Roseville. At the beginning of the third grade, I again just read and hold warm memories of selecting books from the teacher's in-class library. Things changed dramatically at the end of my third-grade year when I changed schools again. I received a workbook that required me to mark long and short vowel sounds. I did not know this language of instruction and certainly did not understand the task. I tried looking at my neighbor's paper who was marking away (a gentle way of saying I tried to cheat). It still didn't make sense. I could correctly pronounce every word in the work-book but failed miserably at this task. In that year of my schooling, reading was not about making meaning from print. It had been reduced to something that for me was unnecessary and foreign. Fortunately/unfortunately, I got quite sick and missed a great deal of school, returning only in time to attend the annual picnic. That summer, I got my first library card, walked to my local library, and checked out four to five books at a time. I returned to reading. In the fourth grade, my teacher did not have me mark words on a workbook page. I did not even have a workbook. I was allowed to just read. And, read I did.

Reducing the act of reading unnecessarily to a piece of reading (saying words), regardless of its helpful potential, can strip reading of its joy. As one of my middle level students said to me at the onset of our school year, "I love to read, but I hate reading in school." Too many students beginning the middle grades share this sentiment. The following examples indicate the limitations and intrusions that accompany well meaning but unnecessary instruction. Teachers, too, need to adopt flexibility.

On the first day of classes, Kevin, a student in my seventh-grade reading class, quietly introduced himself to me with the admission: "I can't read." I tried to allay his concerns. Nothing in his academic record alerted me to his plight. I always started my year by using informal measures to determine a student's reading achievement and identify areas for improvement. Kevin was the only student I ever encountered who had no instructional reading level. I later learned that his mother was allowed to read his standardized reading tests to him which masked his reading needs. When left without this support at the word level, understanding the most basic of texts escaped him. He had three strengths: He held a deep desire to read, a strong oral vocabulary, and the ability to understand texts read to him. For Kevin to read better, he needed to expand his reading vocabulary and capitalize on his oral vocabulary. He needed mediating strategies to help bridge this gap. Kevin had been repeatedly and exclusively taught phonics and tried to use it for all words. I vividly recall a day when he balked at pronouncing *the*. He meticulously and painstakingly attempted to provide the sound for each letter and say them quickly. After several unsuccessful attempts I asked him, "What word would you expect that to be?" He quickly said, "the." That was his introduction to another strategy that maximized his strength and placed his problematic use of phonics as a backup. Over time he became adept in using the question, "What word makes sense here and matches its spelling?" This question entailed a flexible and combined use of strategies that worked well for Kevin to correctly say words. By January of that year, his instructional reading level was grade 3. He remained dramatically behind his age and grade placement, but he was a reader.

Phonics can matter, but not for all students. Phonics can assist with the pronunciation of words, but only if the words follow its generalizations and if students know and can apply them to unknown words. Phonics works best when it is used flexibly. For Kevin, when unknown words did not get in the way, his ability to obtain meaning from print rapidly improved. His exclusive use of phonics constrained his growth as a reader in earlier grades. He needed a broader range of options and a flexible mindset that encouraged him to explore them. As Epstein (2019) stresses, "One good tool is rarely enough in a complex, interconnected, rapidly changing world" (p. 51).

When saying words quickly and accurately defines early reading and the use of decodable texts limits the type of texts young learners read, the natural complexity of reading disappears and the main point of reading, enjoying, and comprehending text can quickly dissipate. These unintended consequences can negatively impact novice readers and linger to impact them in the middle grades.

Another premise that haunts middle level reading success involves the oft heard adage that divides reading into two stages: learning to read, applicable to grades K–3, and, around grade four, a shift to reading to learn. That unfortunate distinction postpones attention to comprehension in a rich and age-appropriate way and prevents students who still need assistance at the word level from getting it.

From the onset of learning to read, all readers deserve an appropriate introduction to the cognitive complexity of reading. This does not eliminate the requisite benefit that young readers receive from that just right instruction and the opportunity to assemble and flexibly use a range of important strategies – strategies that will continue to matter at the middle grades. Young readers benefit from interactions with real books (whether presented on-line or off-line). Real books for our youngest readers maintain reading's complexity and set the stage for readers to better manage the increased complexity of texts they encounter in later years. As Spiro and his colleagues (2019) indicate, early simplification impedes later attainment of complexity. This potential disadvantage must be avoided.

All readers eventually encounter hiccups and benefit from using cognitive flexibility when they encounter one. All readers read to learn – or should. Readers benefit from teachers who provide a range of options across the contributors of importance for them – whether saying a word, inferring the meaning of an unknown word, or negotiating connected text (e.g., making inferences, recognizing the important differences between narrative and expository text structures, or understanding their lack of prior knowledge for understanding a text). Readers profit from teachers who from the start of their reading journey encourage cognitive flexibility. Across the elementary grades, an omission of cognitive flexibility as a priority literacy practice reduces the effective use of any strategy – and that unintended consequence continues to impact older, middle level students. Kevin and too many others offer living proof.

The importance of the psychological contributions to reading cannot overshadow the affective dimensions. The early instillment of the skill to read remains insufficient without the will to do so. Motivation, engagement, and interest contribute to a reading habit and must share the stage in these antecedent years (Roe, 1997). Both illiteracy and aliteracy must be avoided. This joint consideration of literacy's affective and cognitive dimensions becomes extremely important as students enter their middle school years when a decrease in motivation to read strikes (Lepper et al., 2005). A healthy start with a high regard for the benefits of reading can lessen or perhaps even forestall this slump.

A good start for students' middle grade literacy success includes areas beyond the boundary of their schooling. This would include things known to affect success such as access to preschool, childhood nutrition and health, individual and neighborhood poverty and segregation.

The antecedents for middle level success are broad and ripe with challenges. Acknowledging their impact beyond the early grades underscores the ongoing need for collaborative and fruitful exchanges within and across the historical divisions of grade level and age boundaries.

## Needs for the Here and Now

In *Alice in Wonderland* (Carroll, 1865), Alice and the Cheshire Cat have the following conversation:

> Alice begins. "Would you tell me please, which way I ought to go from here?"
> "That depends a good deal on where you want to get to," said the Cat.
> "I don't much care where," said Alice.
> "Then it doesn't matter which way you go," said the Cat.

This important exchange holds guidance for middle level students' literacy progression and the teachers who serve them. As O'Day and Smith (2019) admonish, "Change efforts can indeed start from a host of different 'somewheres;' the choice of where to begin should come with some thought behind it" (p. 218).

With so many needs and challenges that spring up in the middle grades, settling on a starting point proves perplexing. (See Kleinsasser and Roe, 2021, for a selection process they propose to assist in identifying starting points.) Students ultimately provide the guidance and deserve the agency to become a partner in their literacy curriculum. O'Day and Smith (2019) further remind us that teaching and learning are too complex to succumb to bureaucratically defined rules and routines no matter how well designed or intended they are. Teachers, administrators, and local school board members need to guard against handing off a responsibility to determine what matters most within the context of their schools and for their students' achievement. I again proffer my encouragement to always hold in mind the benefits of cognitive flexibility and principled eclecticism in a combined consideration of the cognitive, affective, and, especially during the middle years, the social dynamics of being a learner and a reader (Pijeira-Díaz et al., 2018). Middle level literacy involves a joint venture regardless of the selected path and especially for wicked problems. I temporarily return to the cognitive contributors.

In discussing earlier literacy events that continue to hold sway for the middle grades, I singled out phonics as problematic when used inflexibly. I now propose it as an important consideration for some middle level students. I have long held a strong belief in strategy instruction (Roe, 1992) as well as the rightful inclusion of phonics in a reader's tool kit for word identification strategies (Roe, 2004). I still promote its potential to matter when certain conditions apply.

### Condition One

Students' reduced comprehension of text needs verification that it stems from an inability to negotiate the words on the page. Word identification matters when it impedes comprehension, the goal of reading. It does not become an independent goal.

## Condition Two

Students need to understand that the underlying concepts and principles linked to phonics apply to syllables. Too often, middle level students attempt to apply phonic generalizations to whole words and meet with frustration. Applying phonics appropriately to multisyllable words (the type of words that typically befuddle middle level readers) requires an ability to identify a word's syllables. A practice often seen in the early grades to identify syllables requires students to clap syllables for spoken words. Readers, however, need to rely on a visual inspection to identify the letters that usually represent vowel sounds and, therefore, suggest the number of syllables a word contains. An application of syllabication generalizations to identify the individual syllables follows and continues with a use of phonics to pronounce each syllable, and so it goes. Whew. This becomes a tedious task involving a lot to know, much to do, and an unpredictable outcome. The end result can be worthwhile, but entails a time consuming and effortful approach in obtaining an approximation of a word's pronunciation. As Kevin learned, whether the word makes sense and matches the spelling of the word are final determiners of correctness.

## Condition Three

Finally, and perhaps of most importance, students and their teachers need to highlight the importance of cognitive flexibility. Generalizations do not equate with a rule. Generalizations do not represent single and always accurate paths. If a reader encounters a false start, a flexible orientation encourages the use of a different choice or set of choices. Teachers of all levels, but especially those of middle level students who struggle to say words, need to mindfully, strategically, and flexibly use syllabication and phonics alongside and in concert with other approaches (e.g., context and structural analysis).

Other middle level students have strong word identification and vocabularies yet still have difficulty understanding text. In fact, understanding connected text is often considered the biggest challenge that middle level students face (McGee, 2020). When I think of this reality, I hark back to a conversation I had with a parent about her son, Jerry. An older brother and a strong reader had also been my student. I had great concerns about telling this mom that Jerry had reading needs. Her response surprised me. "I have been telling his teachers since he was in grade four that he didn't understand a word he was reading." She was relieved by my confirmation of her concern and hopeful that her son's needs would be addressed. Again, reading is about understanding text rather than saying words fluently and with prosody or understanding a word's meaning. Middle level students like Jerry require instruction and support systems to address the various things that interfere with understanding connected text. As Epstein (2019) reminds us, "no tool is omnicompetent. There is no such thing as a master key that will unlock all doors" (p. 51). Holding that caveat in mind, two tried and true practices continue to matter: attending to text structure and grasping the source of information for responding to questions. I hope that teachers will receive two important messages from their selection: (1) seminal work can maintain currency and a rightful inclusion in a teacher's selection of things to do and (2) a new term accompanied by a more recent publication date does not necessarily point to a new concept. Take, for example, the concept of personalizing instruction. This need to attend to the needs of an individual reader dates back to calls for one-to-one instruction (deemed too time intensive) to calls for tracking (too many unintended consequences), to flexible grouping, to differentiation and on (Roe, 2010). The subtle variations that might accompany these terms do not greatly change the end goal: modifying the selection and delivery of instruction and wisely selecting texts to read that coincides with a student's needs and interests at that time. The following suggestions maintain their same label, core information, and level of pervasive confidence regarding their benefits.

Although elementary teachers have increased their attention to expository text, reading exposition continues to stump too many middle level students. I was always surprised at the number of content area teachers who would come to me and say, "_____can't read." The overlooked piece in most of these conversations was that the student could read narration, but stumbled with expository texts. A careful attention to text structure has proven helpful across grade levels, but remains too often overlooked as an instructional target for middle level readers. Teaching text structure well takes time and ongoing attention. It begins with a careful analysis of the assigned reading to understand the types of structure(s) used by the author. Then, following the explanation of the attributes of these structures and their usefulness in learning, a gradual release of responsibility model (McVee et al., 2019)) can ensue for moving from teacher assistance to student independence. Only those students who need this assistance should join the instructional group. The concept of flexible grouping coincides with the promotion of an overall flexible mindset. The instruction must also attend to the many shifts that an author often makes when writing exposition. This ability to shift thinking from a descriptive passage to one that explains cause and effect requires the appropriate knowledge and a nimble mind. It fares best with cognitive flexibility included in its instruction and promoted in its use.

Question Answer Relationship (QAR) (Raphael & Au, 2005) offers another well-worn practice that still warrants inclusion in a middle level reader's arsenal. This strategy helps students identify three bases for responding to questions: (1) right there, the answer is explicitly stated in one sentence from the text; (2) think and search, the answer requires a joining of information across the text; or (3) on your own, the answer comes from what's in a reader's head rather than in the text. These categories were later expanded to include author and you where an answer depends upon text information and the reader's prior knowledge. Too many students don't understand the necessity of going to your head while other students fall short of the appropriate use of text information. These categories can help teachers direct their students' thinking and shed light on the sources of information they overuse, use inappropriately, or ignore. Students can benefit from directing their efforts in the right direction. Students are often encouraged to look closely at a text. As one middle level student responded during a class I was observing, "I keep looking but nothing's there." Understanding the relationship of a question to the mental thinking it requires offers specific assistance.

This section would be remiss without mentioning the importance of the school climate and the ongoing battle for equity. As Adams and Palmer (2017) remind us,

> Without positive and effective learning environments for all students coupled with appropriate interventions where needed and a continuous process of school improvement, too many students, especially those from low-income families and those exposed to traumatic experiences, will fall through the cracks, lose confidence about how they are doing in school, and try to avoid notice until they are old enough to leave school.
>
> (p. 116)

Students differ. Every middle level student differs. Dyasi (2014) compares them to "an unruly spark of meaning-making energy on a voyage of discovery and surprise" (p. 87). They deserve an environment that honors them as people and learners. Listen to Coates's (2015 account of his experience: "I was a curious boy, but the schools were not concerned with curiosity. They were concerned with compliance" (p. 26). An overly restrictive environment that douses rather than fans their interests can and should be a thing of the past. An attention to the classroom and school environments closely links to another important piece that surrounds everything that teachers and schools do: a quest for social justice.

Inequities surround the middle school experience whether it be the availability of computing capabilities, the school's infrastructure, a curriculum that sorts and labels students, or the sparse opportunities a school experience affords. Schools and teachers strive to compensate for these shortfalls. They seek opportunities to create a worthwhile curriculum by identifying issues important to their students. They seek a goal to create independent learners, critical thinkers, productive people, and thoughtful, caring citizens (Schultz, 2017). They use the Internet to connect with ideas and experts worldwide. These attempts must be strengthened and supported – small steps followed by leaps and bounds. Other issues are more systemic, such as funding variabilities and the advantages they support and the drawing of school boundaries. They, too, must be faced. As Meier and Gasoi (2017) maintain,

> We will have to face our historic and enduring demons – our entrenched legacy of classism and racism, among many other isms, as well as our

national obsession with efficiency and quantification – if we hope to begin to truly wrestle with and perhaps even, someday, overcome those demons.

(p. 169)

Lichtman (2014) provides an important encouragement to "stop talking and start doing" (p. 259).

This section began by noting the confluence of social, affective, and cognitive domains in the promotion of middle level students who can and do read. I end it with that important reminder.

### Future Hopes and Possibilities

James Baldwin once said, "Not everything that is faced can be changed, but nothing can be changed until it is faced" (cited in Meier and Gasoi, 2017, p. 162). The above sections remain areas to consider and perhaps reconsider. In turning to the middle level students waiting in the wings and other middle level students moving forward to their future, I now take a broader look at a familiar topic, technology, and other less prominent topics stemming from it that hold relevance for future inclusion in our hopes for middle level literacy.

Technology holds current affordances for the areas previously explored and future advantages yet to be invented. Technology, especially during the recent years of pandemic adaptations, became a must for students and teachers. Teachers taught on-line whether ready or not. As our nations' schools slowly return to in-class learning, teachers will again have the space to carefully consider their use of technology instead of a need to completely supplant in-person teaching. An initial consideration involves determining tools important and appropriate for advancing an instructional need – whether affective or cognitive. These tools are currently numerous and will continue to explode in number and use. Staying current with this fast-paced technology will not be easy. Technology's promise, however, goes beyond tools to use in the service of reading better or locating information via Google searches. Its real promise lies in the ability to impact true learning. This broader hope requires an acknowledgement of the limitations of educational software and search engines.

As Spiro (2021) recently suggested, "Google can make you stupid." Since most teachers and students profitably rely on it, how can that be? Users often forget that search engines come with a web of filters. This reality places a user as a passive rather than active participant. The middle grades present the perfect place to reposition a student's use of computing assistance to a more active role. Spiro and his colleagues (2019) use the metaphor of LICRA, Learner Initiated Complex Reciprocally Adaptive Searching to frame this shift. I see the application of this metaphor as comparing licra's elasticity to seeing the web as flexible and promoting the user's obligation to adopt this same flexibility. Students would need support to maximize their use of hypertext environments instead of defaulting to the sites prompted by a search engine. Middle schools, especially those that are currently successful, might be prone to complacency. Times are simply moving too quickly to rest on current laurels dependent upon a static definition of success and competency overall and specifically in a use of technology.

What better time to impact literacy learning and student interest by nudging learning away from fact finding to developing questions and engaging in critical and reflective searching rather than deferring to the web's choices? What better time to take the lead in framing digital literacy for middle level students as a flexible, cognitive, and engaging advancement for literacy and true learning? A focus on technology (and independent of the label used for it) cannot become a goal separated from deepening middle level students' literacy. Technology use and literacy achievement are hand-in-hand considerations rather than competing silos.

Making these advancements and adjustments, whether in the use of technology or other arenas selected to increase students' literacy achievement, teachers might benefit from the pose, wobble, and flow framework proposed by Garcia and O'Donnell-Allen (2015) and its focus on educational equity. Briefly explained, in this framework, teachers assume various poses or roles. They experience spurts of wobbling where they change their roles and engage in learning, reflection, and professional growth in order to successfully function in these new roles. A feeling of flow ends this process with a harmonious and effortless state of satisfaction. Teachers can embrace their positive shifts toward a culturally responsive literacy instruction and their benefits for students. This is not a linear process, but one that evolves over time and with much support and deliberation.

As teachers wobble, they might consider instructional design. As explained by Nash (2019), "design thinking provides a process that gives school leaders permission to imagine what the future might look like and then empathetically, respectfully and compassionately find out" (p. 152). Teachers who tap design thinking would collaborate, understand the needs of others, value hunches, and act on and learn from them. Cognitive flexibility would continue to apply. As Nash minds us, "When ideas are taken from other districts, they are not, by their nature, well suited to address the unmet needs in another district" (p. 137).

Efforts promoting middle level literacy must continuously include factors that contribute to psychological wellness such as happiness, life satisfaction, sense of belonging, and sense of purpose in life. As Osher et al. (2016) assert, "literacy, after all, is a whole person progression and deserves an attention to that reality" (p. 227). Middle level educational leaders live in the right moment to seize an opportunity to "address and transform the grammars of schooling and instruction, produce more equitable outcomes for students, and most important, better equip all students to handle life's challenges, build and maintain quality relationships, thrive personally, collectively, and professionally, and become engaged citizens" (Osher et al., 2016, p. 67). What does the future for middle level students hold? We simply don't know and most likely can't even imagine their future worlds. With uncertainty swirling around, middle level students need to be equipped to read well, use technology actively and thoughtfully, and maintain a disposition to maintain flexibility in thought and action. Educational stakeholders, too, benefit from the willingness to change their minds and loosen the grip of narrow thinking that too often flourishes. Planning forward is the only direction to go.

## Concluding Comments

The American Psychological Association (2020) cautions writers against the overuse of quotes. I like them and keep a writer's notebook containing them. I step away from that APA suggestion to include the words of others to capture my hesitations, hopes, and intentions that imbue these pages:

> From Cohen (2013): "My ideas come with a healthy dose of doubt and uncertainty… doubt is my friend. I don't mean that I've stopped having beliefs, or stopped being passionate about those beliefs; it's just that I'm more and more certain, when it comes to the free life of the mind, of the importance of uncertainty".
>
> (p. 105)

> I also harken to the words of Wittgenstein (n.d.): "I should not like my writing to spare other people the trouble of thinking. But, if possible, to stimulate someone to thoughts of his (or her) own".
>
> (n.p.)

> Nunez et al. (2014) offers an important reminder about seeking solutions: "We will not arrive at our answers by traveling a straight road".
>
> (p. 2)

> From my recent project: "Nothing is simple, permanent, or the same".
> (Kleinsasser & Roe, 2021, p. 13)

> Fleischer and Garcia (2021) contribute an important consolation: "There are no perfect practices or people in education".
> (Fleischer & Garcia, p. 274)

> And finally, the words of Michie, which I first read in his text, *Holler If You Hear me* (1999), and that he used again in the final page of his latest text, *Same as it Never Was* (2019), where he recounts his return to the role of a teacher: "At the core of our work [as teachers] is the belief, despite the distressing signs around us, that the world is indeed changeable, that it can be made into a better, more just, more peaceful place, and that the kids who show up in our classrooms each day not only deserve such a world, but can be instrumental in helping to bring it about. Their voices are

abiding reminders that there is something to hope for in spite of the hope-lessness that seems to be closing in around us – something tangible, some-thing real, something in the here and now".

(p. 137)

The literacy education of our middle grade students matters for them and the nation. They deserve our best efforts to provide practices, policies, and experiences that positively influence their opportunities to learn and enjoy a literate life. A flexible and informed mindset might best prepare them for their time in the care of their middle level teachers and for their unknown future. Onward.

## References

Adams, C. M., & Palmer, A. H. (2017). Toward a positive explanation of student differences in reading growth. *Teachers College Record, 119*(080308), 1–30.

American Psychological Association. (2020). *Publication manual of the American Psychological Association.* American Psychological Association.

Carroll, L. (1865. *Alice adventures in wonderland.* Retrieved from https://www.cs.cmu.edu/-rgs/alice-VI.html

Cartwright, K. B. (Ed.). (2018). *Literacy processes: Cognitive flexibility in learning and teaching.* The Guilford Press.

Coates, T. (2015). *Between the world and me.* Spiegel and Grau.

Cohen, L. H. (2013). *I don't know: In praise of admitting ignorance.* Riverhead Books.

DiCamillo, K. (2013). *Flora and Ulysses.* Candlewick Press.

Durkin, D. (1993). *Teaching them to read.* Allyn & Bacon.

Dyasi, H. M. (2014). Giving childhood a chance to flourish. In H. M. Dyasi, C. T. Laura, & R. Ayers, (Eds.). *Diving in.* (pp. 86–94). Teachers College.

Epstein, D. (2019). *Range: Why generalists triumph in a specialized world.* Riverhead Books.

Fleischer, C., & Garcia, A. (2021). *Everyday advocacy: Teachers who change the literacy narrative.* Norton & Company.

Garcia, A., & O'Donnell-Allen, C. (2015). *Pose, wobble, flow: A culturally proactive approach to literacy instruction.* Teachers College Press; National Writing Project.

Homer, B. D., & Hayward, E. O. (2008). Cognitive and representational development in children. In K. B. Cartwright (Ed.), *Literacy processes: Cognitive flexibility in learning and teaching,* (pp. 19–41). The Guilford Press.

Kander, F., & Roe, M. F. (2018). Teacher as advocate for social justice: Integrating advocacy into the theory and pedagogy of literacy education. In S. Hochstetler (Ed.), *Re-forming literacy education: History, effects, advocacy* (pp. 171–180). Routledge.

Jordan, M., Kleinsasser, R., & Roe, M. F. (2014). Wicked problems: Inescapable wickedity. *Journal of Education for Teaching, 40*(4), 415–430.

Kleinsasser, R., & Roe, M. F. (2021). Selecting teacher education issues: Research-creation as a process for their wickedity [Manuscript submitted for publication].

Lepper, M. R., Corpus, J. H., & Iyenger, S. S. (2005). Intrinsic and extrinsic motivational orientations in the classroom: Age differences and academic correlates. *Journal of Educational Psychology, 97*(2), 184–196.

Lichtman, G. (2014). *Journey: A roadmap to the future of education.* Jossey-Bass.

McGee, E. O. (2020). *Black, brown bruised: How racialized STEM education stifles innovation.* Harvard Education Press.

McVee, B., Ortlieb, E., Reichenberg, J.S. and Pearson, P.D. (Eds.). (2019). *The gradual Release of responsibility in literacy research and practice.* Emerald Publishing Limited. doi: 10.1108/S2048-045820190000010018Meier.

Meier, D., & Gasoi, E. (2017). *These schools belong to you and me.* Beacon Press.

Michie, G. (2019). *Same as it never was.* Teachers College Press.

Nash, J. B. (2019). *Design thinking in schools: A leader's guide to collaborating for improvement.* Harvard Education Press.

Nunez, I., Laura, C. T., Ayers, R. (Eds.). (2014). *Diving in.* Teachers College Press.

O'Day, J. A., & Smith, M. S. (2019). *Opportunity for all: A framework for quality and equality in education.* Harvard Education Press.

Osher, D., Kidmon, Y., Brackett, M, Dymnicki, A., Jones, S., & Weissberg, R. P. (2016). Advancing the science and practice of social and emotional learnings: Looking back and Moving forward. *Review of Research in Education, 40,* 644–681. doi:10.3102/0091 732X16673595

Pijeira-Díaz, H.J., Drachsler, H., Kirschner, P.A., & Järvelä, S. (2018). Profiling sympathetic arousal in a physics course: How active are students? *Journal of Computer Assisted Learning, 34*(4), 397–408.

Raphael, T. E., & Au, K. H. (2005). QAR: Enhancing comprehension and test taking across grades and content areas. *The Reading Techer, 59,* 206–221.

Rittel, H. W. J., & Webber, M. M. (1973). Dilemmas in a general theory of planning. *Policy Sciences, 4,* 155–169.

Roe, M. F. (2010). The ways teachers do the things they do: Differentiation in middle level literacy classes. *Middle Grades Research Journal, 5*(2).

Roe, M. F., & Egbert, J. (2010a). Four faces of differentiation. *Childhood Education, 87*(2), 94–97.

Roe, M. F. (2004). Real reading interactions: Identifying and meeting the challenges of middle level unsuccessful readers. *Childhood Education, 81*(1), 9–15.

Roe, M. F. (2001). Combining enablement and engagement to assist students who do not read and write well. In J. A. Rycik & J. L. Irvin (Eds.), *What adolescents deserve: A commitment to students' literacy learning* (pp. 10–19). International Reading Association.

Roe, M. F. (1997). Combining enablement and engagement to assist students who do not read and write well. *Middle School Journal, 28* (3), 35–41.

Roe, M. F. (1992). Strategy instruction: Complexities and possibilities. *Journal of Reading, 36*(3), 190–196.

Roe, M. F., & Egbert, J. (2010b). Four faces of differentiation. *Childhood Education, 87*(2), 94–97.

Schultz, B. D. (2017). *Teaching in the cracks: Opportunities for student-centered, action-focused curriculum.* Teachers College Press.

Spiro, R.J. (2021, March 26). *Defining digital literacy and its links to cognitive flexibility theory.* Zoom (recorded). Washington State University.

Spiro, R. J., Feltovich, P. J., Gaunt, A., Hu, Y., Klautke, H., Cheng, C., Clemente, I., Leahy, S., & Ward, P. (2019). Cognitive Flexibility Theory and the accelerated development of adaptive readiness and skill in situation-sensitive knowledge assembly in adaptive response to novelty. In P. Ward, J. M. Schragen, J. Gore, & E. Roth (Eds.), *The Oxford handbook of expertise* (pp. 951–976). Oxford University Press.

Spiro, R. J., Vispoel, W. L., Schmitz, J., Samarapungavan, A., & Boerger, A. (1987). Knowledge acquisition for application: Cognitive flexibility and transfer in complex content domains. In B. C. Britton & S. Glynn (Eds.), *Executive control processes in reading* (pp. 177–197). Lawrence Erlbaum.

Spiro, R. J., & Myers, A. (1984) Individual differences and underlying cognitive processes in reading. In P. D. Pearson (Ed.), *Handbook of research in reading* (pp. 471–501). Longman.

Wittgenstein, L. (n.d.) *Wittgenstein quotes.* Retrieved from 99 Notable Ludwig Wittgenstein Quotes You Must Know (thefamouspeople.com)

# SECTION 3

# Troubling Notions of Student and Teacher Identity

# 7

# I AM THE BODY BEAUTIFUL

## Disidentification and the Queering of the Young Adolescent

*Matthew Thomas-Reid*

## Middle Schoolers Are Queer

The year was 1995 and I was a young still very closeted queer kid fresh out of middle school when I first watched *To Wong Foo, Thanks for Everything Julie Newmar*. I say "watched" but "gawked, slack jawed at the opening sequence before I turned it off in horror" would be the more appropriate retelling of the event. I remember watching in fearful fascination as the gender ambiguous main character, played by Patrick Swayze, pulled their hair back, prepared to apply makeup, put on the SALT N PEPA song "I am the body Beautiful" and declared with queer confidence "ready or not, here comes mama." I will never forget the visceral reaction to the opening bars of that song juxtaposed with the application of makeup on this beautiful queen's face. I was simultaneously repulsed and enthralled as I experienced this, perhaps my first real encounter with queerness.

I open with this window into my personal queer journey because this was my first experience with what José Esteban Muñoz (1999) refers to as disidentification (p. 4). Muñoz (1999) suggests that to disidentify is

> to read oneself and one's own life narrative in a moment, object, or subject that is not culturally coded to connect with the disidentifying subject (p. 12). He further suggest that "disidentification is meant to be descriptive of the survival strategies the minority subject practices in order to negotiate a phobic majoritarian public sphere that continuously elides or punishes the existence of subjects who do not conform to the phantasm of normative citizenship.
>
> (Muñoz, 1999, p. 4)

DOI: 10.4324/9781003171508-10

In other words, this phenomenon describes the experiencing of liminal space around the point of self-discovery and the fear of both what one might become and what one might leave behind. I was drawn to my own first experience of disidentification after reading Muñoz's own childhood experience with this phenomenon:

> My pre-out consciousness was completely terrified by the swishy spectacle of Capote's performance. But I also remember feeling a deep pleasure in hearing Capote make language, in "getting" the fantastic bitchiness of his quip. …I can locate that experience of suburban spectatorship as having a disidentificatory impact on me
>
> (Muñoz, 1999, p. 4)

I relate this experience to my own encounter with "To Wong Foo…" because of the similar duel reaction of terror and pleasure. After this experience, I experimented with counter identities in order to avoid the terror of embracing my queerness. I remember that summer donning a "I might be a redneck if" t-shirt and confederate flag ballcap at camp in order to resist the possibility of being like that confident queen applying makeup to a hip-hop song about beautiful bodies. It took me several years of cognitive dissonance to finally accept some version of queer identity (gay seemed the best word for me in the mid 90s), and a further 20 years to accept a queer gender expression that I would eventually embrace as an amateur drag practitioner.

This story and its intertwined theme of disidentification seems appropriate now as I position middle grades education as a site for a queer analysis, because it occurs to me that young adolescents are actually pretty queer: they are visceral, body bound subjects who are constantly identifying and disidentifying, blurring binary understandings of human development, fluidly negotiating their realities and identities, and generally experiencing the world with a queer angle. They are bodies that are menstruating, popping random erections, experiencing joy and horror almost simultaneously, and trying to reconcile the world as it is with the world as they are experiencing it. In short, if there is a need to queer middle grades education, it is precisely because the middle school student is already queer to begin with.

I have written elsewhere that "If education is a form of activism, queer theory can perhaps inform this activism in ways that extend beyond safe spaces and inclusive curriculum by drawing from the experience of the queer to develop approaches to classrooms that interrupt the colonized classroom space. (Thomas-Reid, 2020, p. 1). I take up this concern again in this chapter by suggesting that to queer middle grades education does not mean adding x identity and stirring or focusing on making a space safe. To queer middle grades education, we ought to consider first, what makes the young adolescent already queer, and second, what hegemonic cultural influences exist that a queer activism could disrupt and undo.

It is with this notion of undoing that I reflect on my previous work where I argue that "Queer pedagogy seeks both to uncover and disrupt hidden curricula, …create safety for queer participants across intersectionality of race, gender, and sexuality, [and develop] an understanding of what a queer pedagogy might be working to undo, and this requires an exploration of the normative, specifically the heteronormative" (Thomas-Reid, 2018, p. 3). Beth Berila (2016) defines heteronormative as the notion that heterosexuality [and I suggest by tacit extension being cisgender] is the only 'proper' and 'natural' …identity. (Berila, 2016, p. 6). The ways in which we will interrogate heteronormativity and cisnormativity in this chapter include two key facets of middle grades curriculum, pedagogy, and assessment: Bodies and development. As with the other chapters in this collection, I will work with theory to consider significant impacts of practice beyond the more superficial concepts of diversity in order to uncover what a theoretical take on middle grades education in this context might look like, boldly recognizing that structures might well be disrupted and preconceived notions of meaning might well be undone. In the pages that follow, I will consider how these two themes of bodies and development might be disrupted and undone by applying a lens of queerness to, as I have mentioned, an already pretty queer subject.

## Are You Sure You Want to Use Queer Theory?

It seems fitting that I first learned about queer theory in middle school. No, we did not read Judith Butler or Eve Kosovsky Sedgewick, but I encountered queer theory in its discursive and disruptive power through a variation of schoolyard football known affectionately to its practitioners as "smear the queer." Lisa W. Loutzenheiser (1996) describes this phenomenon as something like:

> a big red rubber ball was thrown to an individual. Sometimes that person threw it away quickly but other times someone would yell 'Smear the queer' and all the participants would pile on top of the person with the ball. Generally, this person was perceived as weaker or less popular than the others.
>
> (p. 59)

I learned a great deal from this game about the social order of straightness in my school. I learned quickly that straightness reigned supreme and queerness was to be quite literally stamped out by heteronormative practices. Sarah Ahmed (2006) describes this as the notion that "queer or wonky moments are corrected. We could describe heteronormativity as a straightening device, which rereads the 'slant' of queer desire" (p. 562). Smear the queer thus served as one of the first of these straightening devices that I encountered, and the lesson was clear: do not disturb the order of things by being queer, as "the world is already organized around certain forms of living — certain times, spaces, and directions" (Ahmed, 2006, p. 565).

To be queer, I learned, was not simply a state of being, rather a force that did something, that changed things, that was dangerous: "Those who seem uncomfortable think the term queer as a noun or an identity. But the queer and the theory in queer theory signify actions, not actors. It can be thought of as a verb, or as a citational relation that signifies more than the signifier" (Britzman, 1995, p.153). Indeed the queer is still very much framed by many as a danger, as a threat to children, as a threat to innocence, as a force acting upon childhood as opposed to a force of childhood, and that those adults seeking to impose queerness on children should be fought against at all costs (Edelman, 2004, p. 21). Greteman and Wojcikiewicz (2014) further this notion suggesting that considering the queerness of children "in the realm of education… disrupts the innocence of the Child as imagined and portrayed. It challenges the frame that sets the Child up as in need of a proper curriculum, in need of protection" (p. 563).

## Well OK, If You are Sure…

To apply queer theory in a middle grades' context, it might be best understood as a tool of dissent (Greteman, 2014). In this case, dissenting against culturally hegemonic notions of adolescent development, and controlling, ignoring, or distracting the adolescent body are two useful entry points into exploring what a queering of middle grades pedagogy, curriculum, and assessment might look like. Queer theory in the middle grades might also be a vehicle for empowerment, both for queer youth and the educational practitioner and researcher, as it provides a rich site for the exploration "of the practices of theorization that organically develop from experience as well as highlighting the centrality of theory to research" (Mayo, 2007a, p. 80).

Along with the growing understanding that one does not have to be a person of color to participate in antiracist education, one does not have to identify as LGBTQIA+ to participate in queer pedagogies as

> both straight and LGBTQ teachers can benefit from an understanding of queer theory, particularly because simply being queer and having a working knowledge of queer theory are not necessarily related (Zacko-Smith & Pritchy, 2010, p. 6). The most important caveat to doing queer work in education is not one's identity, but one's aims. If an educator's goal is to simply add something to their practice to give a nod to their inclusivity of queer students, then it might be advisable to look elsewhere, as a queered approach will necessarily be disruptive, as to queer that which is straight cannot happen without undoing that which we have traditionally seen as true. This is true not only narrowly in doing queer theory but more broadly in doing any critically conscious, socially just education. As Cris Mayo (2007b) points out, "we don't get to talk about race, gender, class, sexuality, disability sequentially, separately or calmly."
>
> (Mayo, Teaching Homophobia, 2007b, p. 172)

But for those willing to take the risk, the stakes are high, as "LGBTQ students continue to face a hostile environment in school, routinely hearing anti-LGBTQ language and experiencing victimization and discrimination at school (Goldfarb & Lieberman, 2020, p. 21)." Still with me? Ok, let's jump in.

## Thinking Bodies and Embodied Minds

A queered approach to bodies in educational spaces is first to recognize that the body is often neglected in middle school space. To view the mid as distinct and separate from the body presents the body as a problem, rather than indelibly connected to the mind. With this in mind, we might consider Descartes's Mind-body problem as alive and well in middle school. By this I mean to suggest that the body is often viewed as the problem, a barrier to the mind. This is by no means suggesting that middle grades educators are totally ignoring the bodies of the students they are teaching, but rather that the body is often viewed as an obstacle to teaching the mind, as opposed to conceptualizing the mind and body as indelibly intertwined and imagining ways to reach the mind through the body. While "educators have to begin acknowledging that bodies, not just minds, inhabit educational spaces," we are a long way from theorizing, let along enacting, pedagogies, curriculum, and assessment strategies which adequately engage bodies, rather than simply distracting them (Hughes-Decatur, 2012, p. 51). Desk fidget bands and stress balls involve students in tactile activities, but these serve as outlets for movement as opposed to engaging the embodied subjects. Even more sophisticated techniques such as brain gym activities still separate embodied movement from actual content-based curriculum, pedagogies, and assessment. In short, having students touch their elbow to their opposite knee (a common brain gym activity) during a three-minute break in between multiple choice bubbled tests is not sufficiently engaging the entire student, rather paying somewhat superficial lip service to some research on kinesthetic learning.

What might a queered take on bodies in educational setting actually look like, then? Returning to Muñoz, let us consider the disidentified subject and their bodily relationship to space. Muñoz (1999) argues that "Disidentification is about recycling and rethinking encoded meaning" (p. 31). How do we recycle and rethink in our bodies? To return to the example of smearing the queer, I literally learned that visibly queer bodies were subject to physical harm when they intrude into straight spaces. I recycled and rethought about my own bodily presentation as weak or feminine and the repercussions of this presentation on the school playground.

What if a pedagogy informed by a queer disruptive disidentification "scrambles and reconstructs the encoded message's universalizing and exclusionary machinations and recircuits its workings to account for, include, and empower minority identities and identifications" (Muñoz, 1999, p. 31). Consider for example why so many queer-identified students gravitate to the performing arts: the empowerment of the sassy, the queeny, the butch, and the tomboy taps into the fully embodied movement which disrupts the exclusionary heteronorms and cis-norms and frees the queer from the machinations of straightness, if only for one class period. Even thinking about disrupting the activities that students do during physical education can serve as a pedagogy of disidentification: my one great feat of accomplishment in middle school PE was during a field day competition when I dominated the jump rope category while the rest of the boys floundered, only because I had been repeatedly excluded from the more masculine activities for the whole semester and found solace among the girls jumping rope on the margins of the playground.

Muñoz (1999) further exemplifies the power of these types of embodied moves by elucidating the fact that "disidentification is a step further than cracking open the code of the majority; it proceeds to use this code as raw material for representing a disempowered politics or positionality that has been rendered unthinkable by the dominant culture" (Muñoz, 1999, p. 31). Allowing the sissy the spotlight to be successful in a physical activity renders the dominant cultural construct unstable and orchestrates what one might think of as an embodied pedagogical queering. This disidentification in schools happens whether the teacher orchestrates it or not, as it becomes. Matter of survival for the minority identity: It is a response to …power apparatuses that employ systems of racial, sexual, and national subjugation …[and] is about managing and negotiating historical trauma and systemic violence" (Muñoz, 1999, p. 179).

If the queer-minded educator were to engage in active opportunities for disidentificatory embodied learning, they would first have to recognize that the "way we do things" is built around a pattern of straightness. Sarah Ahmed (2006) points out that Spaces become straight, which allow straight bodies to extend into them (p. 563). A pedagogy of disidentification would therefore be predicated on unstraightening the space as "bodies are hence shaped by contact with objects and others, with 'what' is near enough to be reached" (Ahmed, 2006, p. 552). This should not be misconstrued as building safe spaces or adding measures to "accommodate" queerness, rather it necessarily means unstraightening the classroom for all, as simply welcoming queer students into a straight space would only serve to "make them appear oblique, strange, and out of place" (Ahmed, 2006, p. 570). Let us now examine more specifically what pedagogy, curriculum, and assessment that takes into account queer bodies and unstraightens the space might look like.

## Teaching Bodies with Bodies

We perhaps should not delude ourselves into thinking that we take straight bodies into account that much more than we take queer bodies into account in middle grades education. Perhaps what makes the prospect of a pedagogy that actually embraces the body difficult is that we would have to confront all bodies, and the materiality of those bodies that makes some of them queer. Even the embodied acknowledgement that *boys have penises and girls have vaginas* leads to the queer question *what about the girls that have penises and the boys that have vaginas*. Even opening conversation about bodies leads to the possibility of queer moments in space.

Many have probably observed icebreaker activities meant to normalize language around the body, such as repeating words like penis and vagina multiple times to make students more comfortable with the language, but Hilary Hughes-Decatur (2012) goes a step further and wonders "how that would go over as a beginning-of-the-year icebreaker in a seventh grade math or social studies class" (p. 50)? While I am not saying that an embodied pedagogy means normalizing the terms for genitalia in math class, but it seems like a plausible place to start queering the space and opening up room for normalizing the fact that we have genitalia, and perhaps going even further and normalizing the fact that said genitalia sometimes bleeds or becomes engorged.

While this might seem a provocative move, one first step in a pedagogy that embraces all bodies is creating "classrooms that are open to discourses about the body as being relevant to our students and to all of us" (Hughes-Decatur, 2012, p. 57). But this is not where we must end, but rather where we begin. Hilary Hughes-Decatur (2012) actually goes on to make an argument worth queerly dissenting with by suggesting that we ought "to begin valuing what young adolescents think and say about the world and the body and, with our students, learn how we can all be enough in the bodies we have" (p. 57). I choose to dissent and problematize this statement first on the grounds that it feels like trans★ erasure, but perhaps more to our concern, it ignores the subject's potential for disidentification with their own bodies. While body and sex positivity are of great importance, dysphoria is a very real and valid aspect of queerness that deserves space in the queered classroom. Rather than simply telling a student to be happy with the body that they are given, we might open a dialogical space about the history of altering our bodies, the tensions between empowerment and assimilation, and the very real visceral experiences of feeling disconnected with our bodies and how we might make meaning out of this. Being educated and prepared to lead very real discussions about gender dysphoria and its distinct differences from simply being self-conscious about bodies is the type of risky and queer discussion making required to make the leap into queered pedagogies.

Furthering this theme of disidentification with bodies, a queer pedagogy embracing bodies might also explore how we present our bodies. I have written elsewhere that "queering pedagogies will involve a certain amount of experimenting, of prancing and squatting in the academic stage, and some of this will decidedly lead to conflict and even emotional upheaval" (Thomas-Reid, 2020, p. 7). As if discussing bodies was not enough, a queer embodied pedagogy is likely one that would welcome the disruption of traditional gender performance, and, perhaps, even welcome drag into the classroom space. While drag is distinct and different from gender identity, it might well serve as a vehicle to highlight gender performance.

Judith Butler (1993) points out that

> what is 'performed' in drag is, of course, the sign of gender, a sign which is not the same as the body of figures, but which cannot be read without it. (Butler, 1993, p. 28). In other words, activities like drag story hour serve multiple functions: they teach kids that it is ok to be gender creative and disrupt gender roles, but they also teach about gender performance and gender roles in visible and visceral ways (Andrews et al., 2018, p. 5). Imagine a school setting in which drag was normalized a s a form of expression. This is distinctly different from traditional misogynist forms of drag that might be seem in schools, such as womanless beauty pageants and powder-puff football games, which actually serve to reinforce the cisnorms by mocking legitimate gender performativity by having jocks stuff their bras to ridiculous levels and prance around in derogatory stereotypes of femininity. One can, however, observe disidentification even in these practices, as there always seems to be that one boy that does the gender performance *just a little too well*. This ambiguous point might be a nice note on which to end this section considering the propensity for queered pedagogies to acknowledge "the queer aspects of education in relation to not knowing, of the unknown, of the unknowable".
>
> (Wolfgang & Rhoades, 2017, p. 72)

## A Curriculum of Bodies for Bodies

Deb Britzman (1995) writes that queer

> demands for civil rights call into question the stability and fundamentalist grounds of categories like masculinity, femininity, sexuality, citizenship, nation, culture, literacy, consent, legality, and so forth; categories that are quite central to the ways in which education organizes knowledge of bodies and bodies of knowledge.
>
> (p. 152)

In this quote, the author is pointing out that curriculum is at the heart of equality; that civil rights go beyond laws legalizing marriage, adoption, and the use of bathrooms to the restructuring of the knowledge centers that have long been the producers and replicators of straightness and cisness. If school structures are indeed constructed with straightness in mind, then it is curriculum that forms the brick and mortar of normativity and cultural hegemony. Wolfgang & Rhoades (2017) point out that when presuming the status quo, queer aspects of people's lives are ignored, erased, camouflaged, or denied (p. 76). Without curriculum that features queer bodies free from shame or remorse, a queer embodied pedagogy becomes hollow.

First it might be useful to identify what we think of as curriculum in a traditional sense, and how we might even queer what it means to be curriculum in the first place. I suggest elsewhere that we might imagine what constitutes a text to teach with, and how text might, in a postmodern sense, include discourse and bodies in addition to marginal representation in written, spoken, and performed texts (Thomas-Reid, 2020, p. 9). Considering the positionality and embodiment of the teacher in a formal lesson, or how pedagogies of coming out might yield value considering the teacher as text. Formal discussion around "menstruation, sex, eating disorders, or sexuality …[or] how popular culture teaches us what a 'normal body' is" in addition to a critical interrogation of "bodies in media (e.g., ads, television, video games, movies, and music videos)" might serve as curricular material with which to embody queerness (Hughes-Decatur, 2012, p. 55).

Hughes-Decatur (2012) goes on in their article to posit particular curricular examples across multiple content areas, from science classes considering the genetic miracle of bodies or materiality of sex, to social studies classes studying the

> body-related practices of various cultures around the world and how those practices influence cultural beliefs and norms (p. 55). Each of the above curricular examples should not serve as a list or curricular resources, rather a glimpse of how a queer embodied mindset can open up space for something beyond "the "add x and stir" approach to diversity.
>
> (Hughes-Decatur, 2012, p. 56)

To further this point, Barbara Blackburn (2016) concludes that within this queer mindset "sexuality, queer desire, gender creativity, gender independence, and trans inclusivity … can move all of us beyond LGBTQ-inclusivity and inform reading, discussing, teaching, and learning in all of the classrooms and school contexts where we live and work" (Blackburn, 2016, 804).

## Assessing Bodies with Bodies

Having written about queering assessment elsewhere, there is certainly not adequate time to give the subject of assessment as merely a subset of a book chapter, but assessment cannot go entirely ignored here, as with any pedagogy there really ought to be ways to allow students to express what they know. Suffice to say, traditional assessment, much like traditional pedagogy and curriculum, privileges normative bodies through a replication of compulsory heterosexuality and cisness through cultivation of bodies into discrete sexes (Butler, 1988, p. 524). Further, assessment, through its "cis-normative curation of the content to be assessed, the heteronormative and cis-normative curation of the standards to be assessed, and even in the procedures used, which often require trans★ students to deadname themselves (use a name associated with a gender or identity that they do not possess) on a summative examination because this is the name on their permanent record, continues to straighten bodies in classrooms" (Thomas-Reid, 2020, p. 11).

How might we unstraighten assessment? What if, counterintuitively, we started from a rather conventional notion of aligning assessment with the curriculum and pedagogy? If we are doing embodied teaching, would embodied assessment not simply require students to find ways to engage their bodies in demonstrating what they know? If we know that "to acknowledge the body in education would mean recognizing that it is through the body and through bodily experiences that our students are making meaning in their learning processes," what if assessment actively engaged bodies to make meaning, to encourage the performative in our students? (Hughes-Decatur, 2012, p. 53). What would a performative assessment look like that takes bodies into account, from those who are differently abled to those who are gender non-conforming? These are some of the questions that might guide the queer-minded educator in the development of embodied assessment.

## Development

Adolescent development has long been at the heart of theoretical approaches to middle grades curriculum, pedagogy, and assessment (Mee et al., 2012, p. 9), but to what extent is this simply. Continuation of Ahmed's notion of the creation of straight spaces? The inculcation of the objective scientific truth of development has largely served to further reinforce the hegemony of straightness and cisness as developmental norms and puts strict expectations on bodies and marginalizes those bodies that do not conform to this development. As Ahmed points out,

> Spaces are oriented around the straight body, which allows that body to extend into space…Repetitive performances of hegemonic asymmetrical gender identities and heterosexual desires congeal over time to produce the appearance that the street is normally a heterosexual space…Spaces become straight.
>
> (Ahmed, 2006, p. 563)

What follows in this section is a critique of the cisnormative and heteronormative power of thinking through a lens of development and further posits how a disidentification of development might shape curriculum, pedagogy, and assessment.

The critiques of both the limits of development and the overemphasis of development are not exactly new, nor are the suggestions that poststructuralist theories might provide a robust reimagining of adolescent development (Vagle 2015, pp. 1–2) (Brinegar, 2019, p. 4). What makes disidentification a useful theme for considering development is that it leans into contradictions and "a disidentifying subject works to hold on to [lost] object and invest [them] with new life" (Muñoz, 1999, p. 12). In this sense, disidentification might be thought of as a hermeneutic through which one might "shuffle back and forth between reception and production …from the perspective of a minority subject who is disempowered in such a representational hierarchy" (Muñoz, 1999, p. 25). In other words, for development to be an objective measurement, there has to be an objective measure of what ought to be developed into. Traditionally this has meant developing into cis, straight, neurotypical, and able bodies (and probably white as well). If one disidentifies with the end product of developmental models as the normative ideal, then, one might well be able to disidentify with any apparently objective developmental milestone along the way.

## Undeveloped Pedagogy

The teachers who claim not to see race, class, gender, or sexuality still see development. It is through the lens of hegemonic developmental milestones that these teachers tacitly discriminate against those students "whose racial, cultural, socio-economic, and gender identities do not conform to developmental norms" (Brinegar, 2019, p. 4). A pedagogy that actively seeks to disidentify developmental norms as a guidepost for teaching might be able to conceive of both student and teacher classroom performances that contradict regulatory regimes, hierarchies and constraints (Butler, 1993, p. 21). Kevin Kumashiro (2002) conceives of pedagogies that reveal and confront our own prejudices and acknowledge "the harmful list of practices that unintentionally perpetuate the stereotypes or are complicit with institutionalized oppression" (Kumashiro, 2002, p. 64). Thus, a pedagogy that actively disidentifies with development would call for teachers to "accept their role as mentors who help to define reality for those they are educating, and …commit to redefining that reality as dictated by demands for social justice and equity" (Zacko-Smith & Pritchy, 2010, p. 2).

A pedagogy that actively disidentifies with development is one that also involves what Jon Wargo calls "hacking and mixing" (Wargo, 2017). Hacking and remixing as a form of queering existing literature while working to recontextualize and recharacterize in terms of queerness (Wargo, 2017). This actively turns development on its head as it requires the educator to allow the student to begin to craft their reality, to unstraighten the space of the classroom disconnected from notions of developmental level (Wargo, 2017). Students actively queering stories could draw from the contemporary tradition of slash fiction, which is a subset of fan fiction which focuses on adding queer storylines for existing fictional characters. Imagine what it might look like to hack, mix, or slash in a history class: to allow students to speculate about the imagined and often unverifiable lives of historical figures from a queer perspective.

## Undeveloped Curriculum

If we acknowledge that "historically, developmentalism has been rooted in White, heterosexual, male supremacy," we might acknowledge that a curriculum based in this developmentalism is rooted in the same hegemony (Brinegar, 2019, p. 8). From curriculum of binary gender that erases intersex identities to differentiated learning that ignores the multiplicity of neuro-atypical understandings of the world, we continue to perpetuate inequality by applying universal models of development to bodies that exist outside of the worldview producing and perpetuating these models (Brinegar, 2019, p. 10).

What if the sciences and mathematics employed different curriculum theories to teach their concepts, moving from traditional curriculum scaffolding to having students "answer different kinds of questions and solve different kinds of problems, especially problems relevant to their own lives and communities" (Kumashiro, 2002, p. 60)? Rather than trying to engage disidentified subjects, we might disrupt our curricular choices to find ways for students to identify and apply. Finally, what if we valued multiplicities of identity in curricula as a means to unstraighten that which has been made straight, especially when we know that "curricula designed specifically to reduce homophobia have been found to be successful across grade levels using a variety of approaches both formally within sexuality education and throughout other areas of the curriculum" (Goldfarb & Lieberman, 2020, p. 16)?

## Yup, You Guessed It: Undeveloped Assessment

Assessment might well be the area impacted by the hegemony of development the most. Here is where I would like to truly employ an insurrectionist mindset, much like "the early days of the middle grades movement [which] could be read as revolts, of sorts, against the educational authorities of the times" (Vagle, 2015, p. 1). Vagle (2015) characterizes this as

> the need for a less prescriptive focus on developmental responsiveness that …positions young adolescents in deficit-oriented ways, in favor of a more particularized responsiveness that honors young adolescents in the here and now and that begins to be more responsive…to the ethnic and cultural diversity … of young adolescents.
>
> (Vagle, 2015, p. 3)

This responsiveness seems particularly relevant to the field of assessment, where we long for a universalization instead of a particularization. If it is true that "I will never know how you see red and you will never know how I see it," it seems more important to hear my voice in the description of red than to force your upon me (Merleau-Ponty, 1964, p. 17). Perhaps a queer disidentified assessment calls for a rather radical notion that we have not historically done a very good job of accurately identifying what students know and can do, and that maybe this is because we have not done a very good job of involving our disidentified students in not only the cocreation of meaning, but also in the cocreation of the evaluation of this meaning.

## Violently Undoing Meaning, in a Meaningful Way

Through this chapter, identity and by extension identification has been a clear and present theme tacitly along with disidentification. To close, it seems important to address the unstable, fluidic, and constructed nature of identify that sets at the backdrop of disidentification. It might be easiest to start with a fact: there were no homosexuals prior to the 19th century. While this is clearly somewhat tongue and cheek, through the lens of identification, this statement is absolutely true. You see, the term homosexual was coined in the 19th century not only as a new word, but as a whole new notion of identity (Foucault, 1978, p. 43). Prior to the 19th century, same sex acts were viewed as that-simply acts with no identity connected to them, except perhaps that of one with mental illness (Foucault, 1978, p. 43). Prior to the 20th century there were no gay people, prior to the 1960s there were no people who identified as pansexual, and prior to the 21st century there were no demisexual folks walking about (Berila, 2016, p. 6) (Mayo, 2007a, p. 84).

This is the fluidity and destabilization that occurs with disidentification. No matter how many categories we create, they will never be able to hold the myriad identifications and disidentifications which constantly create new meaning and problematize old. Clearly people roughly fitting the description of each of these categorizations have been around for as long as the human race has, but it is the identifying, disidentifying, and reidentifying that require language to expand to accommodate new identities. Muñoz (1999) suggests that "The fiction of identity is one that is accessed with relative ease by most majoritarian subjects. Minoritarian subjects need to interface with different subcultural fields to activate their own senses of self" (Muñoz, 1999, p. 5). In short, stable identity is very often the privilege of dominant groups.

It is with this in mind that the traditional language of relating to and being a positive role model for middle school students simply does not work in the context of a queer disidentified approach (Mee et al., 2012, pp. 9–10). Ultimately a queer approach to middle grades really must move us past "embodying this notion that just because we are adults, we know more than our students… Instead, we can move toward learning how to listen differently to them and, in doing so, we might better grasp the incredible resilience they embody, for which they seldom receive credit" (Hughes-Decatur, 2012, pp. 51, 57).

Finally, it is to be remembered that queering in general and disidentification specifically are both points of departure; a process, a building. Although it is a mode of reading and performing, it is ultimately a form of building. (Muñoz, 1999, p. 200). While this chapter certainly engages in what Lee Edelman calls "the violent undoing of meaning, the loss of identity and coherence," a queer response would be to look forward openly to the ever-moving horizons of possibility, never really knowing what might come next (p. 132). What could possibly be more *middle school* than that?

## References

Ahmed, S. (2006) Orientations: Toward a Queer Phenomenology. *GLQ: A Journal of Lesbian and Gay Studies*, 12(4) 543–574.

Andrews, G., Moulton, M., & Hughes, H (2018). Integrating social justice into middle grades teacher education. *Middle School Journal*.

Berila, B. (2016) Mindfulness as a healing, liberatory practice in queer anti-oppression pedagogy. *Social Alternatives* 35 (3) 5–10

Blackburn, M.V. (2016). Investigating LGBT-themed literature and trans informed pedagogies in classrooms. *Discourse Studies in the Cultural Politics of Education*, 37(6), 801–806.

Brinegar, K. (2019). *Equity & Cultural Responsiveness in the Middle Grades*. Information Age Publishing.

Britzman, D. (1995). Is there a Queer Pedagogy? Or, Stop Reading Straight. *Educational Theory*, 45(2), 151–165.

Butler, J. (1993). *Bodies that matter: On the discursive limits of sex*. New York, NY: Routledge.

Butler, J. (1988). "Performative Acts and Gender Constitution: An Essay in Phenomenology and Feminist Theory, *Theatre Journal*, 40(4), 519–531.

Edelman, L. (2004). *No future: Queer theory and the death drive*. Durham, NC: Duke University Press.

Foucault, M. (1978). *The history of sexuality volume 1: An Introduction*. New York, NY: Pantheon.

Greteman, A. J. (2014). Dissenting with queer theory: Reading Rancière queerly. *Studies in the Cultural Politics of Education*. 35(3), 419–432.

Goldfarb, E., & Lieberman, L. (2020). Three Decades of Research: The Case for Comprehensive Sex Education. *Journal of Adolescent health* 68, 13–27.

Greteman, A. J., & Wojcikiewicz, S. K. (2014). The Problems with the Future: Educational Futurism and the Figural Child. *Journal of Philosophy of Education*, 48(4), 559–573.

Hughes-Decatur, H. (2012) Red flags are blowin' on The Tyra Show: Acknowledging the body in middle grades education *Middle School Journal*.

Kumashiro, K. (2002). *Troubling education: Queer activism and anti-oppressive pedagogy*. New York, NY: Routledge Falmer.

Loutzenheiser, L. W. (1996). How schools play "Smear the Queer". *Feminist Teacher*, 10(2), 59–64.

Mayo, C. (2007a). Queering foundations: Queer and lesbian, gay, bisexual, and transgender educational research. In *Review of research in education, Vol. 31. Difference, diversity, and distinctiveness in education and learning* (pp. 78–94). Washington, DC: American Educational Research Association.

Mayo, C. (2007b). Teaching Against Homophobia without Teaching the Subject. In S. Springgay and D. Freedman (Eds.). *Curriculum and the Cultural Body* (New York: Peter Lang, 2007), 163–173.

Mee, M., Haverback, H., & Passe, J. 2012. For the love of the middle: A glimpse into why one group of preservice teachers chose middle grades education. *Middle Grades Research Journal*, 7(4), 1–14.

Merleau-Ponty, M. (1964). *Primacy of Perception*. Evanston: Northwest University Press.

Muñoz, J. (1999). *Disidentifications: Queers of Color and the Performance of Politics*. University of Minnesota Press.

Thomas-Reid, M. (2018). Queer pedagogy. In G. Noblit (Ed.). *Oxford Research Encyclopedia of Education*. New York: Oxford University Press.

Thomas-Reid, M. (2020). Queer Pedagogical Theory. In Cris Mayo. (Ed). *Oxford Encyclopedia of Gender and Sexuality in Education*. New York: Oxford University Press.

Vagle, M. (2015) Reviving theoretical insurrection in middle grades education. *Middle Grades Review*, 1(1) http://scholarworks.uvm.edu/mgreview/vol1/iss1/2

Wargo, J. (2017). Hacking heteronormativity and remixing rhymes: Enacting a [Q]ulturally sustaining pedagogy in middle grades english language arts. *Voices from the Middle*, 24(3).

Wolfgang, C. N., & Rhoades, M. J. (2017). First fagnostics: Queering art education. *Journal of Social Theory in Art Education*, 37, 72–79.

Zacko-Smith, J. D., & Pritchy G. S. (2010). Recognizing and utilizing queer pedagogy. *Multicultural Education*, 1(1). 2–9.

# 8

# MULTILINGUALISM IN MIDDLE SCHOOL EDUCATION

*Katie Walker*

## Multilingualism in Middle School Education

Multilingual education often conjures images of America as "the melting pot," and ideals of the opportunity for all people of all backgrounds to engage meaningfully in the American society, economy, and civic-life. Indeed, this very American ideal lives at the very heart of middle level education, as we acknowledge the value of attending to the development of students' physical, intellectual, moral, psychological, and socio-emotional development (Bishop & Harrison, 2021). However, I would argue that it is equally relevant to consider a sixth dimension, linguistic development (Cummins, 1981; Faltis, & Hudelson, 1994).

Currently, schools worldwide are taking the opportunity to engage in a self-assessment of current instructional practices as they prepare to address the COVID-gap that students have experienced during the pandemic (Economic Policy Institute, 2020). While our society has experienced a traumatic event, it has offered educators the chance to take stock of our current practices and to start fresh in the coming year. We are beginning to see recommendations for school districts to adopt practices that accelerate learning that aligns the best practices from the past 20 years in a way that supports districts in managing implementation (Darling-Hammond & Edgerton, 2021; TNTP, 2018; U.S. Department of Education, 2021). We know from many years of research in the field of second language acquisition, that students learn best when their first language (L1) and cultures are leveraged (Au, 1980; August, Shanahan, & Escamilla, 2009; García, 2017; Gutiérrez, Baquedano-López, & Turner, 1997). It is my hope that within these recommendations for improvement, we, as educators, will take that opportunity to incorporate the best practices related to second language acquisition.

DOI: 10.4324/9781003171508-11

This chapter connects current issues related to serving multilingual early adolescents with strategies that support language and literacy development within a culturally and linguistically sustaining context. I will first provide the reader with the context for understanding who multilingual early adolescents are and what English as a Second Language (ESL) instruction is. Next, I will provide specific strategies that middle grade teachers can use to support the language and literacy development of multilingual early adolescents while providing students with the space to sustain their current cultural, linguistic, and literacy practices.

## Understanding the Multilingual Adolescent

Socio-cultural instruction is valuable when addressing the needs of emergent bilinguals (Cruz, 2008; Gee, 2004). Through the use of socio-cultural methods, classroom teachers can ensure that they are creating culturally responsive classrooms that are conducive to a positive sense of community (Haneda, 2008). These environments are inherently valuable for all students but are essential for students from marginalized groups such as immigrant populations and language minorities (Gutiérrez, 2008). Classrooms that value socio-cultural methods would consider instructional activities that encouraged students to take a critical stance in their reading and learning and also take advantage of students' experiential knowledge to increase comprehension (Alford, 2001; Faltis, Arias, Ramirez-Marin, 2010; Fredricks, 2012).

One key way to help students from marginalized groups find their voices in the classroom is to encourage students to utilize their prior, or experiential knowledge (Fu & Graff, 2009). According to de Jong, Harper and Coady (2013), "teachers in ELL-inclusive classrooms build on and extend their ELLs' linguistic and cultural experiences and scaffold instruction appropriately to ensure ELLs access to grade-level content learning" (p. 93). When working with emergent bilinguals, teachers experience wide ranges of language proficiency, both in heritage and additional languages, cultures, schooling, and experiences (Fu & Graff, 2009; Gutiérrez, 2008; Martinez-Roldan & Franquiz, 2009). This dynamic within a classroom makes the use of students' prior knowledge particularly useful. By meeting students where they are, teachers allow students the freedom to utilize biliteracy strategies, social knowledge, cultural knowledge, and experiential knowledge to help bring meaning to new and difficult concepts and texts (Franquiz & Salinas, 2011; Skerrett & Bomer, 2011).

Similarly, students possess varying political and historical knowledge from schooling in other countries. This knowledge can often help students in content-area classrooms by making meaning from their prior political-historical knowledge (Pacheco, 2009; Ramirez, 2012). This not only increases the likelihood of academic success but also helps emergent bilinguals to develop the 21st century skills needed for the workplace such as considering multiple perspectives, collaborative skills, and bilingualism (Beaufort, 2009; National Governors Association

Center for Best Practices & Council of Chief State School Officers, 2010). When teachers design learning environments that leverage the linguistic and cultural strengths of students, learning outcomes are improved.

## Culturally Responsive Instruction

At the core of the work of leveraging adolescent's socio-cultural and linguistic capital is the idea that all students carry with them a complex world of knowledge that has been influenced by experiences, culture, race, languages, literacies, familial values, spiritual lives, gender, and behaviors (Au, 1998; Khalifa, Gooden, & Davis, 2016; Paris, 2012). Therefore, it is logical that this work must be situated within the context of culturally responsive pedagogy (Au, 2007).

Multiple terms have been suggested to capture the spirit of what CRT educators are trying to accomplish, including "culturally responsive" (Cazden & Leggett, 1976), "culturally relevant" (Ladson-Billings, 1995), and "culturally sustaining" (Paris, 2012). While the terms "culturally responsive" and "culturally relevant" are very similar in meaning, the more recent term, "culturally sustaining," takes a detour from the goal of responding to the unique needs of marginalized students. Paris (2012) defined "culturally sustaining" pedagogy as:

> The term culturally sustaining requires that our pedagogies be more than responsive of or relevant to the cultural experiences and practices of young people – it requires that they support young people in sustaining the cultural and linguistic competence of their communities while simultaneously offering access to dominant cultural competence. Culturally sustaining pedagogy, then, has as its explicit goal supporting multilingualism and multiculturalism in practice and perspective for students and teachers. That is, culturally sustaining pedagogy seeks to perpetuate and foster – to sustain – linguistic, literate, and cultural pluralism as part of the democratic project of schooling.
>
> (p. 95)

However, Khalifa, Gooden, and Davis (2016) stated that each of these terms shared "a common, central point: the need for children's educators and educational contexts to understand, respond, incorporate, accommodate, and ultimately celebrate the entirety of the children they serve" (p. 1277).

For the purposes of this chapter, I will use the term "culturally responsive" to refer to the pedagogies and learning environments that are necessary for capitalizing on students' diverse socio-cultural and linguistic repertoires. Culturally responsive instruction is defined as:

> using the cultural knowledge, prior experiences, frames of reference, and performance styles of ethnically diverse students to make learning

encounters more relevant to and effective for them. It teaches to and through the strength of these students. It is culturally validating and affirming.

(Gay, 2000, p. 29)

I will use the term culturally responsive for two reasons. First, the term culturally responsive is the most recognizable of the three and is most consistently applied across literacy and language educational research (Au, 1998, 2007, 2018; Cazden & Leggett, 1976; Forman & Cazden, 1986; Gay, 2003, 2018). Secondly, the term culturally responsive puts the onus on the educator to take on-going actions to be critically conscious of changing student demographics and learning needs when selecting, incorporating, designing, and implementing instruction.

Often, schools narrowly conceptualize what it means to be culturally responsive to students, by focusing on easily accessible stereotypes of the larger minority cultures represented in the school (Banks, 1993; Gay, 2018). This narrow conceptualization is often visible in schools as single events during Black History Month, Cinco de Mayo, or as stand-alone units within larger curricular contexts (Banks, 1993). The goal of culturally responsive instruction is not to simply acknowledge that other cultures exist, but to leverage the unique characteristics and funds of knowledge that adolescents bring with them to school to improve learning outcomes. For this to occur requires that educators take a broader perspective of culturally responsive instruction that extends from cultures and communities represented in the school down to relationships with students that honor and value the singular experiences of the individual.

According to Ladson-Billings (1995), teachers that adopted a broad conceptualization of culturally responsive instruction "kept the relations between themselves and their students fluid and equitable. They encouraged the students to act as teachers, and they, themselves, often functioned as learners in the classroom" (p. 163). In fact, Gay (2018) extended upon this idea by stating that students should be Gay, 2018 "seen as co-originators, co-designers, and co-directors" (p. 111) of their education if learning was not to be restricted. At the level of school leadership, Madhlangobe and Gordon (2012) identified several characteristics that support the development of culturally responsive campuses including (a) caring for others; (b) building relationships; (c) persistent and persuasiveness; (d) present and communicative; (e) modeling cultural responsiveness; and (f) fostering cultural responsiveness among others.

For professional educators to accept the charge of becoming culturally responsive, it is necessary to become self-reflective on their daily pedagogical practices and personal relationships among staff, students, families, and community members. Effective culturally responsive instruction cannot be achieved in one day or through one event, it must be an on-going process.

## Funds of Knowledge in Literacy and Play

As demonstrated in the previous sections, leveraging adolescents' socio-cultural and linguistic capital requires teachers to take a critical, reflective, and fluid stance toward literacy development and instruction. In the instruction of adolescents, third spaces extend into areas of play, as well as culturally responsive classroom environments. The third space is defined as "a particular social environment … in which students begin to reconceive who they are and what they might be able to accomplish academically and beyond" (Gutiérrez, 2008, p. 148).

This third space is an important theoretical concept in understanding how to incorporate students' funds of knowledge, because this space inherently provides students with an environment that not only is safe but also legitimizes students' in- and out-of-school literacies as mutually beneficial to new learning. Many studies have focused on the importance of academic support for marginalized student groups, but these studies often negated the importance of the family's non-traditional academic ways of knowing and doing on the learning outcomes for students in schools. Delgado-Gaitan (1992) described the importance of the role of the family as follows:

> I argue that parents train their children to adapt to the social order which they understand and with which they identify. Children learn about the nature of the world in which they live through parental socialization. An important aspect of socialization is the transmission of values, which vary from culture to culture and from family to family. Research has shed light on the strengths of the family through the study of cultural continuity and discontinuity as well as the cultural ecology of the family. Cultural difference such as religion, moral values, recreation, and education are reflected in the ways in which people raise their children. Parents transmit their culture to the young by teaching them how to think, act, and feel. Part of this process is the act of socializing children to value education.
>
> pp. 497–498

As we engage students in academic learning, creating a third space in which these funds of knowledge are leveraged can result in improved success for students.

Activities such as drawing, storytelling, and role-playing have long been accepted as activities that promote emergent literacy skills and recent studies have found that play can serve as a link between home and school cultures, literacies, and learning by creating a third space for students to construct meaning from cultural capital within an across in- and out-of-school spaces (Yahya & Wood, 2017). In fact, Alvarez (2018) found that emergent bilingual adolescents frequently utilized multimodal depictions to bring insight into their funds of knowledge and cultural values from their home lives into the classroom. Acknowledging the wealth of information that adolescents are attempting to share through their drawing, writing, and play will require teachers to think differently about how to assess these indicators of emergent literacy development. Kim and Covino (2015) suggested, "two alternative ways of looking at adolescent's narratives that make visible adolescent's strengths and funds of knowledge implicated in their written stories: intertextual analyses and interactional analyses" (p. 358).

Additionally, storytelling can serve as a third space for literacy learning in the classroom. In Taylor, Bernhard, Garg, and Cummins' (2008) study, they found that storytelling emerged as a prominent practice of multilingual literacy and oracy. In the early childhood and elementary classrooms, storytelling may take the form of imaginary play (Yahya & Wood, 2017) or it may take the more formal academic structure of a read-aloud (May, Bingham, & Pendergast, 2014).

Read-alouds, at all levels, serve as an instructional tool for providing students with access to texts that may be above their independent competency level and to engage students in higher-level thinking skills around the text. This space for higher-level thinking can also serve as a third space for bridging home and school competencies when texts are selected intentionally to provide students with stories that build upon their funds of knowledge. In Walker's (2017) study, teachers intentionally selected and maintained balanced materials that reflected the current demographics of the class. The teachers considered the background of the creator of the texts, interests of students, gender, experiences, and relevant topics.

May, Bingham, and Pendergast (2014) found that "cultural competence was displayed in culturally relevant read-alouds, in part, through the way the teacher makes space for student sense-making and facilitates discussions in which classroom members are responsive to that sense-making" (pp. 213–214). The discussions that supported cultural competence focused on relevant topics and encouraged students to participate in whichever language they felt most comfortable.

Another way for educators to build literacy learning environments that leverage students' funds of knowledge is to consider the resources that parents use at home. Taylor, Bernhard, Garg, and Cummins (2008) found that parents often relied on heritage language classes, packages from abroad, newspapers and books, communication with family and friends abroad, and libraries and religious institutions for supporting the heritage language in the home. More recent studies have also found that older students also rely on social media and entertainment as ways of engaging in heritage language literacy practices (Colwell, Woodward, & Hutchinson, 2018; Stewart, 2014; Velázquez, 2017).

Several studies explored the strategies that teachers have used to put these strategies into action. In Pacheco and Miller's (2016) study, a few key examples in which teachers grounded the lesson in key literacy standards and developed culturally responsive activities that required students to explore the standard through a variety of perspectives, including in a variety of languages. One teacher in the study asked students to explore text features such as titles, captions, and headings by providing students with newspapers written in a variety of languages.

The students were first asked to identify the text features in the papers and were then asked to evaluate the similarities in the text features across the texts. Another teacher in the study used a text that centered on a relevant topic and encouraged students to discuss the text in whatever language they felt most comfortable. The students were then asked to write about the text by developing a linguistically accessible book report that any reader could understand, regardless of the language they spoke. Correspondingly, the teacher in Jiménez, et al.'s (2015) study believed in recognizing students as experts of linguistic knowledge and encouraged them to, "think about reading as a process of making meaning" (p. 411). The examples in Pacheco and Millers' (2016) and Jiménez, et al.'s (2015) studies are particularly useful, because teachers often struggle with understanding how to implement strategies that value students' heritage language when the teacher is not fluent in that language (Gay, 2018).

In fact, some researchers now believe that complex literacy skills required in translation activities may support academic success (Orellana, 2003). This is not to suggest that emergent bilinguals should be provided with a series of direct translation tasks, but rather that the complexity of acting as language brokers at home and in school provides students with a wide array of vocabulary and language use within authentic settings. García and Kleifgen (2010) took this a step further by conceptualizing translanguaging as the natural and regular use of an individual's entire language repertoire in sense-making. Guzula, McKinney, and Tyler (2016), stated that translanguaging is a powerful tool in learning, because it enhances multilingual and multimodal meaning-making, elicits prior knowledge, teaching, reinforcing, and deepening understanding, as well as serving as a reservoir of writing inspiration.

Emergent bilinguals often have greater difficulty in writing informational texts that they often have slower retrieval time, that the cultural context or topic of the writing impacts success, and that social interaction has a large impact on writing outcomes (Harklau & Pinnow, 2009). We also know that emergent bilinguals utilize biliteracy skills such as code-switching and cognate searching when writing (Harklau & Pinnow, 2009).

According to Harklau and Pinnow (2009) much of the research suggests that there is a strong link between multimodal writing opportunities and the writing development of emergent bilinguals. Teachers in monolingual classrooms should consider allowing emergent bilinguals the opportunity to work with partners or small groups, particularly during pre-write and revision and editing, allowing extra processing time, and encouraging students to use biliteracy strategies in their writing (Haneda, 2014; Harklau & Pinnow, 2009).

Just as the process of writing is personal, so are the ideas and voice contained within (Rief, 2007). On its face, this idea seems fairly straightforward. However, when faced with classrooms that are increasingly diverse, the need for masterful, reflective teachers grows (Harklau & Pinnow, 2009). Teachers of emergent bilinguals and students from other diverse backgrounds must consider issues of dialect, euphemism, and style that are indicative culture but may fly in the face of traditional English forms. Harklau and Pinnow (2009) said that "many mainstream writing teachers' attitudes toward English learners, with equating bilingualism with linguistic and even cognitive deficiency," (p. 131) is still a problem in today's educational environment. The only way to help teachers to change these attitudes and to value the voices of all students is to encourage reflective practices of their teacher, but also their own writing.

Rief (2007) and Murray (2007) have suggested that writing makes us vulnerable. They said that teachers often are afraid of making errors in their writing, but that sharing their own experiences with a class full of students was frightening to some teachers. Interestingly, this is what writing teachers ask their students to do every day. Students are asked to share their stories, to trust their peers, and to trust their teachers with deeply meaningful and often emotional pieces. If this is something teachers ask of students, then the teacher must begin that trust relationship, but showing themselves as willing to be vulnerable and open in the search for growth (Murray, 2007; Rief, 2007). Writing teachers who do not write are robbing themselves of the opportunity to talk about writing processes of real writers, what strategies they use when they are stuck, the ability to have honest conversations about frustrations and celebrations, models to provide for students, and, worst of all, the opportunity to build meaningful relationships with students that will open the door for growth. Teachers cannot hope to develop a culturally responsive literacy learning environment without honoring the voices within.

## Discourse as Culturally Responsive Instruction

For decades, researchers have explored and proven the value of meaningful talk in the classroom (Barnes, 2010; Forman & Cazden, 1986; Nystrand, Wu, Gomoran, Zeiser, & Long, 2003; Wegerif, Littleton, Dawes, Mercer, Rowe, 2004). The type of classroom utilized the explicit teaching of accountable, purposeful talk as an avenue for exploring questions and concepts through inquiry-style instruction came to be known as dialogic classrooms (Mercer & Dawes, 2008). Despite the efforts of researchers to encourage policy-makers and schools to adopt dialogic inquiry as a valued instruction method, direct instruction and purposeful development of oral language is still largely missing from schools (Mercer & Dawes, 2008).

Part of this issue stems from an incomplete definition of literacy by policy-makers. Through examination of the skills assessed through high-stakes testing, it is clear that policy-makers define literacy as proficiency in reading and writing. In response to this issue, researchers have begun to shift their efforts from proving the value of talk to changing the thinking of policy-makers as to what "counts" as literacy (Mercer & Dawes, 2008; Wendt, 2013).

Purposeful talk in the classroom has been proven to increase the reasoning and literacy skills of all students (Barnes, 2008; Nystrand, Wu, Gomoran, Zeiser,

& Long, 2003; Wells & Mejia Arauz, 2006). However, the research has also shown that talk alone is insufficient. From the perspective of talk as a socio-cultural tool of learning, purposeful talk is a skill that must be explicitly taught (Nystrand, Wu, Gomoran, Zeiser, & Long, 2003; Rojas-Drummond & Mercer, 2004). When purposeful, literate talk is modeled and framed for students; it can be used as a platform to increase community within a classroom (Gilles, 2010; Howell, Thomas, & Ardasheva, 2011), value and explore multiple perspectives (Richardson, 2010), develop argumentation skills (Rojas-Drummond & Peon Zapata, 2004), and promote inquiry and exploration of difficult concepts and genuine questions (Barnes, 2008; Mercer & Dawes, 2008; Mercer & Dawes, 2010).

When considering a shift to a dialogic classroom, practitioners might consider what implications this would have on their instruction. The primary characteristics of dialogic classrooms are that they are inquiry-focused and student-centered. This could mean that teachers would consider instructional strategies that supported inquiry, such as problem-based learning (PBL) (Shahini, & Mehdi Riazi, 2011) and that supported student-centered instruction, such as gradual release of responsibility and genuine guiding questions (Adler, Rougle, Kaiser, & Caughlan, 2003).

A powerful finding of the research into dialogic inquiry is that students' cognition and reasoning skills increase (Forman & Cazden, 1986; Mercer, 2008; Soter, Wilkinson, Murphy, Rudge, Reninger, & Edwards, 2008). Studies at multiple grade levels and across multiple cultures have proven that providing students with explicit instruction and a framework for talk increases reasoning skills (Haneda & Wells, 2008; Rojas-Drummond & Peon Zapata, 2004). Hashemi and Ghanizadeh (2012) suggested that instruction leading students to critical discourse helped to increase critical thinking abilities through activities such as the analysis of texts for underlying messages and bias and discussion that considered multiple perspectives. Studies have also suggested that allowing students the opportunity to reason together can widen access to learning for all adolescents and increase their reasoning skills through asking genuine questions, exploring concepts deeply, and considering multiple perspectives while coming to a group consensus (Wells & Mejia Arauz, 2006; Wegerif, Littleton, Dawes, Mercer, & Rowe, 2004).

Oral discourse has been proven to promote the literacy development of students, including the disciplinary literacies that are highly valued in secondary education (Hansen, 2009; Wendt, 2013). In close relation to the findings above, dialogic classrooms have been shown to support reading and writing skills by allowing students an opportunity to explore and develop ideas in a collaborative setting (Haneda, 2000). In Wolf, Crosson, and Resnick's (2005) study, the major findings focused on the types of talk occurring during reading instruction. Ultimately, the study found that the academic rigor of the lessons was only "slightly beyond the level of comprehending the storyline… close to the level of analyzing and interpreting the text" (Wolf, Crosson, & Resnick, 2005, p. 37).

The importance of a socio-cultural approach to literacy instruction is particularly important when discussing the increase of literacy skills through a focus on oral discourse (Case, Ndura, & Righettini, 2005; Mercer, 2004; Prawat, 1995; Wegerif, Mercer, & Dawes, 1999). When assuming a socio-cultural perspective for instruction, the teacher would create safe spaces for students to use their prior knowledge and personal experiences to examine new topics (Grant, Wong, & Osterling, 2007; Gutiérrez, 2008; Prawat, 1995).

In the following section, I will provide an examination of a scenario from multilingual classrooms with related discussion questions.

## Multilingualism in Small Group Instruction

A 6th grade language arts teacher has two English learners (ELs) in her classroom and they both speak Vietnamese. The girls attend Vietnamese school every Saturday. The teacher requests that the students bring a copy of their materials that they use in their Vietnamese school. Upon studying the resources, she discovers that the workbook looks very similar in structure to an early grades primer workbook or a workbook for an introductory foreign language class. In fact, the materials look so familiar that she is able to discern what skills are being targeted in each lesson.

The teacher decides to compare the skills in the workbook with the skills in the ESL leveled readers in her guided reading library. As she works through this task, she discovers that she can easily align the majority of the skills. The teacher has recently attended a training on reciprocal teaching and this sparks an idea. After discussing this discovery with her cooperating teacher and her principal, she decides to create an instructional sequence for her guided reading lessons with these two students, in which she will use both the materials from the workbook and the ESL leveled readers.

Once the teacher has completed her lesson preparations, she introduces her idea to the girls. She explains that she would like to try something new. When they meet for their daily guided reading lessons, the girls will teach her the target skill in Vietnamese and she will teach them the skill in English. The students are very excited about the idea and cannot wait to get started!

During the first lesson, the girls are very animated and find a lot of humor in the teacher's botched pronunciation attempts. The teacher laughs good naturedly along with the girls and gives it her best try. The roles then shift and the girls engage in the English lesson. The teacher is shocked to see that, in her first attempt, the girls are much more engaged and master the skill much faster than they did in previous lessons. At the end of the lesson, they discuss their progress toward skill mastery. The girls decide that they feel pretty confident, but they would like more practice with pronunciation and with finding examples in their books. They agree that the teacher needs more practice and assign her a short homework exercise that they think will help.

Discussion Question #1: What evidence do you see of research-based best practices for multilingualism in this scenario?

Discussion Question #2: Why do you think the students were able to master the task faster than they had in previous lessons?

Discussion Question #3: How might the teacher build on this practice to develop a broader multilingual community within her classroom?

Discussion Question #4: What implications would approaches like this have for accelerated learning in response to COVID recovery?

## Conclusion

As global migration trends become increasingly complex (Sasnal, 2018), so do the student populations that professional educators are responsible for serving. To successfully serve a population that is experiencing on-going change, educators must be willing to adapt their daily interactions and pedagogies to be culturally responsive to the current population they are serving. This can be a difficult challenge for teachers, because it requires on-going critical reflection, fluid roles, and the consistent development of caring relationships with parents, students, and staff members. However, the benefits of leveraging children's socio-cultural and linguistic capital is undeniable. When children are provided a space in which the all experiences, languages, literacies, cultures, and knowledge are valued, a third space can emerge in which children can experiment with language and knew ideas, eventually leading to growth in both literacy and reasoning skills (Fu & Graff, 2009; Gutiérrez, 2008; Khalifa, Gooden, & Davis, 2016; Yahya & Wood, 2017).

## References

Adler, M., Rougle, E., Kaiser, E., & Caughlan, S. (2003). Closing the gap between concept and practice: Toward more dialogic discussion in the language arts classroom. *Journal of Adolescent and Adult Literacy, 47*(4), 312–322.

Alford, J. (2001). Learning language and critical literacy: Adolescent ESL students. *Journal of Adolescent & Adult Literacy, 45*(3), 238–242.

Alvarez, A. (2018). Drawn and written funds of knowledge: A window into emerging bilingual children's experiences and social interpretations through their written narratives and drawings. *Journal of Early Childhood Literacy, 18*(1), 97–128. doi:10.1177/1468798417740618

Au, K. (1980). Participation structures in a reading lesson with Hawaiian children: An analysis of a culturally appropriate instructional event. *Anthropology & Education Quarterly, 11*(2), 91–115.

Au, K. (1998). Social constructivism and the social literacy learning of students of diverse cultural backgrounds. *Journal of Literacy Research, 30,* 297–319.

Au, K. (2007). Culturally responsive instruction: Application to multiethnic classrooms. *Pedagogies, 2,* 1–18.

Au, K. (2018). Culturally responsive instruction and literacy learning. *Journal of Literacy Research, 50*(2), 141–166.

August, D., Shanahan, T., & Escamilla, K. (2009). English language learners: Developing literacy in second-language learners—Report of the National Literacy Panel on Language-Minority Children and Youth. *Journal of Literacy Research, 41*(4), 432–452.

Banks, J. A. (1993). Multicultural education: Historical development, dimensions, and practice. *Review of Research in Education, 19,* 3–49.

Barnes, D. (2008). Exploratory talk for learning. In N. Mercer & S. Hodgkinson (Eds.), *Exploring talk in schools: Inspired by the work of Douglas Barnes* (pp. 1–15). London: Sage.

Barnes, D. (2010). Why talk is important. *English Teaching: Practice and Critique, 9*(2), 7–10.

Beaufort, A. (2009). Preparing adolescents for the demands of the 21st-century workplace. In L. Christenbury, R. Bomer, & P. Smagorinsky (Eds.), *Handbook of adolescent literacy research* (pp. 239–255). New York: Guilford Press.

Bishop, P. A., & Harrison, L. M. (2021). *The successful middle school: This we believe.* Association for Middle School Education.

Case, R. E., Ndura, E., & Righettini, M. (2005) Balancing linguistic and social needs: Evaluating texts using a critical language awareness approach. *Journal of Adolescent & Adult Literacy, 48*(5), 374–391.

Cazden, C. B., & Leggett, E. L. (1976). *Culturally responsive education: A response to LAU remedies II.* Washington, DC: U.S. Department of Health, Education, and Welfare.

Colwell, J., Woodward, L., & Hutchinson, A. (2018). Out-of-school reading and literature discussion: An exploration of adolescents' participation in digital book clubs. *Online Learning, 22*(2), 221–247. doi:10.24059/olj.v22i2.1222

Cruz, C. (2008). Notes on immigration, youth, and ethnographic silence. *Theory into Practice, 47,* 67–73.

Cummins, J. (1981). Empirical and theoretical underpinnings of bilingual education. *Journal of Education, 163*(1), 16–29.

Darling-Hammond, L., & Edgerton, A. K. (2021, April 5). *Accelerated learning as we build back better.* Learning Policy Institute. https://learningpolicyinstitute.org/blog/covid-accelerated-learning-build-back-better

de Jong, E. J., Harper, C. A., & Coady, M. R. (2013). Enhanced knowledge and skills for elementary mainstream teachers of English language learners. *Theory into Practice, 52*(2), 89–97. doi:10.1080/00405841.2013.770326

Delgado-Gaitan, C. (1992). School matters in the Mexican-American home: Socializing children to education. *American Educational Research Journal, 29*(3), 495–513. doi:10.2307/1163255

Economic Policy Institute. (2020). *COVID-19 and student performance, equity, and U.S. education policy: Lessons from pre-pandemic research to inform relief, recovery, and rebuilding.* https://files.eric.ed.gov/fulltext/ED610971.pdf

Faltis, C., Arias, M. B., & Ramirez-Marin, F. (2010). Identifying relevant competencies for secondary teachers of English learners. *Bilingual Research Journal, 33,* 307–328.

Faltis, C., & Hudelson, S. (1994). Learning English as an additional language in K-12 schools. *TESOL Quarterly, 28*(3), 10–21.

Forman, E. A. & Cazden, C. B. (1986). Exploring Vygotskian perspectives in education: The cognitive value of peer interaction. In J. V. Wertsch (Ed.), *Culture, Communication, and Cognition: Vygotskian Perspectives* (pp. 323–347). Cambridge: Cambridge University Press.

Franquiz, M. E. & Salinas, M. E. (2011). Newcomers developing English literacy through historical thinking and digitized primary sources. *Journal of Second Language Writing, 20,* 196–210.

Fredricks, L. (2012). The benefits and challenges of culturally responsive EFL critical literature circles. *Journal of Adolescent & Adult Literacy*, *55*(6), 494–504.

Fu, D., & Graff, J.M. (2009). The literacies of new immigrant youth. In L. Christenbury, R. Bomer, & P. Smagorinsky (Eds.), *Handbook of adolescent literacy research* (pp. 400–414). New York: Guilford Press.

García, O. (2017). Translanguaging in schools: Subiendo y bajando, bajando y subiendo as afterword. *Journal of Language, Identity & Education*, *16*(4), 256–263.

García, O., & Kleifgen, J. A. (2010). *Educating emergent bilinguals: Policies, programs, and practices for English language learners*. New York, NY: Teachers College Press.

Gay, G. (2000). *Culturally responsive teaching: Theory, research, and practice*. New York, NY: Teachers College Press.

Gay, G. (2018). *Culturally responsive teaching: Theory, research, and practice*. Teachers College Press.

Gay, G., & Kirkland, K. (2003). Developing cultural critical consciousness and self-reflection in pre-service teacher education. *Theory into Practice*, *42*(3), 181–187.

Gee, J. (2004). *Situated language and learning: A critique of traditional schooling*. New York, NY: Routledge.

Gilles, C. (2010). Making the most of talk. *Voices from the Middle*, *18*(2), 9–15.

Grant, R. A., Wong, S. D., & Osterling, J. P. (2007). Developing literacy in second-language learners: Critique from a heteroglossic, sociocultural, and multidimensional framework. [Review of the book Developing Literacy in Second-Language Learners: Report of The National Literacy Panel on Language Minority Children and Youth, by D. August & T. Shanahan]. *Reading Research Quarterly*, *42*(4), 598–609.

Gutiérrez, K. (2008). Developing a sociocritical literacy in the third space. *Reading Research Quarterly*, *43*(2), 148–164.

Gutiérrez, K., Baquedano-López, P., Turner, M. G. (1997). Putting language back into language arts: When the radical middle meets the third space. *Language Arts*, *74*(5), 368–378.

Guzula, X., McKinney, C., & Tyler, R. (2016). Languaging-for-learning: Legitimising translanguaging and enabling multimodal practices in third spaces. *Southern African Linguistics and Applied Language Studies*, *34*(3), 211–226. doi:10.2989/16073614.2016.1250360

Haneda, M. (2000). Modes of student participation in an elementary school science classroom: From talk to writing. *Linguistics and Education*, *10*(4), 459–485.

Haneda, M. (2008). Contexts for learning: English language learners in a US middle school. *International Journal of Bilingual Education and Bilingualism*, *11*(1), 57–74.

Haneda, M. (2014). From academic language to academic communication: Building on English language learners' resources. *Linguistics and Education*, *26*, 126–135.

Haneda, M., & Wells, G. (2008). Learning an additional language through dialogic inquiry. *Language and Education*, *22*(2).114–136.

Hansen, J. (2009). Multiple literacies in the content classroom: High school students' connections to U.S. History. *Journal of Adolescent & Adult Literacy*, *52*(7), 597–606.

Harklau, L., & Pinnow, R. (2009). Adolescent second-language writing. In L. Christenbury, R. Bomer, & P. Smagorinsky (Eds.), *Handbook of adolescent literacy research* (pp. 126–139). New York: Guilford Press.

Hashemi, M., & Ghanizadeh, A. (2012). Critical discourse analysis and critical thinking: An experimental study in an EFL context. *System*, *40*(1), 37–47.

Howell, P. B., Thomas, S., & Ardasheva, Y. (2011). Talk in the classroom: Meeting the developmental, academic, and cultural needs of middle school students. *Middle Grades Research Journal*, *6*(1), 47–63.

Jiménez, R. T., David, S., Pacheco, M., Risko, V. J., Pray, L., Fagan, K., & Gonzales, M. (2015). Supporting teachers of English learners by leveraging students' linguistic strengths. *The Reading Teacher*, *68*(6), 406–412. doi:10.1002/trtr.1289

Khalifa, M. A., Gooden, M. A., & Davis, J. E. (2016). Culturally responsive school leadership: A synthesis of the literature. *Review of Educational Research*, *86*(4), 1272–1311. doi:10.3102/0034654316630383

Kim, M., & Covino, K. (2015). When stories don't make sense: Alternative ways to assess young children's narratives in social contexts. *The Reading Teacher*, *68*(5), 357–361. doi:10.1002/trtr.1334

Ladson-Billings, G. (1995). But that's just good teaching!: The case for culturally relevant pedagogy. *Theory into Practice*, *34*(3), 159–165.

Madhlangobe, L., & Gordon, S. P. (2012). Culturally responsive leadership in a diverse school: A case study of a high school leader. *NASSP Bulletin*, *96*(3), 177–202.

Martinez-Roldan, C. M., & Franquiz, M. E. (2009). Latina/o youth literacies: Hidden funds of knowledge. In L. Christenbury, R. Bomer, & P. Smagorinsky (Eds.), *Handbook of adolescent literacy research* (pp. 323–342). New York: Guilford Press.

May, L. A., Bingham, G. E., & Pendergast, M. L. (2014). Culturally and linguistically relevant readalouds. *Multicultural Perspectives*, *16*(4), 210–218. doi:10.1080/15210960.2014.952299

Mercer, N. (2004). Sociocultural discourse analysis: analyzing classroom talk as a social mode of thinking. *Journal of Applied Linguistics*, *1*(2), 137–168.

Mercer, N. (2008). Talk and the development of reasoning and understanding. *Human Development*, *51*(1), 90–100.

Mercer, N., & Dawes, L. (2008). *The value of exploratory talk: Exploring talk in school*. London: Sage.

Mercer, N. & Dawes, L. (2010). Making the most of talk: Dialogue in the classroom. *English Drama Media*, *16*, 19–26.

Murray, D.M. (2007). Teaching writing your way. In K. Beers, R. Probst, & L. Reif (Eds.), *Adolescent literacy: Turning promise into practice* (pp. 179–188). Portsmouth, NH: Heinemann.

National Governors Association Center for Best Practices & Council of Chief State School Officers. (2010). *Common Core State Standards*. Washington, DC: Authors.

Nystrand, M., Wu, L. L., Gomoran, A., Zeiser, S., & Long, D. A. (2003). Questions in time: Investigating the structure and dynamics of unfolding classroom discourse. *Discourse Processes*, *35*(2), 135–198.

Orellana, M. F. (2003). Responsibilities of children in Latino immigrant homes. *New Directions for Youth Development*, *100*, 25–39. doi:10.1002/yd.61

Pacheco, M. (2009). Expansive learning and Chicana/o and Latina/o students' political-historical knowledge. *Language Arts*, *87*(1), 18–29.

Pacheco, M. B., & Miller, M. E. (2016). Making meaning through translanguaging in the literacy classroom. *The Reading Teacher*, *69*(5), 533–537. doi:10.1002/trtr.1390

Paris, D. (2012). Culturally sustaining pedagogy: A needed change in stance, terminology, and practice. *Educational Researcher*, *41*(3), 93–97. doi:10.3102/0013189X12441244

Prawat, R. S. (1995). Misreading Dewey: Reform, projects, and the language game. *Educational Researcher, 24*(7), 13–22.

Ramirez, A. D. (2012). Latino cultural knowledge in the social studies classroom. *Journal of Hispanic Higher Education,* 11(2), 213–226.

Richardson, A. E. (2010). Exploring text through student discussions: Accountable talk in the middle school classroom. *The English Journal, 100*(1), 83–88.

Rief, L. (2007). Writing: Commonsense matters. Effective teachers, effective instruction. In K. Beers, R. Probst, & L. Reif (Eds.), *Adolescent literacy: Turning promise into practice* (pp. 189–208). Portsmouth, NH: Heinemann.

Rojas-Drummond, S., & Mercer, N. (2004). Scaffolding the development of effective collaboration and learning. *International Journal of Educational Research, 39,* 99–111.

Rojas-Drummond, S., & Peon Zapata, M. (2004). Exploratory talk, argumentation and reasoning in Mexican primary school children. *Language and Education, 18*(6), 537–557.

Sasnal, P. (2018, June 18). Domesticating the global giant: The global governance of migration. Retrieved August 8, 2018 from https://www.cfr.org/report/domesticating-giant-global-governance-migration

Shahini, G., & Mehdi Riazi, A. (2011). A PBLT approach to teaching ESL speaking, writing, and thinking skills. *English Language Teachers Journal, 65*(2), 170–179.

Skerrett, A., & Bomer, R. (2011). Borderzones' in adolescents' literacy practices: Connecting out-of-school literacies to the reading curriculum. *Urban Education, 46*(6), 1256–1279.

Soter, A. O., Wilkinson, I. A., Murphy, P. K., Rudge, L., Reninger, K., & Edwards, M. (2008). What discourse tells us: Talk and indicators of high-level comprehension. *International Journal of Educational Research, 47,* 372–391.

Stewart, M. A. (2014). Social networking, workplace, and entertainment literacies: The out-of-school literate lives of newcomer Latina/o adolescents. *Reading Research Quarterly, 49*(4), 365–369.

Taylor, L. K., Bernhard, J. K., Garg, S., & Cummins, J. (2008). Affirming plural belonging: Building on students' family-based cultural and linguistic capital through multiliteracies pedagogy. *Journal of Early Childhood Literacy, 8*(3), 269–294.

TNTP. (2018). *The opportunity myth: What students can show us about how schools are letting them down and how to fix it.* https://tntp.org/assets/documents/TNTP_The-Opportunity-Myth_Web.pdf

U.S. Department of Education. (2021). *ED COVID-19 Handbook: Roadmap to reopening safely and meeting all students' needs.* https://www2.ed.gov/documents/coronavirus/reopening-2.pdf

Velázquez, I. (2017). Reported literacy, media consumption and social media use as measures of relevance of Spanish as a heritage language. *International Journal of Bilingualism, 21*(1), 21–33.

Walker, M. K. (2017). *Texas schools to watch and middle-level ESL programs: A multiple case study* (Order No. 10598931). Available from Dissertations & Theses @ Texas Woman's University; Pro-uest Dissertations & Theses Global. (1937577399). Retrieved from http://ezp.twu.edu/docview/1937577399?accountid=7102

Wegerif, R., Littleton, K., Dawes, L., Mercer, N., & Rowe, D. (2004). Widening access to educational opportunities through teaching children how to reason together. *Westminster Studies in Education, 27*(2), 143–156.

Wegerif, R., Mercer, N., & Dawes, L. (1999). From social interaction to individual reasoning: An empirical investigation of a possible socio-cultural model of cognitive development. *Learning and Instruction, 9,* 493–516.

Wells, G., & Mejia Arauz, R. (2006). Dialogue in the classroom. *The Journal of the Learning Sciences, 15*(3), 379–428

Wendt, J. L. (2013) Combating the Crisis in Adolescent Literacy: Exploring Literacy in the Secondary Classroom. *American Secondary Education, 41*(2), 38–49.

Wolf, M. K., Crosson, A. C., & Resnick, L. B. (2005). Classroom talk for rigorous reading comprehension instruction. *Reading Psychology, 26*, 27–53.

Yahya, R., & Wood, E. A. (2017). Play as third space between home and school: Bridging cultural discourses. *Journal of Early Childhood Research: ECR, 15*(3), 305–322. doi:10.1177/1476718X15616833

# 9

# WHAT DO WE BELIEVE ABOUT MIDDLE GRADES LITERACY AND RACE?

## Interrogating Practices and Pedagogies of Middle Grades Literacy Education through the Lens of Critical Race Theory

*Kristie White Smith*

When we consider the middle grades educational setting of the 21st century, a range of ideas are important. We think about the needs and nature of the young adolescent and how these needs are honored in the context of schooling. We think about the essence of the middle grades concept given the historical context of the 21st century. And we still think about the qualities and characteristics of thriving middle schools, those that nurture the intellectual identities of young adolescents while wholly honoring them in the socioemotional and developmental in-between. When we turn our attention to teaching and learning in the middle grades context of the 21st century, we think about the curricula, pedagogies, and practices that are most pervasive.

Probing descriptors of middle school success, Bishop and Harrison (2021) noted that among other attributes, successful middle schools include attention to culture, community, curriculum, instruction, and assessment, with curricula that are "challenging, exploratory, integrative, and diverse" (p. 27). Further, Bishop and Harrison (2021) described ideal middle grades curricula as those which "expos[e]students to multiple viewpoints" (p. 31), those curricula which "encourag[e] young adolescents to explore diverse perspectives," (p. 31), and those which empower middle grades learners to "consider new ideas and to question old ones" (p. 31). These and other concepts that Bishop and Harrison (2021) presented in *The Successful Middle School: This We Believe* articulate guiding principles, not only for successful middle schools at large, but also for effective teaching and learning in the middle grades.

Launching with these descriptors, and working to consider how the principles of successful middle schools (Bishop & Harrison, 2021) are embodied by middle grades curriculum and instruction, it is important to consider work in the content areas, asking targeted questions. Honing a particular focus on middle

DOI: 10.4324/9781003171508-12

grades literacy and language arts education, a variety of questions abound, not only about content choices and best practices, but also about the extent to which content and curricula represent, reflect, and address the needs of a diverse 21st century learning populace. In a consideration of the modern educational landscape of American public schools, Love (2020) delved into race, discussing that not only is there a growing number of students of color, but there is also an immensely white teaching force. About this, Love (2020) noted the following:

> Six decades later (after Brown vs. Board of Education), researchers have found that students of color make up a majority of public school enrollment, while White students make up more than half of the nation's overall enrollment; most White students attend a school where three-quarters of their peers are White too. Currently, less than 2 percent of teachers are Black men; White men and women make up more than 80 percent of the teaching force....
>
> (p. 29)

Further, Love (2020) discussed the impact that having had a "white gaze" (Morrison, 2013) across one's formative education and training, noting, "many of these teachers are unaware of how their lily-White communities were established and have upheld Whiteness. This lack of awareness…leads them to measure their communities against the urban school communities they teach in, mak[ing] subscribing to stereotypes easier" (p. 29). The impacts of shifting demographics juxtaposed against an overwhelmingly White teacher population undoubtedly permeates curriculum and instruction across all content areas, to include middle grades literacy and language arts.

Given these factors, along with other characteristics of the 21st century educational landscape, a few of the targeted questions that might arise around literacy and language arts curriculum and instruction for the 21st century are the following:

- What are common pedagogies and practices in middle grades literacy and language arts?
- What are the critical conversation points at the intersection of 21st century middle grades literacy pedagogies and the realities of a larger social setting, such as racial diversities?
- Using points of Critical Race Theory to frame analysis, how do common principles, practices, and pedagogies in middle grades literacy and language arts instruction fit the complexities of a 21st century instructional context? What are the recommendations in this area?

Through these questions and others, this chapter presents an analytical examination of prevailing principles, practices, and pedagogies in middle grades literacy education using key ideas drawn from Critical Race Theory (CRT) to frame points of discussion, inquiry, and critique. In a connection between theory and practice, this chapter includes a point-by-point consideration of common extant framings of literacies and literacy pedagogies for the middle grades with evaluations and instructional considerations through a CRT lens. The chapter concludes with a principled call to action, constructing and amplifying the need for extended critical conversations about middle grades literacy curricula, practices, and pedagogies with a lens toward instructional equity.

## Considering Critical Race Theory and Critical Race Theory in Education

While the ideas of CRT are relevant across many disciplines, including education, the ideas that shape CRT as theory have intellectual origins in legal scholarship. As defined by Cornel West (1995)[1], in a consideration of CRT in the legal context, "in short Critical Race Theory is an intellectual movement that (is) part of a long tradition in liberation" (Crenshaw et al., 1995, p. xi). West (1995) further noted that "Critical Race Theorists put forward novel readings of a hidden past that disclose the flagrant shortcomings of the treacherous present in the light of the unrealized--though not unrealizable-- possibilities for human freedom and equality" (Crenshaw et al., 1995, pp. xi–xii)[2]. Even at its origins in legal thinking, definitions and tenets of CRT are a broad theoretical body. In characterizing some of the key ideas of CRT, Crenshaw et al. (1995)[1] discussed that while there is not a "canonical set of doctrines or methodologies to which (all CRT theorists) subscribe" (p. xiii), there is an overarching frame. Within this, the work of Critical Race Theorists "changes the way in which race and racial power are constructed and represented…" (Crenshaw et al., 1995, p. xiii). Also, through the lens of CRT, there is a focus on understanding the impacts of white supremacy (Crenshaw et al., 1995).

Putting forth other definitions of CRT, and in the context of education, Ladson-Billings and Tate (1995) noted that CRT involves the work of "theorizing race and us[ing] it as an analytic tool for understanding school inequity" (p. 12). They argued that historically, students of marginalized racial and ethnic groups, such as African Americans, find spaces of educational affirmation beyond, not within, the construct of traditional schooling. Ladson-Billings and Tate (1995) also discussed race as a continued "factor in inequity" (p. 12), significantly so, and maintained the idea of "race as endemic and deeply ingrained in American Life" (p. 18), directly challenging "claims of neutrality, objectivity, color-blindness, and meritocracy" (p. 20) in the realm of education and race. Ladson-Billings and Tate (1995) also argued the existence of white normative ideas at the foundation of traditional education systems, noting that CRT involves the liberation of "naming one's own reality" (p. 20) and rejecting "a paradigm that attempts to be everything to everyone and consequently becomes nothing for anyone, allowing the status quo to prevail…" (p. 25). Similarly, Carbado (2011) concluded that CRT illuminates race as social construction and acts in concert with other aspects of society.

As Dixson et al. (2017) discussed, it was the seminal work of Gloria Ladson-Billings and William Tate that brought together education and Critical Race Theory (CRT) in their 2004 presentation for the American Education Research Association (AERA). About this, Dixson et al. (2017) noted Ladson-Billings and Tate's work stood on the previous research of scholars such as Derrick Bell, Kimberlé Crenshaw, and Richard Delgado, among others. Further, Dixson et al. (2017) highlighted the ideas of Milner and Howard (2013) around counter narratives, Crenshaw's et al. (1995) work on intersectionality, and Pierce (1970) and Huber and Solorzano's (2015) work to define microaggressions, as all being important in the intellectual lineage of CRT in education. Thus, while CRT had its intellectual creation in the legal discipline, the ideas of CRT are aptly applied to other disciplines, particularly education.

## Standards and Skill Domains for the English/Language Arts

In the work of middle grades literacy education, while there is a vast range of nuanced and localized curricula, there are some broadly acknowledged domains of learning and skill. These domains are often referred to as "core" standards and include reading literature and informational text, writing, speaking/listening, and language (Ryan et al., 2012). In addition to common skill and instructional domains, there are also overarching standards for the preparation of literacy educators. As shown in Table 9.1, both the National Council of Teachers of English (NCTE) and the International Reading Association (IRA) put forth comprehensive standards for student learning and competencies in English/Language Arts.

These standards, which integrate the domains of reading, writing, speaking, and listening, also give broader guidance about what students, through literacy and language arts education, should know and be able to do.

In addition to the standards for student learning, there are standards that delineate expected outcomes and competencies for literacy educators. For example, according to International Literacy Association (ILA) standards (2017) for the preparation of literacy professionals, in terms of foundational competencies, "candidates (should) demonstrate knowledge of the theoretical, historical, and evidence-based foundations of literacy and language and the ways in which they interrelate and the role of literacy professionals in schools" (ILA, 2017). Core skill domains and teacher preparation standards give shape to common practices and pedagogies for literacy and language arts education. These influences are intended to guide teachers with care and pedagogical responsibility; thus, it is important to note how they fare when considered through the lens of a 21st century educational setting.

**TABLE 9.1** National Council of Teachers of English (NCTE)/International Reading Association (IRA) 2017 for English/Language Arts

*NCTE/IIRA Standards for English/Language Arts*

1. Students read a wide range of print and non-print texts to build an understanding of texts, of themselves, and of the cultures of the United States and the world; to acquire new information; to respond to the needs and demands of society and the workplace; and for personal fulfillment. Among these texts are fiction and nonfiction, classic and contemporary works (NCTE, IRA, 2017)[a].

2. Students read a wide range of literature from many periods in many genres to build an understanding of the many dimensions (e.g., philosophical, ethical, aesthetic) of human experience (NCTE, IRA, 2017).

3. Students apply a wide range of strategies to comprehend, interpret, evaluate, and appreciate texts. They draw on their prior experience, their interactions with other readers and writers, their knowledge of word meaning and of other texts, their word identification strategies, and their understanding of textual features (e.g., sound-letter correspondence, sentence structure, context, graphics) (NCTE, IRA, 2017).

4. Students adjust their use of spoken, written, and visual language (e.g., conventions, style, vocabulary) to communicate effectively with a variety of audiences and for different purposes (NCTE, IRA, 2017).

5. Students employ a wide range of strategies as they write and use different writing process elements appropriately to communicate with different audiences and for a variety of purposes (NCTE, IRA, 2017).

6. Students apply knowledge of language structure, language conventions (e.g., spelling and punctuation), media techniques, figurative language, and genre to create, critique, and discuss print and non-print texts (NCTE, IRA, 2017).

7. Students conduct research on issues and interests by generating ideas and questions, and by posing problems. They gather, evaluate, and synthesize data from a variety of sources (e.g., print and non-print texts, artifacts, people) to communicate their discoveries in ways that suit their purpose and audience (NCTE, IRA, 2017).

8. Students use a variety of technological and information resources (e.g., libraries, databases, computer networks, video) to gather and synthesize information and to create and communicate knowledge (NCTE, IRA, 2017).

9. Students develop an understanding of and respect for diversity in language use, patterns, and dialects across cultures, ethnic groups, geographic regions, and social roles (NCTE, IRA, 2017).

10. Students whose first language is not English make use of their first language to develop competency in the English language arts and to develop understanding of content across the curriculum (NCTE, IRA, 2017).

11. Students participate as knowledgeable, reflective, creative, and critical members of a variety of literacy communities (NCTE, IRA, 2017).

12. Students use spoken, written, and visual language to accomplish their own purposes (e.g., for learning, enjoyment, persuasion, and the exchange of information) (NCTE, IRA, 2017).

a National Council of Teachers and English/International Reading Association 2017 Standards for English/Language Arts

## Middle Grades Curricula and Literacy Education for the 21st Century

Considering the attributes of 21st century middle school curricula at large, Bishop and Harrison (2021) discussed successful middle schools as being representative of diverse thinking. About this they noted, "middle grades curriculum is most meaningful when it exposes students to multiple viewpoints and encourages young adolescents to explore diverse perspectives… encourag[ing] young adolescents to consider new ideas and to question old ones" (p. 31). This practice of asking questions aligns with core 21st Century Competencies (Partnership for 21st Century Skills, table 2009), which articulate "real world" skills such as critical thinking, problem solving, communication, and collaboration. Bishop and Harrison (2021) further argued that through curricular exposures to multiple viewpoints, young adolescents strengthen 21st century competencies, such as " an increased awareness of diversity and… a heightened understanding of how power and privilege results in differences among groups of people… (even being able to) question how their own cultural and social identity groups…are in position to other groups" (p. 31). Within this, it is important to hold in view the ways commonly sanctioned curricula support critical interrogation, present positive representative images across diversities, and invite students' challenges to "what is" and opportunities to co-construct new meaning.

Honing in on the work of teaching middle grades literacy and language arts, specifically, Burke (2013) discussed 21st century literacy as a resource, essentially a body of skills and knowledge that we leverage, not only to negotiate meaning, generally, but also to socially engage, to obtain employment, and to broadly navigate life. Further, Burke (2013) argued that literacy education for the 21st century undoubtedly integrates digital literacies and competencies. Thus, it follows that it is important to examine the extent to which common middle grades literacy curricula incorporate opportunities for students to exercise and to refine these intelligences.

## The "Why" of CRT for Middle Grades Literacy Education in the 21st Century

In consideration of the "why" of using a lens of CRT to assess the practices and pedagogies of middle grades literacy and language arts education, it is important to note the realities of the current historical moment. Members of the Middle Level Research Special Interest Group (MLER SIG) of AERA wrote the following in their living statement on dismantling racism:

> The recent racial injustices, including the murders of Ahmaud Arbery and George Floyd, have elevated our awareness that our research and practices can no longer essentialize or stereotype the young adolescent experience;

we must recognize the harm that doing so causes to all, but especially Black youth".

(MLER SIG, 2020)

Similarly, Whitmarsh et al. (2020) discussed the insufficiency in having conversations about racism without explicit antiracist educational action.

Carrying a similar charge of commitment to action, with a specific focus on English Education, Baker-Bell et al. (2017) discussed, not only their personal stories around the trauma of racial injustice, but also some of the actions that they would take in their teaching as a result. In their collective piece, *The Pain and the Wounds: A Call for Critical Race English Education in the Wake of Racial Violence*, Baker-Bell et al. (2017) presented a clear and actionable commitment to amplify racial topics in his teacher education work. Within this, he noted his plan to "center racial violence… (and to) discuss emancipatory theories and pedagogies that move the experiences and multiple languages and literacies that Black and Brown youth bring to classrooms from the margins to the center" (p.126). Given these and other ideas, it follows that using CRT to frame conversations about middle grades literacy is one way to ground critical thinking about relevant practices and pedagogies. It may also help to spark transformation and revisions in curricula and instructional approaches.

## Using CRT to Frame the Critical Conversation about Middle Grades Literacy Education

This section presents an overview of major skill domains that are commonly used in literacy and language arts education. The skill domains discussed align with the organization of broadly used academic standards for English/Language Arts in the middle grades. Within each domain, there is a discussion of some of its common practices and pedagogies, focused in the middle level, followed by a discussion of the domain using CRT to frame points of critical conversation. The domains discussed are the following: Reading and Literature, Writing, Speaking/Listening and Language.

### *Reading and Literature*

By the time readers reach the middle grades, they have often developed and are growing to understand their reading identities. For example, as Kiefer et al. (2019) and Kittle (2013) discussed, middle grades readers have a sense of their reading likes and dislikes and often present personal preferences about their reading tastes. Additionally, middle grades readers are developing an analytical lens for their reading experiences. About middle grades students' developmental abilities in their responses to reading, by the middle grades, Kiefer et al. noted the following:

Older children go beyond categorizing stories toward a more analytical perception of why characters behave as they do, how the story is put together, or what the author is trying to say. They begin to test fiction against real life and understand it better through the comparison. They use some critical terminology, although their understanding of terms may be incomplete. In talk and writing, children who are encouraged to express ideas freely begin to stand back from their own involvement and take an evaluative look at literature.

(p. 54)

Thus, in thinking about readers in the middle, it is important to note that along with their developing sense of self, middle grades readers are also developing a critical lens for literature. As Keene and Zimmermann (1997)[3] discussed, middle grades readers might already be doing the work of making text connections, such as text-to-text, text-to-self, and text-to-world, important to note in defining the middle grades literary classroom literary canon.

## Traditional Literary Canons in the Middle Grades

One of the critical issues that arises in the discussion of middle grades literature is text choice, both for students' independent reading and for classroom libraries or shared reading. Despite the classification of literature for middle grades starting in the years of upper elementary and moving through middle school (Kiefer et al., 2019), it is important to acknowledge the blurred lines between middle grades literature and young adult literature (YAL). This is particularly important as it relates to the influence of the traditional literary canon in teachers' text choices for middle grades readers. Thein and Beach (2013) discussed the ways that canonical mindsets inevitably encroach upon the instructional landscape of the middle grades setting. About this, they noted the following:

While the classic literary canon is a force more often encountered by high school teachers, middle grade teachers must frequently confront numerous other canonizing forces. For instance, literary-recognition programs such as the Newbery Medal and the Printz Award are particularly influential in determining which children's and young adult texts come to be valued and taught in the classroom. Although those awards certainly recognize many high-quality books, those who select the winners are not without particular biases or agendas.

(pp. 10–11)

While the inclusion of traditional literary canons in the middle grades may acknowledge some readers' preferences and the range of readers' skill journeys along the reading continuum (Fountas & Pinnell, 2017), it is important to consider the cultural frameworks that traditional literary canonical literary choices affirm.

## Literary Theories in the Middle Grades

Similar to the blurring that happens between middle grades literature and YAL, middle grades literary analysis curricula often blend into the work of secondary literary analysis, to include instruction found in common literary theories. Using a historical perspective, Beach and Swiss (2011) discussed the lineage of literary theories as being derived from socio-political definitions and ideals about institutionalized schooling. About this, they noted the grounding of literary theories in "moral socialization" and a focus on the "didactic role of literature." Further, Beach and Swiss (2011)[4] summarized four categories of literary theory, about which they pointed out that historical influences and context are important in the framing of each theory, and they offer a brief description of the emphases of each. Table 9.2 summarizes the ideas Beach and Swiss (2011) put forth about this.

**TABLE 9.2** Excerpts from Lapp and Fisher (2011) discussion and summaries about categories of literary theory.

| Theory | Discussion |
| --- | --- |
| Textual literary theories | "…emphasize acquisition of literary conventions for interpreting texts, ways of applying knowledge of conventions that are often modeled by teachers as expert readers." |
| Reader-based literary theories | "…emphasize valuing individual differences in readers' aesthetic experiences of texts, leading to an emphasis on classroom sharing or enactment of students' unique responses." |
| Socio-cultural literary theories | "…highlight the importance of the social and cultural contexts shaping the text-reader transaction, resulting in a focus on critical analysis of social-cultural forces shaping both characters and readers' practices, for example, critical analysis of representations of race, gender, and class in texts." |
| New Media literary theories | "…emphasize the interactive, multimodal, and hypertextual aspects of digital literature requiring instruction in often-unfamiliar interpretive strategies specific to understanding these texts." |

These theories become particularly important in conversations about influences upon curricula and about hidden curricula, "those aspects of the learned curriculum that lie outside of the boundaries of the school's intentional efforts" (Glatthorn et al., 2019, p. 24). Similarly, definitions of these common literary theories beg questions about teacher culture and identity in leading literacy instruction through these lenses.

## Middle Grades Reading, Literature, and CRT

Thinking about reading and literature for the middle grades, and using the lens of CRT, a variety of considerations and instructional possibilities arise. Among them are diversifying middle grades classroom libraries, flipping traditional literary theories, and actually using CRT as a lens for literary analysis. In the next sections, each of these ideas are considered in discussion.

### Diverse Middle Grades Classroom Libraries

In November, 2015, Marley Dias was a young adolescent when she decided that she wanted to collect "1000 Black Girl Books" (Dias, 2021) in protest of enduring a marked pattern of having been assigned to read books that were not representative of her culture or identity. What Marley articulated about reading too many books about "white boys and their dogs" was a challenge to a noticeable lack of representation in her classroom canon. This idea that young readers need both representation and diversity in their reading was described by scholar Rudine Sims Bishop (1990) as the need for readers to encounter "windows, mirrors, and sliding glass doors" in their reading. Bishop (1990) explained this metaphor in the following way:

> Books are often windows, offering views of worlds that may be real or imagined, familiar or strange. These windows are also sliding glass doors, and readers have only to walk through in imagination to become part of whatever world has been created or recreated by the author. When lighting conditions are just right, however, a window can also be a mirror. Literature transforms human experience and reflects it back to us, and in that reflection, we can see our own lives and experiences as part of the larger human experience. Reading, then, becomes a means of self-affirmation, and readers often seek their mirrors in books.

Inherent in Bishop's (1990) ideas is the need for all students, not only students of color, to experience diversities in their literary experiences. Similarly, Adichie (2009)[5] discussed "the danger of a single story," and organizations such as We Need Diverse Books (WNDB, 2021) showcase and publish books that celebrate a range of diversities. Tatum (2009) and Muhammad (2020) both emphasize the need for readers to see themselves in books, which speaks directly to CRT as it relates to disrupting color blindness. Tatum (2009) discussed the idea of black male adolescents interrogating identity through the work of textual lineages. Muhammad (2020) put forth the following suggestions for teachers selecting texts for the classroom: "When selecting texts for the classroom, teachers need to consider the curriculum (what we teach) and the instruction (how we teach)" (p. 145). Muhammad (2020) further suggested that teachers' theoretical framing will impact both what and how teachers teach – both curriculum and pedagogy.

### Flipping Traditional Literary Theories and Using a CRT Lens for Literary Analysis

The idea of flipping traditional literary theory takes the approach of working within extant instructional frames for middle grades/secondary literary instruction, using critical interrogations and counter narrative approaches as tools that challenge racist implications. In the tradition of CRT, it provides a lens through which dominant narratives might be challenged. In *Letting Go of Literary Whiteness*, Borsheim-Black and Sarigianides (2019)[6] offered instructional suggestions for "unearthing Whiteness in canonical texts about racism" that include "ensuring students understand how a text critiques racism" (p. 58) and "investigating canonicity with students" (p. 59). Borsheim-Black and Sarigianides (2019) also presented questions meant to prompt a "racialized reader response," that interrogate context, text, and readers, such as the following:

- Context: What are your purposes for reading this text? How do these purposes inform your experience with this text? How is a critical race analysis relevant to your purposes? (p. 47)
- Text: What are the major themes? In what ways do the themes reinforce or interrupt dominant ways of thinking about race or racism? (p. 47)
- Reader: What is your racial identity? How does your racial identity shape your reading of this text?

(p. 47)

Questions such as these might provide a starting place for middle grades teachers' consideration of text choices, illuminate racist ideas in the classroom canon, and offer opportunities to revise text choices in response to new understandings.

### *Writing Instruction in the Middle Grades*

Writing instruction in the 21st century middle grades classroom is characterized by its complexity. Not only do middle grades teachers shoulder the responsibility of bridging the writing instruction and skill work of elementary to high school, but there is also the consideration of the multiple modes of writing in

21st century communication. As Calkins (2014) discussed in consideration of writing instruction the middle grades,

> the information age of today makes it especially imperative that young people…develop skills that are significantly more complex than those required of them in the past…As ways of communicating---text messaging, email, social media, search engines---seep into every nook and cranny of our day.
>
> (p. 1)

Calkins (2014) further emphasized the importance of middle grades students honing critical writing skills, such as synthesis, organization, reflection, and response to data, writing across genres such as narrative, argumentative, and informational.

In addition to its complexity, it is important to acknowledge that writing work in the middle grades is given context by the nature of the young adolescent student. As Burke (2013) discussed, "all writing is personal, an extension of ourselves, a record of the process by which we create ourselves, discover our ideas; it is a performance of ourselves" (p. 65). This concept of writing as such a personal, identity grounded process is relevant, particularly as it might interact with the young adolescent student writer. In terms of effective practices in writing instruction, Burke (2013) put forth a traditional writing cycle, to include the work of "inventing, focusing, ordering, revising, and editing (p. 76)." Within this, middle grades and secondary students might move through, working on single or multiple drafts of assigned or chosen topics for writing.

Middle school teachers of writing also know the importance of tapping into practices and routines that support young adolescents' work as focused, reflective writers. For example, Atwell (2015) discussed her reliance on the teaching of routines in the middle grades writing workshop, noting, "writing workshop doesn't come naturally to kids. They need to be taught and retaught its routines until they internalize the rhythms…Once students have a sense of what to do next, they can regulate how to use their time" (p. 103). Atwell further discussed the foundational role played by the teaching of routines in the flow and organization of the middle grades writing workshop, while Ehrenworth and Vinton (2005) argued the potential of teaching writing to be not only reflective, but also speculative. About this, Ehrenworth and Vinton (2005) noted, "in teaching writing, we teach that students' lives are worth writing about and that writing is one way to observe current conditions and imagine others" (p. 8).

In addition to teaching routines and practices, middle school teachers of writing tap into teacher/student conferences, particularly during the writing workshop. About his work in this area, Anderson (2019), discussed the power of conferences in teacher-to-student relationship building and as a tool for teachers to interrogate student needs throughout the workshop. About this, he said, "conferring…makes an essential contribution to students feeling that the curriculum reflects who they are as writers and to our teaching actually meeting their needs"(p. 12). Anderson (2019) further discussed the embedded opportunities for instructional differentiation within writing workshop, along with opportunities to build independence in adolescent writers, by inviting their thoughtful reflection about their writing and giving them opportunities for choice-making about their continued writing work.

## Middle Grades Writing and CRT

Applying a CRT lens to middle grades writing work unveils opportunities for further differentiation and broadened perspectives that challenge dominant narratives with attention to instructional form.

### Instruction for Various Literacy Styles

Turning a CRT lens toward writing instruction for the middle grades, it might be important to notice places in the curriculum where there are opportunities for intentional differentiation. Delpit (2006) discussed the existence of "culturally based differences in language use and writing…," (p. 61), calling out rhetorical norms and idea organization as creating writing styles that may differ from those commonly considered traditional in the writing classroom. Delpit (2006) also argued that in many ways the institutionalized rules of writing and other forms of classroom-instructed communication are inherently racialized, as they are encoded with "the rules for participating in power…a culture of power" (p. 25). Further, Delpit (2006) suggested that students of color, particularly, be instructed in ways that not only nurture their ways of knowing in written communication, but in ways that are also explicit about the rules and organizational form that shape the writing traditions within cultures of power.

### Storytelling

Another way to use the lens of CRT as it pertains to writing instruction for the middle grades is to consider the value of storytelling in its varied forms, to include counter storytelling and to open opportunities in the curriculum. As Delgado (1989)[7] noted about CRT in its legal roots, "storytelling offers a cure to oppression" (p. 2414). About this, he noted that "stories can challenge complacency and status quo," (p. 2414) especially those stories told by minoritized group members. About this, Delgado (1989) offered the following:

> Most who write about storytelling focus on its community-building functions: stories build consensus, a common culture of shared understandings, and deeper, more vital ethics. Counterstories, which challenge the received wisdom, do that as well. They can open new windows into reality, showing us that there are possibilities for life other than the ones we live. They enrich

imagination and teach that by combining elements from the story and current reality, we may construct a new world richer than either alone. Counterstories can quicken and engage conscience. Their graphic quality can stir imagination in ways in which more conventional discourse cannot.

(pp. 2414–2415)

Thus, it follows that in a consideration of middle grades writing curricula, it is important to identify opportunities for non-traditional storytelling both in form and content. Similarly, it is important to evaluate tools of writing assessment for bias against non-traditional forms of storytelling and against counter narratives.

## Broadened Perspectives: Cultivating the Skills of Literacy Societies

As it relates to broadened perspectives around middle grades literacy and writing, one important area of influence is in the traditions of the literate societies of racialized groups, such as African Americans. Muhammad (2020) and Perry et al. (2004)[8] referenced historical traditions of the African American literate, noting patterns of liberation and transcendence in and through writing. Perry et al. (2004) juxtaposed the criminalization of enslaved people who learned to read and write against the existence of Black narrative, even in the form of slave narratives/narratives of the enslaved. Perry (2003) noted about the value of literacy for the enslaved, "…literacy was more than a symbol of freedom; it was freedom. It affirmed their humanity, their personhood. To be able to read and write was an intrinsic good, as well as a mighty weapon in the slave's struggle for freedom" (p. 13). Similarly, Muhammad (2020) explained the cultivation of writing skills that was part of the work accomplished in literary society in times of African American enslavement. Muhammad noted the following:

> Historically, writing was the ultimate intellectual and literary skill because it entailed the act of reading something, thinking about the content, considering new ideas to set to paper, and then communicating those words to the intended audience. After something was written, it was usually discussed, debated, and used to address the public.

(p. 83)

Muhammad (2020) further discussed the work of writing as a process that happened in literacy societies, wherein works of writing were not only critiqued, but also revised. Contemplating this historical perspective about the role of writing in early American communities of color helps to bring into view 21st century ways to broaden instructional ideas, origin story narratives, and curricular perspectives about writing instruction in the middle grades. Amplifying aspects of CRT that support liberatory pedagogies, there is space to conceive culturally responsive pedagogical approaches to writing instruction in the middle.

## Speaking, Listening, and Language

### Speaking and Listening

As it relates to instructional work in the domains of speaking/listening and language for the middle grades, there are a variety of layered competencies and pedagogical expectations both for teaching and for learning. Aquino-Sterling (2014) pointed out some of the complexities in middle grades standards for speaking and listening. About this, Aquino-Sterling (2014) noted, "learning to speak beyond the sentence level has reached the curricular spotlight as the demand of …standards in the middle grades require that young adolescents perform language tasks in increasingly complex and organized ways, (such as) discursive practices…" (p. 30).

In thinking about the nature of speaking and listening skill instruction in the 21st century middle grades setting, it is important to acknowledge where speaking and listening instruction pulls across domains of literacy and language and to notice named characteristics of its effectiveness. For example, in characterizing 21st century speaking and listening skills, Burke (2013) noted the varied context of speaking and listening, about which he said, "effective speaking these days depends as much on what you say as on what you use to say it: video, images, software applications, audio, infographics, and stories" (p. 203). Further, Burke (2013) characterized the speaking and listening exchanges between adolescent students and teachers as dialogic. About this he noted that dialogue, both teacher:student and student:student are part of a healthy language arts classroom's functioning and learning culture. Burke (2013) provided pedagogical examples such as reciprocal teaching, literature circles, and Socratic seminars, which, he argued, provide students with opportunities to sharpen and exercise the following speaking and listening skills as shown in Table 9.3:

**TABLE 9.3** An excerpt from Jim Burke's *The English Teacher's Companion* wherein Burke (2013) provides examples of speaking and listening skills.

- Asking authentic questions (p. 218)[a];
- Explaining, elaborating, or defending positions (p. 218);
- Posing follow up questions (p. 219);
- Generating and making room for multiple, even contradictory perspectives (p. 219);
- Discussing topics that are meaningful (p. 219);
- Learning the skills, conventions, and background knowledge to participate in and contribute to the class or small-group discussion (p. 219);
- Provided adequate time to develop ideas through the discussion; use the discussion as a "medium of instruction (p. 219);
- Use a variety of discussion formats (think-pair-share, reciprocal teaching, Socratic Seminar) and strategies (questions, passages, graphic organizers, sentence stems) to ensure that discussion deepens over time, is purposeful, and, in general, improves students' understanding of the text or subject being discussed (p. 219).

a From Jim Burke's *The English Teacher's Companion* pp. 218–219.

Burke's (2013) noted that the skills of speaking and listening articulate the layers of learning that happen through comprehensive pedagogical practices across literacy domains.

## Language

In language instruction, adolescents' study of grammar and conventions persists but is considered through various perspectives within 21st century standards and competencies. For example, there is a school of thought that students need practical instruction in traditional grammar and conventions in order to write correctly. For example, Burke (2013) noted that "to explore those elements of language---vocabulary, grammar, usage, and style---that students must master as readers, writers and speakers to develop in them not just a consciousness of these elements but a conscience about their correct and effective use" (p. 257). Along similar lines, but shifting a bit in the "why" of language instruction, it might be said that language instruction in the middle grades serves the purpose of building students' agency and independence over their conventions in writing. For example, Atwell (2015) noted about language-focused minilessons in the middle grades writing workshop that "conventions minilessons should help students take responsibility for perfecting their writing before it goes public" (p. 142). Atwell (2015) further warned against decontextualized conventions instruction that is formed with the intention of reviewing conventions fundamentals, but not grounded in students' real-time, real-world conventions work in their writing.

In addition to other ideas about language instruction, there is the perspective of traditional grammatical frames being part of a culture of power (Delpit, 2006; Ehrenworth and Vinton, 2005) but not explicitly and necessarily correlating to improved student writing (Yatvin, 2016)[9]. About this, Ehrenworth and Vinton (2005) wondered, through the lens of 21st century instruction, if grammar, in the current context is "a matter of taste, a personal or communal preference" (p. 3), and further discussed the teacher's work in grammar instruction to include leading students to shape meaning in their own voices. About this, they discussed grammar instruction with an intention to "examine and teach language as cultural code…(doing so) in such a way (that) maintain[s] the potential for interrupting the very codes we study" (p. 7). Further, Ehrenworth and Vinton (2005) noted that teachers "can teach grammar organically this way if [their] literacy work is informed by certain critical reading and liberating writing practices" (p. 7). To consider language instructional practices as opportunities for the interruption of traditional cultural coding moves toward the ideas that might emerge through the lens of CRT and middle grades language practices.

## Middle Grades Listening/Speaking, Language, and CRT

One of the key ideas that helps to bring into focus thinking about middle grades listening, speaking, and language through the lens of CRT is thinking about "White Mainstream English" (Baker-Bell, 2020) as belonging to the culture of power (Delpit, 2006) and other Englishes being, subjugated, and beyond the bounds of the English traditions upheld within a culture of power. Dillard (1973)[10] called out the chasm between "Black English" and what Baker-Bell (2020) referred to as "White Mainstream English." Dillard (1973) noted the following: "The most notable group of unabsorbed persons consists of American Blacks; it is clear that many of their folkways have remained after more than three hundred years in this country" (p. 5). Dillard (1973) further argued that despite time and an intermingling of cultures, Black English "remains distinct from those of any large group of whites" (p. 5). Despite the distinction, "Black English" as Dillard (1973) referred to it, or "Black Language" as Baker-Bell (2020) termed it, contains "… highly complex linguistic codes and rules one must know before being able to speak it with fluency…" (Emdin, 2016, p.11).

In applying a CRT lens to middle grades work in this area, educators might consider the liberatory nature of acknowledging Black grammars, conventions, and even histories as they relate to speaking and language. Drawing upon these histories, the black literary societies during the era of enslavement are prominent in the historical conversation (Perry et al., 2004; Muhammad, 2020, Price-Dennis et al., 2017). As Price-Dennis et al., (2017) discussed, "within these literary societies, literacy was not only skill-driven, but also a tool used to define their identities, advocate for their rights to better themselves, and address issues of inequity for the wider society" (p. 3), underscoring the idea of the use of speaking and language in a liberatory capacity and uncovering a framework through which 21st century teachers of middle grades language arts might pursue instructional pathways that embody the ideas of CRT and language, while disrupting the "Anti-Black Linguistic Racism" (Baker-Bell, 2020, p. 11) inherent in many teaching and assessment forms.

## Conclusion, A Call to Action for the Middle Grades Literacy Community

The ideas presented in this chapter are not comprehensive, as there is vastly more to consider in the conversation about middle grades literacy and language arts through the lens of CRT. However, these considerations offer a springboard for critical contemplation and curricular action. As (Dixson et al., 2017) noted,

> there is a focus in CRT on praxis, a commitment not only to scholarship but also to social action towards liberation and the end of oppression… CRT requires that scholars utilize their insight and knowledge to work on the ground to resist and disrupt… .

(p. 4)

Thus, as it relates to literacy and language arts in the middle, these disruptions might come in the form of amended curriculum and revised instructional practices with CRT in focus.

In order to avoid what Ladson-Billings refers to as "intellectual death" (p. 17), liberatory pedagogies for literacies (Muhammad (2020)[11]; Price-Dennis (2019)[12]; Perry (2003) must be part of the conversation. Love (2020) argued that "teachers must embrace theories such as CRT…to interrogate anti-Blackness and (to) frame experiences with injustice…" (p. 12). With CRT in focus, particularly for middle grades literacies and the language arts, educators must be keenly on the lookout for curricular color blindness, perpetuation of dominant narratives, and the cultural neglect of some students. As Delpit (2006) suggested, the culture of power is important to realize and code switch to as long as it frames the dominant narrative. However, as Picower (2021) put forth, a continued use of "curricular tools of whiteness" (p. 27), such as "White Out, No One is to Blame, Not That Bad, All Things Being Equal, White Gaze, Embedded Stereotypes, and Racist Reproduction" (p. 27) negatively perpetuate dominant ideologies and leave some students out of high impact teaching and learning.

Rather than acquiescing to literacy practices and pedagogies that unevenly represent the collective literacy genius and histories of students of color, it will be important in the middle grades literacy education community of the 21st century to disrupt. Within this challenge, there is an urgent call to action, for as Dewey (1916)[13] noted, "education is not preparation for life. Education is life itself" (p. 239). An earnest consideration of education as life itself leads to complex thinking about the frames that shape instructional practices, particularly for students in the middle.

Finally, in striving to be highly effective middle grades educators of literacy and language arts, we cling to "what we believe" about successful middle schools. As Bishop and Harrison (2021) wrote, middle school teachers "critically examine materials to identify what is missing or misrepresented in order to provide a more inclusive and anti-racist curriculum…" (p. 28), an idea that is of particular importance within the humanities-based work of literacy and language arts instruction. As we continue to interrogate the principles, practices, and pedagogies that define middle grades literacy and language arts instruction in the 21st century, we should also continue the critical conversations leading to outcomes of action. All middle school students deserve to learn in the light and opportunity of curricular "mirrors, windows and sliding glass doors" (Bishop, 1990). *This* we believe.

## Notes

1 In *Critical Race Theory: The Key Writings that Formed the Movement*
2 *Critical Race Theory: The Key Writings that Formed the Movement*
3 *Mosaic of Thought: Teaching Comprehension in a Reader's Workshop*

4 "Literary Theory and The English Language Arts" in *The Handbook of Research on Teaching the English Language Arts*
5 TED Talk: *The Danger of a Single Story*
6 *Letting Go of Literary Whiteness: Antiracist Literature Instruction for White Students*
7 Storytelling for Oppositionists and Others: A Plea for Narrative
8 Young, Gifted, and Black: Promoting High Achievement Among African American Students
9 Is Teaching Grammar Necessary?
10 *Black English: Its history and Usage in the United States*
11 *Cultivating Genius: An Equity Framework for Culturally and Historically Responsive Literacy*
12 What happens here can change the world: Preparing Literacy Teachers in the Digital Age
13 *Democracy and Education: An Introduction to the Philosophy of Education*

## References

Adichie, C.N. (2009). *TED Talks: Chimamanda Adichie--the danger of a single story*. https://www.ted.com/talks/chimamanda_ngozi_adichie_the_danger_of_a_single_story?language=en.

Anderson, C. (2019). Let's put conferring at the center of writing instruction. *Voices from the Middle, 26*(4), 9–13.

Aquino-Sterling, C. (2014). Speaking and listening in a new key: Discursive performances in light of Common Core. *Voices from the Middle, 22*(1), 30–35.

Atwell, N. (2015). *In the middle: A lifetime of learning about writing, reading, and adolescents*. Heinemann.

Baker-Bell, A. (2020). *Linguistic justice: black language, literacy, identity, and pedagogy*. Routledge, Taylor & Francis Group.

Baker-Bell, A., Butler, T., & Johnson, L. (2017). The pain and the wounds: A call for Critical Race English education in the wake of racial violence. *English Education, 49*(2), 116–129.

Beach, R., & Swiss, T. (2011). Literary theories and teaching of English language arts. In D. Lapp, & D. Fisher (Eds.), *Handbook of research on teaching the English language arts* (3rd ed.). Routledge. Credo Reference: http://ezproxy.gardner-webb.edu/login?url=https://search.credoreference.com/content/entry/routengart/literary_theories_and_teaching_of_english_language_arts/0?institutionId=5562

Bishop, P., & Harrison, L. M. (2021). *The successful middle school: this we believe*. Association for Middle Level Education.

Bishop, R. S. (1990). Mirrors, Windows, and Sliding Glass Doors. *Perspectives: Choosing and Using Books for the Classroom, 6*(3), ix–xi.

Borsheim-Black, C., & Sarigianides, S. T. (2019). *Letting go of literary whiteness: Antiracist literature instruction for white students*. Teachers College Press.

Burke, J. (2013). *The English teacher's companion: a completely new guide to classroom, curriculum, and the profession*. Heinemann.

Calkins, L. (2014). *A guide to the common core writing workshop, middle school grades*. Heinemann.

Carbado, D. W., (2011). Critical what commentary: Critical race theory: A commemoration: Afterword *Connecticut Law Review*, 127. https://opencommons.uconn.edu/law_review/127

Crenshaw, K., Gotanda, N., Peller, G., & Thomas, K. (Eds.). (1995). *Critical race theory: the key writings that formed the movement*. The New Press.

Delgado, R. (1989). Storytelling for Oppositionists and Others: A Plea for Narrative. *Michigan Law Review*, 87(8), 2411–2441. doi:10.2307/1289308

Delpit, L. (2006). *Other people's children: cultural conflict in the classroom*. New Press.

Dewey, J. (1916). *Democracy and education: An introduction to the philosophy of education*. New York: MacMillan.

Dias, M. (2021, April 6). *About*. Marley Dias. https://www.marleydias.com/about/.

Dillard, J. L. (1973). *Black English: Its history and usage in the United States*. Vintage Books.

Dixson, A. D., Anderson, C. R., & Donner, J. K. (2017). *Critical race theory in education: all God's children got a song* (2nd ed.). Routledge.

Ehrenworth, M., & Vinton, V. (2005). *The power of grammar: unconventional approaches to the conventions of language*. Heinemann.

Emdin, C. (2016). *For white folks who teach in the hood… and the rest of y'all too: Reality pedagogy and urban education*. Beacon Press.

Fountas, I. C., & Pinnell, G. S. (2017). *The Fountas & Pinnell literacy continuum: a tool for assessment, planning, and teaching*. Heinemann.

Glatthorn, A. A., Boschee, F., Whitehead, B. M., & Boschee, B. F. (2019). *Curriculum leadership: strategies for development and implementation*. SAGE Publications, Inc.

Huber, P. L., & Solorzano, D. G. (2015). Visualizing everyday racism. *Qualitative Inquiry*, 21(3), 223–238. https://doi.org/10.1177/1077800414562899

International Literacy Association. (2017). *Standards for the Preparation of Literacy Professionals 2017*. International Literacy Association. https://www.literacyworldwide.org/get-resources/standards/standards-2017.

Keene, E. O., & Zimmermann, S. (1997). *Mosaic of thought: teaching comprehension in a reader's workshop*. Heinemann.

Kiefer, B. Z., Tyson, C. A., Barger, B. P., Patrick, L., & Reilly-Sanders, E. (2019). *Charlotte Huck's children's literature: a brief guide* (3rd ed.). McGraw-Hill.

Kittle, P. (2013). *Book love: developing depth, stamina, and passion in adolescent readers*. Heinemann.

Ladson-Billings, G., & Tate, IV, W. F. (1995). Toward a Critical Race Theory of Education. *Teachers College Record*, 97(1), 47–68. https://doi.org/10.4324/9781315870557-7

Lapp, D., & Fisher, D. (2011). *Handbook of research on teaching the English language arts*. Routledge.

Love, B. (2020). *We want to do more than survive: Abolitionist teaching and the pursuit of educational freedom*. Beacon.

Middle Level Education Research Special Interest Group. (2020). *MLER SIG Research Agenda*. Middle Level Education Research. https://mlersig.net/research/mler-sig-research-agenda/.

Milner, H. & Howard, Tyrone. (2013). Counter-narrative as method: Race, policy and research for teacher education. *Race*, 16. 10.1080/13613324.2013.817772.

Morrison, T. (2013). *On Language, Evil and 'The White Gaze'*. Sam. https://www.sam-network.org/video/on-language-evil-and-the-white-gaze.

Muhammad, G., (2020). *Cultivating genius: an equity framework for culturally and historically responsive literacy*. Scholastic.

NCTE, & IRA. (2017). *NCTE / IRA Standards for the English Language Arts*. NCTE. https://ncte.org/resources/standards/ncte-ira-standards-for-the-english-language-arts/.

Partnership for 21st Century Skills. (2009, December). *P21 framework definitions*. Battelle for Kids.

Perry, T., Hilliard, A. G., & Steele, C. (2004). *Young, gifted and black: promoting high achievement among African American students*. Beacon Press.

Picower, B. (2021). *Reading, writing, and racism: disrupting whiteness in teacher education and in the classroom.* Beacon Press.

Pierce, C. (1970). Offensive mechanisms. In F. B. Barbour (Ed.), *The Black seventies* (pp. 265–282). Boston, MA: Porter Sargent.

Price-Dennis, D., Muhammad, G., Womack, E., McArthur, S., & Haddix, M. (2017). The Multiple Identities and Literacies of Black Girlhood: A Conversation About Creating Spaces for Black Girl Voices. *Journal and Language and Literacy Education, 13*(2), 2–15.

Price-Dennis, D. (2019). "What happens here can change the world": Preparing literacy teachers in the digital age. In V. Kinloch, T. Burkhard, & C. Penn (Eds.). *Research on Race, Justice, and Activism in Literacy Teacher Education* (pp. 23–34). New York, NY: Teachers College Press.

Ryan, S., Frazee, D., & Kendall, J. (2012). *Chapter 1. About the common core English language arts standards for middle school.* About the Common Core English Language Arts Standards for Middle School. http://www.ascd.org/publications/books/113012/chapters/About-the-Common-Core-English-Language-Arts-Standards-for-Middle-School.aspx.

Tatum, A. W. (2009). *Reading for their life: (re)building the textual lineages of African American adolescent males.* Heinemann.

Thein, A. H., & Beach, R. (2013). Critiquing and constructing canons in middle grade English language arts classrooms. *Voices from the Middle, 21*(1), 10–14.

We Need Diverse Books. (2021, January 24). *About WNDB.* We Need Diverse Books. https://diversebooks.org.

Whitmarsh, B., Ahmed, S. K., Cherry-Paul, S., & Minor, C. (2020, June 5). *On the Podcast: Dismantling Racism in Education (Rebroadcast).* https://blog.heinemann.com/the-heinemann-podcast-dismantling-racism-in-education.

Yatvin, J. (2016). Is Teaching Grammar Necessary? [web log]. https://ncte.org/blog/2016/10/teaching-grammar-necessary/.

# 10

# DIS-ORIENTING PEDAGOGY

## Teaching Critical Engagement with Orientalism and Islamophobia

*Fatima van Hattum*

In 2015, Ahmed Mohamed, a 14-year-old in Houston, Texas, was arrested after bringing a homemade alarm clock to school to show his engineering teacher (Fernandez & Hauser, 2017). After another teacher saw the clock and thought it was a bomb, the school notified the police and the youth was handcuffed, interrogated, and suspended from his school. Later, a federal judge dismissed the family's lawsuit claiming discrimination on the basis of race and religion (Criss, 2017). The case—wherein a teenage American-Sudanese Muslim in South Texas was arrested due to his purported terrorist intentions and his identity as a Muslim and Arab—spans both real and imagined racialized and orientalist identities and belies how they are enacted in the classroom. Similarly, Abu El-Haj (2015) described a Palestinian-American Muslim high school student who was disciplined by his teacher for wearing an Osama bin Laden t-shirt. In fact, the shirt actually featured an image of *Bob Marley*. Based on their perceptions of the student and broader socio-political context and discourses surrounding Muslims, Islam, Arabs, and Palestinians, it is possible the teacher genuinely thought they saw Osama bin Laden instead of Bob Marley. These examples demonstrate how the interpretation of an image or person is not an isolated phenomenon but is rooted in one's historical context, cultural knowledge, and is part of a broader system of intertextual meanings related to the image or person at hand (Watt, 2012). They also highlight, first, that one does not look and see neutrally and, second, that the visual matters and there are deep implications in the classroom and beyond, based upon how people are visually represented.

Within this context, this chapter provides an overview of orientalism and how it is expressed within curricular materials including textbooks. The chapter also shares pedagogical responses that educators and students can participate in as a counter-curriculum. Middle school is typically when students begin to study

DOI: 10.4324/9781003171508-13

Islam and the Middle East. However, by the time students study these topics in depth, they have already received a lifetime of negative and biased media schooling about them through cultural pedagogies (Sensoy, 2010). Textbooks then reinforce negative messages through orientalist content (Jackson, 2014). Visual representations of Muslims and people from the Middle East are a key means through which these messages are conveyed (Matthews, 2005). This chapter provides educators with examples and resources to build critical visual literacy for middle school students through exploring what orientalism is and how it operates to perpetuate stereotypes. It provides example activities, and graphic novel texts for students and educators to engage with about Muslims and the Middle East, alongside textbooks. In our visually saturated society, wherein one is surrounded by biased representations of Muslims and people from the Middle East (Jackson, 2014; Kinchelo et al., 2010; Kincheloe & Steinberg, 2004; Said, 1997; Sensoy, 2016), visual narratives offer a powerful pedagogical opportunity to engage middle school students in discussions of racial and religious difference and representation.

## Call to Action

Due to media exposure and social media use, our daily lives and senses are saturated with images and information—mass culture is a hyper-visual culture (Rose, 2014b). In this context of prolific visual stimulation, the current political and public discourse in the United States surrounding Muslims has become increasingly biased, pejorative, and rhetorically violent (Alim et al., 2016). For example, a study of media coverage of terrorist attacks in the US between 2006 and 2015 found that attacks by Muslims received 357% more coverage than any other attacks (Kearns et al., 2019). Muslims and Arabs are overrepresented in the news and media in particular ways. This inflammatory rhetoric has real consequences. Each time presidential candidates in the 2016 election cycle expressed anti-Muslim sentiments, there was a rise in violence and hate crimes against Muslims and those who were mistaken for them (Alim et al., 2016). Ultimately, the stereotyping of Muslims and people from the Middle East as frightening enemies "affects *real* Muslim bodies" (Arjana, 2015, p. 3). This discourse surrounding Muslims, and the places with which they are associated, precedes the war on terror and has deeper roots in orientalism.

Within education, a lifetime of media and cultural pedagogy propagating particular ideas about Muslims (Sensoy, 2010) often results in orientalist and Islamophobic views in the classroom (Jackson, 2014; Kincheloe & Steinberg, 2004; Said, 1978). Similarly, textbook representations largely connect Muslims and the Middle East to violence and terrorism, perpetuating stereotypes, and rarely encouraging students to adopt a critical analysis about this diverse population comprising a quarter of the world (Jackson, 2014). In this broader sociopolitical context with constant visual stimulation, as educators, it is essential to adopt pedagogies that equip students to critically interpret images and information. While visual communication is a key source of knowledge in society, little curricular attention has been paid to visual literacy in the classroom, undervaluing it as an essential knowledge source (Ali-Khan, 2011). Students are often not equipped with the analytical tools with which to effectively interpret images (Ali-Khan, 2011). While treated as marginal, in fact, the visual develops earlier than the verbal (Avgerinou & Pettersson, 2011) and children formulate their earliest understandings of the world through seeing and looking (Albers, 2008).

## Background on Orientalism

Before turning to the practical application of pedagogy, I will provide an overview of orientalism as a theoretical framework through which to analyze representations of Muslims and the Middle East. First, it is important to first clarify and define the geography and people discussed here. In Said's (1978) conception, "the Orient" primarily referred to the areas of West Asia and North Africa, also known as the Middle East, but at times included areas of South and East Asia. Significantly, understandings and boundaries of what is considered part of the Middle East, or even an "Islamic" nation are contested. The Middle East is a political term and the countries included within its boundaries vary depending upon who is using it and how it is used. Some countries included within the so-called Middle East are not Arab countries (e.g., Turkey and Iran). Within Arab countries, not all Arabs are Muslim. Finally, countries globally with the largest Muslim populations—Indonesia, India, and Pakistan—are not Arab nations (Diamant, 2019).

However, Western portrayals and understandings of Muslims often conflate Muslims with Arabs and even use the two terms interchangeably, creating an imagined racialized religious identity (Abu El-Haj, 2015; Arjana, 2015; Jarmakani, 2015; Jiwani, 2010; Said, 1978; Thobani, 2008; Watt, 2012). The unique challenge of considering representations of Muslims lies in the breadth of Islam as a religion with adherents in countries from Indonesia, Saudi Arabia, Senegal, Bosnia, to the US. These adherents are often defined by a limited set of politicized ideas, while actually believing, practicing, and expressing their Muslimness across an immensely wide spectrum. Religious, racial, and cultural identity, their definitions, and relationships to place and citizenship are, of course, deeply layered and nuanced. However, the very essence of orientalist discourse is to cast "the Orient" and its peoples as one simplistic place that is "Islamic" in character (Said, 1978). For the purpose of this chapter, given the overlapping identities and political discourse of the Middle East as a region and Islam as a religion, I will specifically examine how Muslims and people from the Middle East are represented through orientalist and Islamophobic lenses in the US.

In his influential book, *Orientalism*, Said (1978) described orientalism as both a discourse and systematic discipline for "…dealing with the Orient…by making statements about it, authorizing views of it, describing it, by teaching it, settling it, ruling over it" (p. 3). This discourse became a means for imperial Europe, and later the United States to dominate and have authority over "the Orient" politically, sociologically, scientifically, and imaginatively (Said, 1978). Said's work in *Orientalism* (1978) and *Covering Islam* (1997) traced a repetitive and deeply engrained genealogy of representations of Arabs and Muslims from the late 18th century through the 20th century as brutal, unstable, sensual, and overly sexual with a "tendency to despotism" (1978, pp. 205–206) and overall "aberrant mentality" (1978, pp. 205–206). Said (1978) argued that, far from a blithe "fantasy about the Orient" (p. 6), these representations serve to reproduce a Western discourse and belief that "the Orient" and its people require Western governance, occupation, modernity, control, and, even, redemption. Said's focus was on the consistency of these various ideas that represent "the Orient" whether or not they correspond or relate to actual real places. It is this consistency of ideas and representations that is at the heart of orientalism reflecting its "citational nature" (Said, 1978, pp. 67, 176–177) as it reproduces itself over time, each depiction citing the previous depiction, with truth becoming a learned judgment and not a matter of material reality.

This discourse is inextricable with contemporary politics and the United States' continued military interventions in the Middle East. Ultimately, the defining feature of these representations is a relationship of power and authority, namely European and US domination over "the Orient" and the Middle East specifically (Said, 1978). Thus, orientalism, as a discourse and knowledge project, should always be considered in relation to dominant politics, as it draws upon different imagery and facets at different times to support specific politics and policies. For example, Shaheen (as interviewed in Jhally, 2006) in his research and subsequent documentary, *Reel Bad Arabs: How Hollywood Vilifies a People*, demonstrated how Hollywood portrayals of Muslims and Arabs follow American foreign policy goals with most representations from the 1980s onwards as violent terrorists. As this example highlights, orientalist discourse, while seemingly focused on "the Orient," is usually a projection of Western politics and interpretations of the Middle East (Said, 1978). It is important to note that, more recently, the term neo-orientalism has also been used to denote dynamics associated with the post 9/11 war on terror, Islamophobia, and a neoliberal agenda in the Middle East (Altwaiji, 2014).

### Orientalism and Visual Representation

Visual representations of Muslims and Arabs are then filtered through this same orientalist lens (Said, 1978; Watt, 2012). The visual repertoires associated with the Middle East tend to conform to orientalist tropes with imagery evoking the harem, desert, violence, gender oppression, sexual aggression, and exotified sexuality, reproducing seemingly timeless and simplistic dichotomies of the Western civilized "us" and the strange Eastern brutal "others" (Matthews, 2005; Said, 1978). Poole's (2005) work in visual anthropology contended that images help to craft ideas of racial common sense, particularly in relation to visual representations of colonized peoples. In relation to representations of Muslims, there are particular visual repertoires at work to create racialized and gendered religious differences. For example, Jiwani (2010) described how the prevalent imagery representing such difference is of the aggressive ultra-patriarchal terrorist Muslim man and the passive, oppressed, veiled, hyper-victimized Muslim woman.

In relation to Muslim and Arab men and masculinity, there is often a focus upon men's beards or particular physical traits, such as their noses, and focus upon clothing, such as turbans, as markers of difference. Arjana (2015) has documented how, in the Western imagination, a beard, curved nose, bushy eyebrows, and darker skin, which have come to be associated with Muslims and Arabs, are also indicative of danger, violence, and questionable intelligence or moral character. Similarly, for women, the visual focus is often upon the hijab as a marker of ultimate difference. Popular culture and mainstream media often employ images and commentary around Muslim women's clothing to depict Islamic cultures and societies as strange, absurd, or extreme (Fitzpatrick, 2009). In relation to Muslim women, "Images of…burqa-clad women remain primary markers of the so-called Muslim world" (Watt, 2012, p. 34). Further, Western imaginary of Muslim women often uses tropes related to the harem and exotified sexuality (Jones, 2015). It is important to note how this orientalist discourse also serves to entrench and reproduce gender binaries erasing the true spectrum of Muslim and Arab gender identities and expressions.

Another visual marker is what Memmi (1965) referred to as the "mark of the plural" (p. 85), or how colonized and oppressed peoples are rarely characterized as individuals but are branded as a collective. Similarly, Shohat and Stam (2014), described how a person from a marginalized or oppressed group becomes a synecdoche for the behavior of the entirety of their community. As Jiwani (2010) described, a Black man becomes associated with criminality and a Muslim man with terrorism, and the imagery surrounding them relies upon "specific historically inscribed stocks of knowledge" (p. 63) to perpetuate racism. The mark of the plural is found throughout visual codes of orientalism, as Muslims and Arabs are often portrayed visually in groups (Said, 1978). Muslim men are frequently depicted in angry and violent crowds, Muslim women in severe looking groups wearing black, and Muslims generally worshipping en masse. This casting of racialized people as a collective serves to reduce them to indistinguishable bodies, rather than holistic, complex, and nuanced human beings (Shohat & Stam, 2014).

The result of these orientalist visual codes is a "symbolic universe" (Yeğenoğlu, 1998, p. 70) of intertextual representations that have been distilled over time and across space into a set of essential ideas and specific references regarding the Middle East. Thus, a contemporary editor only needs to show one particular visual representation of the Middle East and Islam and the audience will already have access to a specific, seemingly objective body of knowledge about these topics (Said, 1978).

## Orientalism and Islamophobia in Curriculum and Textbooks

How then does orientalism operate within the context of education? This section is intended to support teachers' understandings of how orientalism and Islamophobia operate in their curricular materials, and particularly textbooks, so they can better engage in critical practice. Most available scholarship has focused on high school textbooks. However, the discourse and imagery within these textbooks is consistent across the middle grades (Apple, 2012; Jackson, 2014; Kinchelo et al., 2010; Kincheloe & Steinberg, 2004). Scholarship examining contemporary textual and visual representations in textbooks from the past 20 years, spanning the pre and post September 11th context, are particularly relevant. Through examining this scholarship, educators will be better able to recognize the hidden curriculum (Apple, 2004, 2012) at work in these textbooks and identify whose stories are silenced.

### *Textbook Orientalism*

Jackson's (2014) work in *Muslims and Islam in U.S. Education*, examined over 12 of the most popular world history and world geography textbooks used over the past 20 years, along with state educational standards for social studies. The textbooks and standards that she analyzed, "position Muslims' significance in the world within the medieval era rather than within contemporary life" (p. 78). For example, she found that imagery portrayed people in the Middle East on camels, or leading donkeys, inaccurately implying that throughout the 1990s, most people in the region primarily used them for transport, in implicit contrast to the developed and modern West. She documented how, when Muslims were portrayed in contemporary contexts, it was usually in relation to violent conflicts in the Middle East and also filtered through the perspective of US foreign policy interests. For example, the texts analyzed included lessons inviting students to compare the "parliamentary democracy of the State of Israel" to the "theocracy of the Islamic Republic of Iran" and "monarchy of the Kingdom of Saudi Arabia" (Jackson, 2014, p. 81) without any accompanying instruction around Israeli apartheid and the occupation of Palestine. While it is indisputable that Saudi Arabia and Iran are deeply repressive, the lesson asked students to compare the two most oppressive countries in the region with a purportedly unproblematic democracy— reproducing a false binary of Israel as a progressive White European civilized modern nation and people, versus backward, repressive, and barbarous Muslim and Arab peoples and nations. As a result, Jackson (2014) described how images, and their captioning, throughout the textbooks, presented a "binary, mutually exclusive, 'clash of civilizations' view" (p. 95) of Islam and Muslims.

Douglass and Dunn's (2003) work reviewed 11 world history textbooks focused specifically on textual coverage of Islam as a religion. They described how, "As a world religion in the twentieth century, Islam comes across as a traditional holdover, as anti-western, and often as merely militant and extremist" (p. 70). They described the chronology of world history textbooks as disorienting for students who would learn about the European Crusades or the Ottoman Empire, as self-contained phenomena, before they learned about the history and rise of Islam. The authors also argued that Islam was explicitly disconnected from other Judeo-Christian religions in most textbooks, although Muslims believe in and venerate most Jewish and Christian prophets.

Abu El-Haj's (2015) research found that the social studies curriculum in a school she observed framed the US as a paragon of democratic freedom in opposition to the "irrational forces of fundamentalist Islam" (p. 124). A common history textbook used, portrayed the US as a force for good, spreading democracy in the Middle East, while countries in the region were described as being angry at the US for undermining their traditional Muslim values (Appleby et al., 2005). In this context, the general framing of Islam in the school Abu El-Haj (2015) observed was as external to the US and possessing values inimical to American values. She argued that this narrative situates the US in the curriculum "as a benign force in the world, rendering its imperial power invisible under the mantle of the good fight to eradicate terrorism and establish democracy everywhere" (p. 124). The textbook further conflated entire regions of the world and the various social movements within them. In an egregious example highlighting regressive Islamic governments, the Iranian government was conflated with the Taliban (Appleby et al., 2005), reducing vast national, political, linguistic, ethnic, and major Islamic sectarian differences to a generalized Middle Eastern Muslim other. Overall, textbooks such as this are deeply politicized and obfuscate the various economic and geopolitical reasons the US repetitively intervenes, overtly and covertly, in the Middle East.

Kincheloe and Steinberg's (2004) edited volume, *The Miseducation of the West: How Schools and the Media Distort our Understanding of the Islamic World*, argued that "A distorted, demonized view of the Islamic world is passed along by a pedagogy much more powerful than traditional academic scholarship. The new cultural pedagogy colonizes consciousness via the pleasure of the entertainment media" (p. 10). Chapters in the volume explore gendered orientalist discourse, educator biases, and how, beyond the classroom, students interact with orientalist and Islamophobic discourse in the media, Internet, games, and movies. The authors argued that while this discourse has "new attire and high-tech modes of transmission" (p. 11), it is effectively a postmodern orientalism that is reliant upon the same medieval orientalist imagery of Islam and Muslims as barbaric and zealous. The works in this volume demonstrated how porous the school, classroom, and curriculum are and how it is essential to adopt an intertextual analysis that acknowledges the importance of public and cultural pedagogy.

Building upon this idea, Sensoy's (2010) chapter in Kincheloe, Steinberg, and Stonebank's edited volume, *Teaching Against Islamophobia*, questioned whether the formal curricular canon of knowledge transmitted in schools about Islam, Muslims, and the Middle East is as enduring, organized, and powerful as the media-based and societal curriculum to which we are exposed. She drew on the work of Hall (1997), Giroux (2004), and others to argue the significance of cultural pedagogy beyond the classroom contending that, "…by the time students study the Middle East and Islam (usually in upper elementary, and at length at the secondary levels), they have already received a lifetime of media-based schooling about it" (p. 113).

It is important to note that there is not a substantial body of educational research specifically examining visual representations of Muslims and the Middle East in the curriculum and related textbooks. The work of Zagumny and Richey (2012, 2013) is perhaps the most thorough. Their research focused on orientalist visual discourse and textbook representations of Muslims, Arabs, and the Middle East and found that textbooks invoked binaries of the modern West and traditional East to explain and describe geography, gender roles, cities, and people. The images they analyzed relied upon simple orientalist visual tropes such as oil-rich Arabs, groups of covered Afghan women, and Muslims worshipping en masse to introduce students to a vast geographic area spanning from North Africa across Southwest Asia.

Across these works, key themes begin to emerge that can help educators and their students to critically engage with textbooks and the orientalist and Islamophobic stereotypes that they may perpetuate. In our politicized educational context (Apple, 2012; Spring, 2016), it is also critical to connect scholarship focused on representation of Muslims and the Middle East, to broader multicultural education debates, struggles, and the representation of other groups. For example, domestically, there are parallels with how Native Americans are portrayed in geography and history curricula in the past tense with stereotypical, essentialized, fixed, and seemingly timeless characteristics (Calderon, 2014). Similarly, textbook portrayals of historical events and international political developments from Cuba to China are all influenced by particular perspectives, ideologies, and, what Apple (2012) terms, the hidden curriculum.

These sources—the textbook and curricular representations described above—largely connect Muslims and Arabs to violence and terrorism, perpetuating orientalist and Islamophobic media stereotypes, with little information provided to the contrary about this diverse group of people representing a quarter of the global population. Of course, students and educators are diverse, creative, and critical in their own right, and I do not wish to overly generalize their knowledge and perspectives. However, ongoing media exposure and cultural pedagogy promulgating particular ideas about Muslims and the Middle East is reinforced within public-school textbooks. Students then leave the walls of the school and enter broader society, culture, and politics with this particular discourse internalized.

In relation to the implications of representation, Shohat and Stam (2014) argued that "The sensitivity around stereotypes and distortions largely arises…from the powerlessness of historically marginalized groups to control their own representation" (p. 184). This lack of control and stereotypical representations may then result in discursive and physical violence. Jiwani (2010) argued that the manners in which people are represented anticipates and nurtures subsequent actions toward them, the consequences of which will be discussed below.

## Implications for Muslim Students: State Surveillance and Discipline

In the US, on a federal institutional level, the curricular discourse toward Muslims and Arabs described above is reflected in programs such as the Countering Violent Extremism Task Force which was developed as a domestic mechanism of the war on terror. The program emphasized that academia and educators are key stakeholders in identifying and countering violent extremism (*What Is CVE?* 2017). For example, an unclassified Federal Bureau of Investigation report titled, "Preventing Violent Extremism in Schools" (2016) stated: "High school students are ideal targets for recruitment by violent extremists seeking support for their radical ideologies, foreign fighter networks, or conducting acts of targeted violence within our borders. High schools must remain vigilant in educating their students…" (p. 1). The report contains images of Muslim and Arab looking people, describes concerning behaviors, and outlines actions for educators to monitor and report students. This focus on Muslim students is striking as most violent extremism and shootings experienced within American schools are not perpetrated by Muslim students. Of importance here is how the discourse pushing the surveillance of Muslims in broader society extends into the schools with educators expected to "remain vigilant" of the perceived threat of Muslim students. Indeed, one of the policy aspects of the war on terror is that "educational institutions are being tasked with threat assessment and the enforcement of antiterrorist measures" (Shirazi, 2017, p. 4).

Simultaneously, in much of the educational research on the topic of Muslim students, educators viewed students' attachment to Islam as a problematic source of oppression and violence (Abu El-Haj, 2015; Abu El-Haj et al., 2017; Jaffe-Walter, 2017; Kinchelo et al., 2010; Kincheloe & Steinberg, 2004; Zine, 2006). For example, educators may frame schooling as a means to liberate their Muslim students from the purportedly violent, intolerant, and oppressive ideologies of Islam (Abu El-Haj, 2015; Jaffe-Walter, 2016). Muslim students have been presumed to be predisposed to extremism, and needing education to become moderate, modern, and democratic Americans (Shirazi, 2017). In addition, Zine (2006) found that these educator biases often framed young Muslim women as oppressed, whereas young Muslim and Arab men may be read through a lens of purported aggression and violence, leading to a harsher disciplinary context for

174 Fatima van Hattum

them (Abu El-Haj, 2015). With this in mind, we return to the opening story of this chapter describing the arrest of 14-year-old Ahmed Mohamed as a result of his engineering enthusiasm, which was erroneously interpreted by educators through the dangerous lens of violent extremism. Mohamed's layered and complex identity as a Muslim, American, Arab, Sudanese, and Texan teenager excited about science were rendered invisible in the context of overarching and deeply entrenched orientalist narratives and the more recent US imperial discourses around the war on terror. In broad terms, Muslims are represented in particularly binarized, violent, and regressive manners in textbooks. Muslim students, in turn, experience the negative outcomes of this problematic institutional discourse within schools and classrooms.

## Theory into Practice: Dis-Orienting Pedagogy

With pervasive orientalist discourse in both mainstream media and textbook representations of Muslims, Arabs and the Middle East, how can educators connect theory to practice and better equip students to critically engage with such representations? This section outlines several pedagogy responses. First, I offer various activities and methods of visual analysis to build critical visual literacy. Next, I outline a text set of graphic novels that offer more nuanced and complex representations.

Of relevance, in terms of moving theory to practice, is Jones' (2015) work on using graphic novels of Muslims to teach critical visual literacy skills. In the context of historical and contemporary visual representations that dehumanize Muslims and Arabs, she proposed that graphic novels can be a useful way to generate discussion about difference and can provide "educators a new way to teach critical literacy skills that honor rather than flatten the complexity and messiness of representing difference" (p. 26). However, in teaching Muslim- and Arab-related graphic novels, it is important for educators to pay attention to the positionality of the authors which variously results in: insider memoir perspectives; outsider journalist perspectives; exoticized and problematic portrayals; and, fictionalized insider portrayals (Jones, 2015). Namely, not all graphic novels are the same, and some may serve to reproduce the very orientalist and Islamophobic narratives one is trying to disrupt.

A potential pedagogical approach to address this, prior to reading graphic novels, is for students to collect images of Muslims, Arabs, and the Middle East from social media, the internet, and news. Students could then be invited to journal about their impressions of the images, as well as their assumptions and ideas about Muslims and the Middle East (Jones, 2015). A first step in building a critical visual analysis is to have students discuss, identify, and articulate the visual themes and patterns across the images and then begin to critically analyze them with attention to stereotypes, accuracy, context, and the motivation of the images (Sensoy, 2010). Key questions to encourage critical engagement are listed in Table 10.1. This critical visual literacy exercise helps students to disrupt the

**TABLE 10.1** Questions to Encourage Critical Engagement with Images

| Thematic Questions | Context Questions | Design and Curation | Audience | Comparison and Analysis |
|---|---|---|---|---|
| What images, words, and phrases are associated most frequently with Muslims, Arabs, and the Middle East? | What was happening politically, socio-economically, and culturally when this image was created? | Who was the designer, photographer, or creator of this image? | Who is the intended audience? Who might also see the image unintentionally? | How does this compare with portrayals of other racial or religious groups? |
| What ideas and emotions do these images and words evoke—are they positive or negative? | How does the image relate to the political, socioeconomic, and cultural context? | Who was the editor who chose to include this image? | Do you think the images used might change depending on the audience? | Are there specific symbols used that you recognize? |
| What will you remember most about this image later and why? | Why do you think the people and places are portrayed in the ways that they are? | Why do their backgrounds matter? | Why does the intended audience matter? | Do you think the image is trustworthy and credible and why? |

normative, begin seeing things in social context, and examine issues from multiple perspectives (Lewison et al., 2002).

In this vein, Sensoy (2010) suggested that studying representation in the classroom be organized around accuracy, context, and motivation. With regards to the accuracy of visual examples, students could be asked to consider, for example, whether portrayals of modern cities in the region are accurate. Sensoy (2010) proposed:

> Try this quick thought experiment: when was the last time you saw a media representation of a major urban centre in the Middle East…in all of its mundane urban glory? Can you picture in your mind's eye Cairenes texting on their smartphones or getting cash from a bank machine? Istanbulites hailing taxis on their way to a rock concert? Tehranians joining friends for dinner out or a football match?
>
> (p. 11)

In terms of context, as outlined in Table 10.1, students should consider the audience, time period, and the setting in which and for whom the imagery was produced. Finally, in terms of motivations, Sensoy (2010) proposed asking students to consider who produces a given representation, for whose consumption, and with what motivations.

**TABLE 10.2** Analyzing for Absence

| *Prompts to Analyze for Absence* |
| --- |
| Whose perspectives are missing or not represented in the images? |
| Which genders are most represented? |
| Are most of the women in hijab? |
| Are the people portrayed mostly Arab? |
| What objects or places are missing? |

To deepen the critical practice and further enable students to examine this topic from multiple perspectives, students should be taught to analyze for absence (Rose, 2014a) using the questions in Table 10.2 as prompts. This exercise brings complexity and nuance around the sociocultural and political context surrounding images and representation. Educators can use this space to bring in other voices and perspectives and challenge the idea of one monolithic type of Muslim or Arab. For example, Black Muslims comprise at least 20% of the American Muslim population (Mohamed & Diamant, 2019) but are often marginalized in mainstream media and curricular content around Islam. Further, globally there are Muslim majority countries in Sub Saharan Africa and many Arabs are also Black. Educators and students should explore whether and how Black Muslims are included in images. This enables a more complex and intersectional conversation about race and religious identity. To start, educators can use the free lesson plan, *Black Muslims in the United States: An Introductory Activity* (Kysia, 2019).

Following this, a page and layout analysis is an exercise to enable students to understand that images and text are never neutral and are presented with a rhetorical purpose. Choose a given textbook page, news site, or page of one of the graphic novels presented below. This practice entails scanning the page in the order the eye has been trained to read it (*Visual Rhetoric: Analyzing Visual Documents*, 2019) and asking the questions outlined in Table 10.3. This will enable students to reflect upon the layout and why images have been arranged in certain ways.

As students develop critical visual practice, graphic novels and other resources suitable for middle grades that complexify and disrupt stereotypes and portray insider perspectives should be introduced. These include the graphic novels outlined in Table 10.4. These texts are all insider perspectives and could be

**TABLE 10.3** Basic Page Analysis

| *Key Questions* |
| --- |
| What is in the center of the page? |
| What is at the top? |
| What is the largest image? |
| Where is your eye drawn to first? |
| How does the way the page is arranged, and the images used, function to convince you of what is important? |

**TABLE 10.4** Graphic Novels and Resources for Middle School Students and Educators

| Title | Author | Year | Description | Pedagogical Purpose |
|---|---|---|---|---|
| *Yes, I'm Hot in This* | Huda Fahmy | 2018 | Instagram comic and book which uses humor and satire to challenge stereotypical portrayals of Muslim women. | Allows the reader to experience a first-hand account of an Arab Muslim woman wearing hijab in America. |
| *Ms. Marvel: No Normal* | G. Willow Wilson and Adrian Alphona | 2014 | A comic book about Kamala Khan, a Muslim teenager from Jersey City who is suddenly empowered with super human gifts. The story traces her and identity struggle as a Muslim child of immigrants from Pakistan. | Broadens notions of Muslim female representation to include other racial perspectives, varying degrees of religiosity, and portrayals of Muslim women who do not wear hijab. |
| *Baddawi* | Leila Abdelrazaq | 2015 | Graphic novel about Ahmad, a boy finding his place in the world as he is raised in a Palestinian refugee camp in Lebanon after the 1948 war that established Israel. | Brings the perspective of a boy and an introduction to Palestine. Muslims are normalized through the quotidian presence of Islam. |
| *Persepolis* | Marjane Satrapi | 2008 | Coming of age story of Satrapi's life in Iran and Austria during the Islamic Revolution and Iran-Iraq war. | Introduces readers to one version of political Islam and the diversity of beliefs and perspectives of people from Muslim countries. |

*(Continued)*

**TABLE 10.4** (Continued)

| Title | Author | Year | Description | Pedagogical Purpose |
|-------|--------|------|-------------|---------------------|
| *Challenge Islamophobia* | Teaching for Change | 2019 | Beyond strictly the visual, this is a series of lessons developed for middle and high school students, designed to be taught by educators without specialized knowledge of Islam. Lessons do not focus on details of the faith and practice. | Invites learners to explore Islamophobia as a type of racism. Lesson plans include: Islamophobia and discrimination, the Muslim NBA player who refused to stand for the national anthem in 1996, an introduction to Black American Muslims, and analyzing the term, terrorism |

compared and contrasted with the images that students collected, along with more stereotypical portrayals, in order to build critical analysis. For example, students could examine *Dust*, the X-Men character from Afghanistan who has been criticized as inaccurate and conforming to orientalist stereotypes through her portrayal wearing a sexualized niqab (Nayeem, 2018). Alongside that comic, students could watch a video featuring artist, Sara Alfageeh (2018), describing her critical response and redrawing of the character. Overall, these graphic novels and the engagement with various images are intended to build critical practice and serve as a basis for discussions around representation of Muslims and Arabs. They offer a pedagogical entrance into discussions around orientalism, stereotypes, and racial and religious identity.

## Conclusion

To return to the Bob Marley t-shirt example presented at the beginning of this chapter, the visual is central to how we make meaning of the world, ourselves, and others within it. Images, and the way we interpret them, are not neutral and they have implications with regards to how we interpret and engage with people. This chapter sought to present a background on orientalism, how it is visually expressed, how it operates within textbook representations of Muslims and the Middle East, and the implications of that representation. Following this, various pedagogical responses and activities were presented to build critical visual literacy skills for middle school students and begin "dis-orienting" (Leonardo, 2018) the curriculum.

Sensoy (2010, 2016) described how, without these active analytic interventions, there are deep and long-lasting pedagogical effects in terms of how Muslims and people from the Middle East are portrayed. In a society saturated with deeply biased representations of Muslims, Arabs, and the Middle East, these resources offer an important pedagogical opportunity to build critical visual literacy skills by engaging students in experiential discussions of difference and representation. The broader purpose of this chapter is to enable middle school educators and students to critically explore how images construct and reflect particular social and political views of the world. The overall goal is to make visible and question the discourses at work in order to build a more just and inclusive educational practice.

## References

Abu El-Haj, T. R. (2015). *Unsettled belonging: Educating Palestinian American youth after 9/11*. University of Chicago Press.

Abu El-Haj, T. R., Ríos-Rojas, A., & Jaffe-Walter, R. (2017). Whose race problem? Tracking patterns of racial denial in US and European educational discourses on Muslim youth. *Curriculum Inquiry*, *47*(3), 310–335. https://doi.org/10.1080/036267 84.2017.1324736

Albers, P. (2008). Theorizing visual representation in children's literature. *Journal of Literacy Research*, *40*(2), 163–200. https://doi.org/10.1080/10862960802411901

Alfageeh, S. (2018). *This illustrator gave Marvel's Dust character a realistic makeover* [Video]. https://www.newsy.com/stories/illustrator-makes-marvel-dust-character-more-accurate/

Ali-Khan, C. (2011). Seeing what we mean: Visual knowledge and critical epistemology. *International Journal of Qualitative Studies in Education*, *24*(3), 303–322. http://dx.doi.org/10.1080/09518398.2011.554450

Alim, H. S., Rickford, J. R., & Ball, A. F. (Eds.). (2016). *Raciolinguistics: How language shapes our ideas about race*. Oxford University Press. https://doi.org/10.1093/acprof:oso/9780190625696.001.0001

Altwaiji, M. (2014). Neo-orientalism and the neo-imperialism thesis: Post-9/11 US and Arab world relationship. *Arab Studies Quarterly*, *36*(4), 313–323.

Apple, M. W. (2004). *Ideology and curriculum* (3rd ed.). Routledge.

Apple, M. W. (2012). *Knowledge, power, and education: The selected works of Michael W. Apple*. Taylor & Francis Group.

Appleby, J. O., Glencoe/McGraw-Hill, & National Geographic Society (U.S.). (2005). *The American vision*. Glencoe McGraw-Hill.

Arjana, S. R. (2015). *Muslims in the Western imagination*. Oxford University Press.

Avgerinou, M. D., & Pettersson, R. (2011). Toward a cohesive theory of visual literacy. *Journal of Visual Literacy*, *30*(2), 1–19. https://doi.org/10.1080/23796529.2011.11674687

Calderon, D. (2014). Uncovering settler grammars in curriculum. *Educational Studies: Journal of the American Educational Studies Association*, *50*(4), 313–338. https://doi.org/10.1080/00131946.2014.926904

Criss, D. (2017, May 22). *Family who sued after a boy's clock was mistaken for a bomb sees suit tossed*. CNN. https://www.cnn.com/2017/05/22/us/ahmed-mohamed-lawsuit-clock-trnd/index.html

Diamant, J. (2019, April 1). The countries with the 10 largest Christian populations and the 10 largest Muslim populations. *Pew Research Center*. https://www.pewresearch.org/fact-tank/2019/04/01/the-countries-with-the-10-largest-christian-populations-and-the-10-largest-muslim-populations/

Douglass, S., & Dunn, R. (2003). Interpreting Islam in American schools. *The Annals of the American Academy of Political and Social Science, 588* (Islam: Enduring Myths and Changing Realities), 22.

Federal Bureau of Investigation. (2016). *Preventing violent extremism in schools*. Federal Bureau of Investigation. https://www.aclu.org/foia-document/preventing-violent-extremism-schools-1

Fernandez, M., & Hauser, C. (2017, December 21). Handcuffed for Making Clock, Ahmed Mohamed, 14, Wins Time With Obama. *The New York Times*. https://www.nytimes.com/2015/09/17/us/texas-student-is-under-police-investigation-for-building-a-clock.html

Fitzpatrick, S. (2009). Covering Muslim women at the beach: Media representations of the burkini. *UCLA Center for the Study of Women*. https://escholarship.org/uc/item/9d0860x7

Giroux, H. A. (2004). Cultural Studies, Public Pedagogy, and the Responsibility of Intellectuals. *Communication & Critical/Cultural Studies, 1*(1), 59–79. https://doi.org/10.1080/1479142042000180926

Hall, S. (1997). The centrality of culture: Notes on the cultural revolutions of our times. In K. Thompson (Ed.), *Media and cultural regulation* (pp. 208–238). Sage Publications.

Jackson, L. (2014). *Muslims and Islam in U.S. education: Reconsidering multiculturalism*. Routledge.

Jaffe-Walter, R. (2016). *Coercive concern: Nationalism, liberalism, and the schooling of Muslim youth*. Stanford University Press.

Jaffe-Walter, R. (2017). "The more we can try to open them up, the better it will be for their integration": Integration and the coercive assimilation of Muslim youth. *Diaspora, Indigenous, and Minority Education, 11*(2), 63–68. https://doi.org/10.1080/15595692.2017.1288616

Jarmakani, A. (2015). *An imperialist love story: Desert romances and the War on Terror*. New York University Press.

Jhally, S. (2006). *Reel bad Arabs: How Hollywood vilifies a people featuring Jack Shaheen* [Documentary]. Media Education Foundation.

Jiwani, Y. (2010). Doubling discourses and the veiled other: Mediations of race and gender in Canadian media. In S. Razack, M. Smith, & S. Thobani (Eds.), *States of race: Critical race feminism for the 21st Century*. Between the Lines.

Jones, R. B. (2015). *(Re)thinking orientalism: Using graphic narratives to teach critical visual literacy*. Peter Lang.

Kearns, E. M., Betus, A., & Lemieux, A. (2019). Why do some terrorist attacks receive more media attention than others? *Justice Quarterly, 36*(6), 985–1022.

Kinchelo, J. L., Steinberg, L., & Stonebanks, C. (Eds.). (2010). *Teaching against Islamophobia*. Peter Lang.

Kincheloe, J. L., & Steinberg, S. R. (Eds.). (2004). *The miseducation of the West: How schools and the media distort our understanding of the Islamic world*. Praeger.

Kysia, A. (2019). *Black Muslims in the United States: An introductory activity (Challenge Islamophobia) [Lesson Plan]*. Teaching for Change. https://www.challengeislamophobia.org/lessons/black-muslims-united-states

Leonardo, Z. (2018). Dis-orienting western knowledge. *The Cambridge Journal of Anthropology, 36*(2), 7–20. https://doi.org/10.3167/cja.2018.360203

Lewison, M., Flint, A. S., & Sluys, K.V. (2002). Taking on critical literacy:The journey of newcomers and novices. *Language Arts, 79*(5), 11.

Matthews, J. (2005). Visual culture and critical pedagogy in "terrorist times". *Discourse: Studies in the Cultural Politics of Education, 26*(2), 203–224. https://doi.org/10.1080/01596300500143179

Memmi, A. (1965). *The colonizer and the colonized*. Beacon Press.

Mohamed, B., & Diamant, J. (2019, January 17). Black Muslims account for a fifth of all U.S. Muslims, and about half are converts to Islam. *Pew Research Center*. https://www.pewresearch.org/fact-tank/2019/01/17/black-muslims-account-for-a-fifth-of-all-u-s-muslims-and-about-half-are-converts-to-islam/

Nayeem, T. (2018, September 3). *This Muslim artist wasn't feeling the sexualized portrayal of a niqabi superhero, so she decided to show us how it's done*. https://twitter.com/ajplus/status/1036780634247704579

Poole, D. (2005). An excess of description: Ethnography, race, and visual technologies. *Annual Review of Anthropology, 34*, 159–179.

Rose, G. (2014a). *Visual methodologies: An introduction to researching with visual materials* (3rd ed.). SAGE Publications.

Rose, G. (2014b). On the relation between 'visual research methods' and contemporary visual culture. *The Sociological Review, 62*(1), 24–46. https://doi.org/10.1111/1467-954X.12109

Said, E. W. (1978). *Orientalism*. Penguin.

Said, E. W. (1997). *Covering Islam: How the media and the experts determine how we see the rest of the world* (Rev. ed., 1st Vintage books ed.). Vintage Books.

Sensoy, Ö. (2010). "Mad man Hassan will buy your carpets!" The bearded curricula of evil Muslims. In J. L. Kinchelo, L. Steinberg, & C. Stonebanks (Eds.), *Teaching against Islamophobia* (pp. 111–133). Peter Lang.

Sensoy, Ö. (2016). Angry Muslim Man: Neo-orientalism and the Pop Culture Curriculum. *Critical Education, 7*(16), Article 16. https://doi.org/10.14288/ce.v7i16.186189

Shirazi, R. (2017). When schooling becomes a tactic of security: Educating to counter "extremism". *Diaspora, Indigenous, and Minority Education, 11*(1), 2–5. https://doi.org/10.1080/15595692.2016.1253555

Shohat, E., & Stam, R. (2014). *Unthinking Eurocentrism: Multiculturalism and the media* (2nd ed.). Routledge, Taylor & Francis Group.

Spring, J. H. (2016). *Deculturalization and the struggle for equality: A brief history of the education of dominated cultures in the United States* (8th ed). Routledge.

Thobani, S. (2008). Gender and empire:Veilomentaries and the War on Terror. In Yuezhi Zhao & Paula Chakravartty (Eds.), *Global communications: Toward a transcultural political economy*. Rowman & Littlefield Publishers.

Visual rhetoric: Analyzing visual documents. (2019). Purdue Online Writing Lab. https://owl.purdue.edu/owl/general_writing/visual_rhetoric/analyzing_visual_documents/index.html

Watt, D. P. (2012). The Urgency of visual media literacy in our post-9/11 world: Reading images of Muslim women in the print news media. *Journal of Media Literacy Education, 4*(1), 32–43.

*What is CVE?* (2017, January 19). Department of Homeland Security. https://www.dhs.
gov/cve/what-is-cve

Yeğenoğlu, M. (1998). *Colonial fantasies: Towards a feminist reading of Orientalism.* Cambridge
University Press.

Zagumny, L., & Richey, A. B. (2012). Textbook orientalism. In H. Hickman & B. J. Porfilio
(Eds.), *The New Politics of the Textbook* (Vol. 1, pp. 195–213). SensePublishers. https://
doi.org/10.1007/978-94-6091-912-1_11

Zagumny, L., & Richey, A. B. (2013). Orientalism(s), world geography textbooks, and
temporal paradox: Questioning representations of Southwest Asia and North Africa.
*International Journal of Qualitative Studies in Education, 26*(10), 1330–1348. https://doi.
org/10.1080/09518398.2012.731534

Zine, J. (2006). Unveiled sentiments: Gendered Islamophobia and experiences of veiling
among Muslim girls in a Canadian Islamic school. *Equity & Excellence in Education,
39*(3), 239–252. https://doi.org/10.1080/10665680600788503

# SECTION 4
# CONCLUDING SECTION

# 11

# THE ROLE OF REFLECTION AND REFLECTIVE CONVERSATION IN SUSTAINING THEORETICALLY-BASED PEDAGOGY IN MIDDLE GRADES

*Jason DeHart*

## Introduction

As noted in the introduction, theory and practice are inextricably linked. In this final chapter, I explore the importance of reflection through the lens of recorded and filmed notes about teaching practices. Based on the voices represented in this work from the teaching field, I turn my attention to the potential for mentorship in further understanding educational processes in middle grades literacy, particularly as a space for continued dialogue and reflection surrounding practice.

In the original study I draw on in this discussion, I defined film as a text and sought to answer the question of how teachers used film as a text for literacy instruction when working with rural adolescent students. In order to conceptualize this work, I drew on Tan's (2006) definition of film as "a series of moving pictures that has been recorded and made available for viewing" (p. 483). The notion of film as a site for teacher reflection acted as a potential influence on the study, as this was Tan's intended focus of their research, and this alignment between the initial study and the current presentation of findings reflect an intentional theoretical symmetry.

Uniting my conceptualization of the materials teachers were using, I further drew on Serafini's (2014) definition of film as a medium specifically including movement as an important feature, but also including image and sound. Part of my work with the teachers in the study was focused on the materials, but a large part of our time together was spent on discussing the steps and stages that teachers went through in developing and realizing their plans for literacy instruction. In spite of my definitional work prior to the study, my initial conversations with teachers included an invitation for their definitions of film as I did not want my understanding of the medium to eclipse their voice in the work. In framing the

DOI: 10.4324/9781003171508-15

work, recorded reflections often took the place of onsite observations as I knew teachers would be showing films and felt that observations might be limited in this way.

Over the course of two months, teachers shared written and audio-recorded reflections focused on the work they were doing. As part of our conversation about instructional design choices and daily experiences, teachers naturally spoke of the process of reflection and noted that this was an experience they rarely had the opportunity to engage with meaningfully in the context of their daily work. Though discussion of the process of reflection was not part of my original focus or intention as part of culminating interviews, the function that reflection served was essential in thinking about teachers' action steps. Moreover, teachers discussed the reflection process naturally in our final interviews without prompting from me. It is now to this sense of reflection practice that I return in an effort to make the case for continued reflection among and between teaching professionals.

In a coda to this collected volume's focus on the critical nexus of theory and practice, I share the stories of these teachers as a way of pointing to reflection in middle grades literacy instruction as an essential component for both recognizing and reifying the merging of educational theory and practice. While the reflections teachers created for this study were more systematic in approach, educators also spoke to the organic friendships and networks of mentorships with which they regularly engaged.

## Review of the Literature

I first offer a review of the literature relative to the processes of reflective teaching, as well as in relationship to the mentoring that teachers noted as they sought communities of practice with which to dialogue before turning my attention back to the teachers who took part in this study.

### Reflective Practice

It has been suggested for some time that reflection is an inextricable variable in effective teaching practice (Calderhead, 1989; Cruickshank, 1985; Pollard & Collins, 2005; Richards, 1995). Calderhead (1989) drew on Dewey's (1933) description of reflective practice as a process of careful consideration, including attention on the present reality and future implications of an action taken or belief held. This researcher went on to suggest that a closer examination of reflective teaching practice in terms of assessment of practices had not been conducted and pointed to the difficulty of ascertaining the knowledge that student teachers drew on in their decision-making. Cruickshank's (1985) work on reflective practice, meanwhile, served as impetus for greater attention to field experiences for teachers. More recently, Scales, Wolsey, and Parsons (2020) suggested that reflection is an essential component of effective practice, and that reflections can vary depending on the situation. Scales et al., (2020) went on to suggest that the complexity of educational work is further complicated by the presence and interaction of multiple stakeholders. These researchers suggested that "Reflection and metacognitive teaching complement each other perfectly" (Scales et al., 2020, p. 19) and that such reflective practice is both proactive and essential for adaptation.

In more recent work, Rowan, Robin, and Correnti (2009) pointed to the efficacy of teacher reflections recorded in instructional logs for their potential for insight into classroom interactions and processes. Rowan et al. (2009) posited this model of data collection as a potential mitigator of the cost and complication, as well as overall issues with efficacy, of classroom observations. In short, these researchers contended that a teacher instructional log might provide insight into the thinking and processing of educators, in the moment, rather than as an after-thought at some undetermined time following the instructional event or routine. These researchers pointed to the flurry of activity that educators engage in each day and throughout the academic year and highlighted teacher logs as a source of data closer to the sense of the "daily rhythms of instructional practice" (Rowan et al., 2009, p. 20). Rowan, Camburn, and Correnti (2004) pointed to a similar method for gathering data regarding the ways in which teachers enacted curriculum, as well.

## Film and Reflection

In the context of the study of film, teacher reflection has been examined in terms of video-based reflections and in terms of film-based professional development. For example, Christ, Arya, and Chiu (2014) described a video-based reflective discussion method (CPVA), in which educators introduced and critiqued videos of one another teaching. Film, in this quantitative study, existed in the form of teacher-created videos in the interest of improving pedagogy. Educators then used the film as a learning tool for their own practice.

Research questions in this study focused on how teachers described their learning, how this learning was applied in teaching, and how teachers connected their sources of learning to their insights from the videoing process. Most of the implication for learning (43%) fell in the category of "teaching methods or materials for instruction" as teachers considered the ways they thought about instruction, and the tools they utilized; "teaching methods or materials for motivation" accounted for 20% of the self-reported learning, and "motivation issues not related to methods or materials" accounting for 10 percent (Christ et al., 2014, p. 362). In the context of this study, it was both method and material that were central to the ways that teachers examined their practice. Similarly, Davidsen and Vanderlinde (2014) used classroom videos as a means of connecting research and practice. Classroom practices were video-taped in this study, and the researchers recommended that these videos could then be used by researchers and practitioners to examine the ways children collaborate in classrooms.

Miller (2009) advocated for the use of video-based conversations among teachers in a one-year longitudinal study, which utilized an ethnographic case study methodology, completed with pre-service teachers in a graduate education program. Miller (2009) noted that "conversations enabled the participants to think like practicing and professional teachers," and that analysis of videotapes opened up opportunities for participants to ask one another questions and explore the complexities of the problems they might face in the classroom (p. 158). In this study, reflection mingled with a sense of collaboration and mentorship.

Film has also served as a site for consideration of identity and culture among teachers as an additional textual space for reflections on bias and worldview. Fontaine (2010) conducted a qualitative case study in which eight themes emerged from pre-service teachers' viewing of the film *Hidalgo*. Participants in this study examined one character's "Caucasian-American/Sioux hybrid and fractured identity" (Fontaine, 2010, p. 40). Concepts of victory in the film were connected to this engagement with ethnic identity.

Finally, in terms of film and reflection, Schleppenbach Bates, Phalen, and Moran (2016) quantitatively examined the top digital video choices educators used for professional development from an online site which hosted such videos. According to these researchers, educators most often chose videos related to classroom management, reflection, and demonstration videos that outlined processes such as setting up centers and establishing classroom routines.

### The Role of Mentorship in Reflection

In addition to reflection, Scales et al. (2020) highlighted the importance of mentorship in the journey to effective, metacognitive instructional practice. These researchers suggested that mentor teachers are, ideally, continuing to shape their own practice, as well. Franklin (2018) reported that an intentional mentorship program is essential to creating opportunities for teacher leadership.

The phenomenon of reflection occurring within a mentor and novice relationship has been examined in research literature (Gratch, 1998; Wang, Strong, & Odell, 2004). Gratch (1998) examined the ways in which teachers are socialized into the teaching environment, and shared dynamics of change, depending on other circumstances. In the ethnographic case that Gratch (1998) presented, a teacher indicated a positive relationship with a cooperating teacher with frequent engagement in critical reflection, while a subsequent mentor/mentee relationship created feelings of isolation. The sense of frustration in this teacher's experience were based on not only busyness and distance from the mentor, but on a sense of criticism that traveled beyond positive critical reflection.

## Methodology and Methods

This study was originally framed as a hermeneutic phenomenological study, examining the use of a particular medium (film) in the classroom, informed by the historical work of Heidegger (1958) and Husserl (1965). Flick (2014) defined phenomenology as, "Careful description and analyses of the subjects' life world and the meaning making and understanding in that life world" (p. 541). Part of my discovery in beginning to investigate phenomenology has confirmed that there is a rich and complex historical background for this methodology, drawing on the academic discipline of philosophy, and this approach lent insight into a specific experience with a particular phenomenon. Spiegelberg (1994) has written a detailed history of the phenomenology movement and traces the methodological stance of phenomenology from a transcendent mode of observation to one of interpretive work on the part of the researcher.

The sense of reflection and mentorship, however, was taken up in detail by three of the five participants in the original study and therefore was held in analysis as these experiences were not universal to the phenomenon of teaching using film. This aspect of the study was one that I returned to as I began to develop a broader understanding of who the educators were that I interviewed, and what impact our initial study had on them.

As an additional form of theoretical framing, I drew on Denzin's (1992) description of symbolic interactionism, with particular attention to examination of meaning in film and visual media. The materiality so present in Davidsen and Vanderlinde's (2014) study provided an additional layer of support for this theoretical focus. In order to consider the interactions of participants with the texts they are using, I hope to draw on the theory of symbolic interactionism. The theoretical framework of symbolic interactionism has been used before in literacy studies (Braund, 1985; Ziegahn & Hinchman, 1999).

Flick (2014) suggested that symbolic interactionism concerns itself with "the subjective meaning that individuals attribute to their activities and their environments" (p. 81) and suggested that symbolic interactionism lends itself to phenomenological work (p. 83). Flick (2014) went on to mention Blumer and Mead as historical figures in the symbolic interactionist movement. Patton (2002) also mentioned Mead and Blumer explicitly when discussing symbolic interactionism.

It was this nexus of person and material that helped to form a sense of theoretical foundation for thinking about the ways that teachers used film and later reflected on their use of the medium.

### Initial and Final Interviews

Following deMarrais's (2008) description of the phenomenological interview, I began with open-ended questions in order to elicit the participant's experience (a "Think about a time when you" question) and iteratively returned to this experience with probes like "Tell me more about" and "What was __ like for you?" (pp. 57–58). In my role as researcher, I asked "short, descriptive questions that lead participants to respond" in what I hoped would be "long, detailed descriptions of the experience being studied" (deMarrais's (2008), p. 58). Recognizing the interviewee as a leader in this process of data collection was essential to the nature of the study.

It was within the scope of the interview process, particularly in the second and final round of iterative interviews, that participants began to more openly describe what the experience of reflection was like for them as we approached the end of the study. This use of iterative interviews (Polkinghorne, 2005) was used to capture experiences at the outset, as well as at the conclusion of the research project. Notably, the process of reflection was not part of my initial interview guide and would have been relegated to unrelated material had I not embarked on a semi-structured approach to interviewing that gave teachers the chance to share about their range of experiences. Kendall (2008) suggested a utility for interviewing when approaching literacy studies and wrote that such interviews include "the active listening process within the interview itself" (p. 137). Kendall (2008) maintained that analysis of participant interviews should include rich description (p. 143).

Once gathered, I coded the data. Saldaña (2016) suggested that coding methods align with the theoretical and methodological nature of the study being conducted and, to that end, I began with in vivo coding to center my thinking in the words of the teacher participants. This coding method aligns with "ontological, epistemological" inquiries that "address the nature of participants' realities" (Saldaña, 2016, p. 70). In vivo coding prioritizes the words of the participant, drawing codes from the very words of the participants themselves. In this way, I hoped to honor the experience of my participants as the primary source of description in the study. As a second round of coding in studies focusing on ontological questions, I used Saldaña's (2016) recommended process coding based on its relevance for pedagogical processes and its alignment with in vivo coding.

### Recorded Reflections

The central feature of this aspect of the study was the recordings of reflections themselves. Each time teachers used film as a text for their instruction, they were encouraged to record reflections using an audio recorder.

It was first to the use of film that I turned my attention as I examined these reflections, with their perceived value on the part of the teachers forming a secondary understanding as we discussed the project in our final interviews.

## Teachers in the Study

The study took place in a rural, Appalachian school district in the southeastern United States. Though rural, the presence of local towns and communities, as well as extensive bus routes, created large middle schools and even larger high schools for the students that teachers worked with. On average, teachers worked with approximately 90–100 students in schools that ranged from 1000 to 1200 total students.

Three of the five educators in the study were noted in this follow-up documentation of teacher responses to the process of reflection due to their commentary on reflection and, in the same thread of conversation, mentorship among each other and with outside sources. Anthony and Adam were both middle school social studies teachers, while Tom was a high school social studies teacher who had taught in previous years with Anthony. An additional participant, Fitzgerald, commented on mentorship but did not construct any reflections throughout the study. This teacher's absence of reflection provides additional insight in discussing reflection, particularly in terms of barriers that sometimes make the practice difficult. Fitzgerald was a middle school English teacher. I have used a pseudonym for each teacher.

## Findings: Reflection and Mentoring

Of first note in the findings is a set of barriers that, at times, kept teachers from engaging in reflection. The second finding I offer is the role of mentorship among the teachers, including mentoring from outside influencers. Finally, I will comment on the organic nature of the teacher relationships and reflections.

Two of the teachers preferred writing their reflections on paper, while two of the teachers preferred to dictate theirs. Over the course of two months, teachers averaged 4–7 reflections. A fourth participant in the study did not record reflections in either mode and cited a busy schedule, sick family members, and additional life demands as barriers to conducting the reflecting process. The greatest number of reflections came from Anthony, who chose to audio-record their responses. Tom shared five reflections, while Adams shared four.

### Barriers to Reflection (and Breakthroughs)

For a number of reasons, teachers identified reflection as a positive experience, but also one which they found difficult at, at times, untenable. For example, Adams noted a sense of privacy as part of a reluctance to reflect, and referred to the process as, in some way, forced and yet effective. They reported that writing reflections were, in some ways, forced but made this teacher think about how effective the work of teaching actually is. Adams added that sometimes reflections are difficult because they consider themselves a "private person," but that reflection does "force you, I guess, to think about what you're doing and why you're doing it" (Interview 2, December 2018).

Adams indicated that he did not do much writing and said "I guess I should. It's, I guess, more it's just a mental thing" (Interview 2, December 2018). Adams said that the drive home was usually at time to decompress and think about teaching decisions made during the day. They added, "I'll wake up in the morning and think about what I'm going to do that day and reflect on it. So, yeah. Those quiet times" (Interview 2, December 2018). For many teachers in the study, including those who did not share reflections, finding quiet time in the midst of busy schedules, along with personal and professional demands, emerged as a significant barrier to accessing an opportunity to write and reflect that teachers indicated that they desired.

In terms of continued practice, Anthony reported, "I definitely would like to utilize that and be more reflective. I've always wanted to, you know, write more of my thoughts down" (Interview, January 2019). Anthony's attention to a desire to write echoed Adams's for written practice, but a new set of challenges were part of this second teacher's experiences. They said, "I have like a dad journal that I write in like once every three months. So, so you know something like a recorder for teaching could definitely be more helpful, could definitely be helpful for me" (Interview 2, January 2019).

In spite of a desire to engage in written practice, Adams indicated that daily life, including just finding a moment of privacy in family life, created barriers. Privacy worked as a dual limitation as a commodity sought, as well as a desired element that made reflection challenging. This need for privacy for Anthony was also expressed in his role as a parent and reflected in his notes that he often finds it difficult to spend time reading and thinking at home. Adams added, "Just a lot of teachers get in their zone and, you know, life happens. You may still like what you do but you just kind of settle in to what you have, so reflection is maybe a rare thing for a lot of teachers who've been in the game for a while" (Interview 2, January 2019). An assumed stance of experience acts as a further limitation in this statement, and it is notable that Adams pointed to the rarity of reflection.

### Dynamics of Mentoring and Friendship

In a continued strand of their conversation about reflection, teachers in the study mentioned that mentorship was a space for sharing ideas and exchanging thoughts about teaching practice. Adams reported that a number of changes had taken place in his school just prior to our time together in the research project and that many of the people he felt were mentors and close colleagues had moved to other schools. Anthony said, "We've got some, we've got a lot of solid folks still, but I definitely miss a lot of my homies that have gone on to high school or even people who are older who retired" (Interview 2, January 2019). This quote indicated a level of friendship that went beyond the traditional mechanisms of a mentoring dynamic and also spoke to the need to maintain teacher teams and relationships as these dynamics are sometimes fragmented.

When asked about the context of change occurring in the school and the impact these changes had on practice, if any, Anthony continued:

> Last year was probably the worst year teaching as far as just the students didn't seem very psyched. A lot of my, you know, coworkers had moved to the high school. I would have lot of collaborating with other people, you know. And some people can, like light their own fire but I can do that somewhat too but, you know, it also really helps if I have somebody who I'm like bouncing ideas off, and working with, collaborating.
>
> (Interview 2, January 2019)

In particular, Anthony mentioned a collaborator named here as Tom. Because the context of the original study I conducted with these teachers focused on film, Adams first noted that Tom was a co-worker in this media-specific capacity. However, their working friendship and collaboration extended beyond a particular medium. Anthony mentioned Tom and how the two teachers were comfortable in one another's classrooms. They said: "Like, literally we were in each other's class like, 'Here's what I'm doing today. What are you doing today?' 'Here's what I'm reading. What are you reading?'" (Interview 2, January 2019). This quote speaks to the powerful relationship and dialogue and also points to the ways that teachers engage with ideas in professional literature outside of what might be considered a typical mode of reflection. Tom and Anthony did not belong to a structured book club, per se, but found motivation to read and grow, as well as discuss ideas together, as a more natural result of their interactions with one another.

Anthony went on to say that their collaborative network extended to other teachers, as well, and that not having these relationships currently in practice "kind of doused the fire a little bit" (Interview 2, January 2019). In spite of this feeling, Anthony indicated that the feeling of collaboration was returning and that these feelings were part of reflections on the previous year. The current year was more positive, and this teacher expressed a sense of hope. Anthony indicated that there were moments in the previous year when the thought of leaving the profession and finding another career did enter their mind. This desire to leave the profession in the absence of reflective dialogue was punctuated by Anthony's note again that the current academic year was progressing in a more positive direction and speaks to the power of both reflection and reflective mentoring relationships in sustaining middle school teachers in their work.

In a follow-up interview with Tom, this teacher in the planning dyad suggested that he had fond memories of collaboration with Adams, calling it "the old days" when they "used to make stuff" (Interview 2, January 2019). Tom added that this collaboration with making film and engaging in professional discussions occurred "outside of school and on weekends" and incorporated members of the two teachers' families. They said, "You know, I mean it was just fun. And maybe that'll occur again" (Interview 2, January 2019). This last statement indicated a mirrored sense of hopefulness on the part of the teacher, and a sense of nostalgia for a partnership that led both parties to moments of reflection and collaboration.

Tom indicated that they had a mentor in their early days of teaching, and so the relationship shared by these teachers had roots in another relationship to predate my work with them. Tom said, "My mentor used to say, everything that [students] write and give to you is a love letter" (Interview 2, January 2019). This teacher then indicated that the value that his mentor gave to the voices of students was a practice that he carried into teaching as a way of inviting the voices of others. This strand of mentorship and relationship suggested an on-going network that, in some cases, was hidden from view as Tom passed along practices and reflective teaching to colleagues.

Adams noted that a college professor acted as a mentor in using film, and an additional teacher in the study, Fitzgerald, shared a similar reflection about their history and influences as a teacher. Like Adams, Fitzgerald indicated that part of their teaching routine was influenced by a college professor as a mentor. Fitzgerald indicated that they elected to take the professor's class in film with the expectation that the content would be easy to navigate and then found that the work that the teacher did was actually complex. These mentor figures served as examples from the past, informing present instructional practices, including the use of particular media and the choice to incorporate writing intentionally in instruction.

Of final note in terms of outside mentors, Anthony mentioned the work of Paolo Friere as essential in the framing of their teaching and goals as an educator, noting the power of the notion of reading the world. For Anthony, this idea was relevant and palpable as they led seventh grade students through world history curriculum in an environment in which racial and ethnic diversity was not particularly notable. Anthony indicated that their practice, influenced by Friere's work, was focused on showing students the wider world of experiences and disrupting the problematic issues raised by stereotypes. Tom mentioned the work of Parker Palmer as an additional influence on his practice, and specifically cited Palmer's ideas about improving practice and continuing to be reflective, as well as the power of the individual's story in community.

## Organic Bonds

Of final note in the findings was the take-away that the reflective practices in which teachers engaged, when they were able to do so, was not solitary work, but involved dyadic and triadic relationships with one another. In some cases, the sense of mentorship and reflection had been lost, and a desire for a return to these practices was voiced. At no point did the theme of a forced or imposed mentorship program arise, and these teachers were not connected in this way. Instead, they navigated together.

The dynamic of Tom as a traveling teacher in his first years enabled them to form a relationship with Anthony and other teachers at the school, unbound by territory and traditional concepts of classroom space. Tom spoke highly of their years as a "roamer" (Interview 1, November 2018) and noted that this opportunity afforded them reflection about the ways in which teachers construct their physical space, having witnessed many examples throughout a school building. Without these moments of communal reflection and "unofficial" mentorship, Anthony felt a lack of passion, and the move to foster relationships with other teachers provided a space for development and growth of the kind that might not occur organically in other professional development spaces. It may be worth restating that Anthony had considered leaving the profession as a result of a fracturing in mentorship.

The schools in which these teachers worked did have unofficial mentoring systems in place, particularly for new teachers. What is striking is that the relationships fostered among the teachers in this study were essential for providing living spaces for reflection but were not the result of an intentional mentor/mentee pairing. Rather, they were the organic bonds that sometimes develop over time in institutions and were much more akin to friendship than a systematic relationship imposed by an administrator or outside entity. This relationship also traveled outside the confines of the school building and became an aspect of family life in the evenings and on weekends, with Tom and Anthony engaging in nature expeditions, sometimes including students along as part of the experience to learn and grow together.

## Discussion

Based on the findings presented in this study, a number of threads emerge for ongoing practice in middle schools. The first of such threads might be that reflective practice, particularly in the context of mentoring relationships, should be an essential feature of the middle school model. At the time of this writing, the notion of the reflection as an essential feature may be intimated but is not directly stated in the Association of Middle Level Education's (2020) published statement on effective instruction, *This We Believe*. Such relationships form the official and unofficial spaces for reflection, discussion about practices, and potential for improvement. Teachers expressed the desire to reflect more, but they experienced the flurry of activity described by Rowan, Robin, and Correnti (2009), and these multiple demands added strain to the possibility of moments of reflection.

This strain provides an additional theme in terms of the sense of a variety of barriers that exist for teachers who want to reflect. It should be noted that extracurricular demands and duties, including administrative duties, and obligations to construct plans, attend meetings, and engage in work with committees all stood in the way of teachers' ability to find times to reflect. While the professional work that teachers did was deemed valuable and no teacher in study spoke in a critical way about their additional responsibilities, administrators and policymakers who wish to ensure teachers have time to reflect on practice might take note of this trend. Apart from these moments of consideration, teachers indicated that they felt tired and were effusive with apologies when they were not able to record reflections. This is an advisement for policy-makers who may or may not have a grasp of the busyness of the lives of teachers.

The mode of reflection might be an additional area of insight into practice. For some teachers, recorded reflections were ideal. For others, it was more feasible to jot notes down during the day. Even still, some educators found difficult in taking time to make notes and none indicated that reflections were certain to continue in written or recorded form, although two teachers in the study did indicate the desire for continued reflection when possible. Flexible thinking in responding to moments in instruction, as well as moments in trauma and crisis in pandemic teaching, might be invitational for teachers who wish to engage with reflection but feel they lack the proper mode or time to do so.

The affordances of the middle school model for team relationships and collaboration serve as the impetus for a final commentary on the need for future research examining the ways in which teachers form and sustain mentoring relationships. The extent to which these relationships are systematically or organically fostered, along with the barriers that exist as they form and reform, might provide an additional range of insights into the role of reflection and the ways in which such reflection plays out over time.

## Conclusions

Teaching is thoughtful work and is composed of myriad decisions from moment to moment. The flurry of activity in middle school instruction does little to mitigate these demands, and many teachers feel additional demands in terms of professional duties and family responsibilities. Coupled with this sense of challenge, teachers have new obstacles to face in pandemic teaching and trauma-informed pedagogy.

Without reflection, the careful attention to texts, concepts of identity, and planning for effective literacy instruction in light of theory that contributors in this volume have called for is daunting, if not impossible. It is with a final sense of hope, but also of appreciation for the work that teachers do at all levels, that I offer one last call: Teachers are professionals who do complex work that combines theory and practice every day, and actions like guarding time, fostering opportunities for dialogue, and making wise political and social decisions to support the education system are not just important – these are essential elements of a healthy social and emotional environment where literacy learning can occur.

# References

Association of Middle Level Education. (2020). *The successful middle school: This we believe.* Retrieved from http://www.amle.org/AboutAMLE/TheSuccessfulMiddleSchool/tabid/1330/Default.aspx

Braund, D. (1985). Teacher-pupil relationships in adult literacy tuition.

Calderhead, J. (1989). Reflective teaching and teacher education. *Teaching and teacher education, 5*(1), 43–51.

Christ, T., Arya, P., & Chiu, M.M. (2014). Teachers' reports of learning and application to pedagogy based on engagement in collaborative peer video analysis. *Teaching Education, 25*(4), 349–374.

Cruickshank, D. (1985). Uses and benefits of reflective teaching. *Phi Delta Kappan, 66*(10), 704–706.

Davidsen, J., & Vanderlinde, R. (2014). Researchers and teachers learning together and from each other using video-based multimodal analysis. *British Journal of Educational Technology, 45*(3), 451–460.

deMarrais, K. (2008). Qualitative interview studies: Learning through experience. In *Foundations for research: Methods of inquiry in education and the social sciences,* (K. deMarrais, & S.D. Lapan, Eds.), 51–68. Mahwah, NJ: Lawrence Erlbaum Associates.

Denzin, N.K. (1992). The Conversation. *Symbolic Interaction, 15*(2), 135–150.

Dewey, J. (1933). *The way we think.* D.C. Health & Co.

Flick, U. (2014). *An introduction to qualitative research* (5th ed.). London: SAGE Publications, Ltd.

Fontaine, H.A. (2010, Winter). The power of film to educate and miseducate pre-service teachers: A phenomenological analysis of *Hidalgo* and cultural representation of Muslims post 9/11. *Multicultural Education, 17*(2), 37–43.

Franklin, D. (2018). 5 ways to foster teacher leadership: Practical ways to build up leaders. *Teachers Matter, 38,* 6–7.

Gratch, A. (1998). Beginning teacher and mentor relationships. *Journal of Teacher Education, 49*(3), 220–227.

Heidegger, M. (1958). *The question of being.* New York, NY: Twayne Publishers Inc.

Husserl, E. (1965). *Phenomenology and the crisis of philosophy.* New York, NY: Harper & Row.

Kendall, L. (2008). The conduct of qualitative interviews. In *Handbook of research on new literacies,* (Coiro, Knobel, Lankshear, Leu, Eds.), 133–149. New York, NY: Lawrence Erlbaum Associates.

Miller, M.J. (2009). Talking about their troubles: Using video-based dialogue to build preservice teachers' professional knowledge. *The Teacher Educator, 44*(3), 143–163.

Patton, M.Q. (2002). Two decades of developments in qualitative inquiry: A personal, experiential perspective. *Qualitative Social Work, 1*(3), 261–283.

Polkinghorne, D.E. (2005). Language and meaning: Data collection in qualitative research. *Journal of Counseling Psychology, 52*(2), 137–145.

Pollard, A., & Collins, J. (2005). *Reflective teaching.* A&C Black.

Richards, J. C. (1995). Towards reflective teaching. *English Teachers Journal Israel, 2,* 59–63.

Rowan, B., Camburn, E., & Correnti, R. (2004). Using teacher logs to measure the enacted curriculum: A study of literacy teaching in third-grade classrooms. *Elementary School Journal, 105*(1), 75–101.

Rowan, B., Robin, J., & Correnti, R. (2009). Using instructional logs to identify quality in educational settings. *New Directions for Youth Development, 121,* 13–31.

Saldaña, J. (2016). *The coding manual for qualitative researchers* (3rd ed.). Thousand Oaks, CA: SAGE Publications, Ltd.

Scales, R.Q., Wolsey, T.D., & Parsons, S.A. (2020). *Becoming a metacognitive teacher: A guide for early and preservice teachers.* Teachers College Press.

Schleppenbach Bates, M., Phalen, L., & Moran, C.G. (2016). If you build it, will they reflect? Examining teachers' use of an online video-based learning website. *Teaching and Teacher Education, 58*, 17–27.

Serafini, F. (2014). *Reading the visual: An introduction to teaching multimodal literacy.* New York, NY: Teachers College Press.

Spiegelberg, H. (1994). *The phenomenological movement: A historical introduction.* Dordrecht, The Netherlands: Kluwer Academic Publishers.

Tan, C. (2006, November). Philosophical reflections from the silver screen: Using films to promote reflection in pre-service teachers. *Reflective Practice, 7*(4), 483–497.

Wang, J., Strong, M., & Odell, S.J. (2004). Mentor-novice conversations about teaching: A comparison of two U.S. and two Chinese cases. *Teachers College Record, 106*(4), 775–813.

Ziegahn, L, & Hinchman, K.A. (1999). Liberation or reproduction: Exploring meaning in college students' adult literacy tutoring. *Qualitative Studies in Education, 12*(1), 85–101.

# INDEX

Page numbers in *Italics* refer to figures; **bold** refer to tables and page numbers followed by 'n' refer to notes numbers

Ingram Content Group UK Ltd.
Milton Keynes UK
UKHW022204030523
421200UK00030B/324